Solve Your Child's Sleep Problems

Richard Ferber, M.D.

A FIRESIDE BOOK
Published by Simon & Schuster
New York London Toronto Sydney Tokyo Singapore

Copyright © 1985 by Richard Ferber, M.D.
All rights reserved
including the right of reproduction
in whole or in part in any form
First Fireside Edition, 1986
Published by Simon & Schuster, Inc.
Simon & Schuster Building
Rockefeller Center
1230 Avenue of the Americas
New York, New York 10020
FIRESIDE and colophon are registered trademarks of
Simon & Schuster, Inc.
Designed by Patricia Girvin Dunbar
Manufactured in the United States of America

3 5 7 9 10 8 6 4
19   20   18   Pbk.

Library of Congress Cataloging in Publication Data
Ferber, Richard.
Solve your child's sleep problems.

"Children's books on sleep and dreams"—
Includes index.
1. Sleep disorders in children.   I. Title.
RJ506.S55F47   1985   618.92'849   84-22132
ISBN: 0-671-46027-7
ISBN: 0-671-62099-1 Pbk.

Contents

Acknowledgments

I am indebted to many people for their support, teaching, ideas, encouragement, and criticism.

I want to thank Dr. Peter Wolff, who first taught me about the states of waking and sleep in the infant and who impressed upon me the importance of observation instead of assumption. My interest in the sleep of children began under his tutelage.

Dr. Wolff introduced me to Dr. Myron Belfer, who shared with me a belief in the need for a sleep center for children. Together we organized the Center for Pediatric Sleep Disorders in 1979.

Special thanks are due to Dr. M. Patricia Boyle, the Center's Co-Director. Her interest, enthusiasm, insight, and caring have contributed greatly to the Center's ongoing success. Her diagnostic expertise is invaluable and has helped lead to a better way of understanding, classifying, and treating sleep disorders in children.

Our sleep laboratory was established within the Seizure Unit at Children's Hospital. This would not have been possible were it not for the support and teaching of Dr. Giuseppe Erba and Dr. Cesare Lombroso.

The initial idea of writing a book came from my conversations with the parents of many of the children I treated, and in the end their experiences provided most of the material for this work. To them I am particularly indebted.

My sincerest thanks also to A. Barry Merkin, who recognized the feasibility of a book such, as this, convinced me of it, and took the steps necessary to ensure that others were similarly convinced. Were it not for his enthusiastic interest and time volunteered on my behalf, this book would not have been written.

Each draft of this book was read over carefully by Martha Cochrane and my wife, Geri. The amount of time they contributed was enormous. They, and my editor, Fred Hills, helped transform a rough draft into a final version that I believe is understandable, readable, and helpful to parents. Any errors in content, of course, remain my own.

Finally I would like to thank the many members of the Association of Sleep Disorders Centers whose enthusiasm for the field of sleep disorders medicine has been infectious.

Preface

Sleep problems are extremely common in children and often cause tremendous worry, frustration, and anger at home. Yet, appropriate help is difficult to find. For these reasons and to learn more about the special problems of diagnosing and treating children with disordered sleep, we opened the Center for Pediatric Sleep Disorders at The Children's Hospital in Boston, in 1979.

My own training had been in pediatrics, psychosomatic medicine, and adult sleep disorders. I had learned how to diagnose and treat sleep problems at a major adult sleep disorders center, but I knew that very different approaches would be required to treat children successfully.

Sleep problems are not the same in children as they are in adults. For example, infants and toddlers who are not sleeping well do not complain—their parents do. Young children are usually more unhappy about having to go to bed than about any inability to fall asleep; in fact they are more likely to fight sleep than they are to count sheep. The significance of other sleep symptoms also depends on age. A four-year-old who wets the bed every night probably has no disorder at all. A seven-year-old who does the same has an annoying problem. But a young adult who wets nightly has a genuinely disturbing disorder. Sleepwalking or sleep terrors may have very different psychological significance at different ages. And loud nightly snoring in children does not usually have the same cause or require the same treatment as it does in adults.

Since opening our clinic, I have learned a great deal from the hundreds of families whose children I have treated. Most of the parents had received varied and often conflicting advice from family, friends, and health professionals, and most had tried several different approaches in an attempt to improve their children's sleep. Many of them had been told, at some point, simply to let their child cry. Or they were advised to lock the child in his or her room, to let the child sleep with them, to have a parent sleep in the child's room, to change the child's diet, to increase nighttime feedings, to warm the milk, to

9

use a pacifier, to rock their child to sleep, to turn on a light or radio or white-noise generator, to drive their child in the car at bedtime, to eliminate a nap, to switch to a water bed, or to give their child sleep medicine. Parents were often told—incorrectly—that there was little they could do but wait for the child to outgrow the problem. Frequently they were unjustly accused of "spoiling" their child, and were made to feel inadequate as parents.

I have found that most of this advice not only doesn't help but will usually make matters worse because it is not based on a full understanding of children's sleep. Fortunately I have been able to gain a much better appreciation of the nature of sleep and sleep disturbances in children, and I have found that the causes of most of these disturbances can be identified fairly readily and then corrected by simple, straightforward techniques.

The most common problem, for example, sleeplessness in young children, has proven to be the easiest to treat: even an infant or toddler who has never slept through the night can begin doing so within a few days with the right assistance from parents. Other problems such as bedwetting, sleepwalking, or sleep terrors need different approaches, but can almost always be alleviated over time. Only occasional disorders such as narcolepsy require the continued use of medication. And only very specific conditions such as sleep apnea ever call for surgery.

At our center I work closely with families. With their help I examine the factors responsible for the child's sleep disruption and then, in most cases, work out treatment methods that the parents can carry out by themselves. For the most part it is still the parents who solve their child's sleep problems, and usually quite successfully.

Since I can work directly with only a limited number of families, it seemed important to find a way to share what I have learned with parents everywhere. It is to this end that this book was written. The material in these chapters should help you to identify and treat your children's sleep disturbances by yourselves or to recognize problems for which you should seek professional advice. I hope this book will provide you with answers to questions about your children's sleep that have not been available elsewhere and will, in the end, help your child —and you—to sleep well at night.

To my children, Matt and Thad,
for teaching me the most about children
and their sleep,
and to my wife, Geri,
for helping me learn

Part One

❧ ❦

YOUR CHILD'S SLEEP

Chapter 1

At the End of Your Rope

The most frequent calls I receive at the Center for Pediatric Sleep Disorders at Children's Hospital in Boston are from a parent or parents whose children are sleeping poorly. When the parent on the phone begins by telling me "I am at the end of my rope" or "We are at our wits' end," I can almost predict what will be said next.

Typically, the couple or single parent has a young child (often their first), who is between five months and four years of age. Their child does not fall asleep readily at night and/or wakes repeatedly during the night. The parents are tired, frustrated, and often angry. Their own relationship has become tense and they are wondering whether there is something inherently wrong with their child, or if they are unfit parents.

In most cases the parents have had lots of advice on how to handle the situation from friends, relatives, even the pediatrician. "Let him cry; you're just spoiling him," they are told, or "That's just a phase; wait until she outgrows it." They don't want to wait but begin to wonder if they will have to, since despite all their efforts and strategies the sleep problem persists. Often the more the parents do to try and solve the problem, the worse it gets. Sooner or later they ask themselves, "How long do I let my child cry—*all night?*" And if he or she gets up four, five, and six times at night, "Will this phase pass before we collapse from our own loss of sleep?"

Everything seems pretty hopeless at first. If your child isn't sleeping well or has other problems—such as sleep terrors, bedwetting, nightmares, or loud snoring—which are sources of worry and frustration, it won't take long for you to feel as if you're at the end of your rope too.

Let me assure you there is hope. With almost all of these children we are able to at least reduce the disturbance significantly, and often we can actually eliminate the sleep disorder entirely. The information in this book will help you to identify your child's particular disorder and will give you practical ways of solving the problem.

At the Sleep Center I meet with the family—parents and child together—and learn all I can about the child's problem. How frequent and long-lasting has it been? What are the episodes like? How do the parents handle the child at bedtime and during the nighttime wakings? Is there a family history of sleep problems, and are there social factors that might be contributing to the problem? With this detailed history, a physical examination, and, in certain cases, after laboratory study, I can usually identify the disorder and its causes. At that point I can begin to work with the family to help them solve their child's sleep problem.

Our methods of treatment for the "sleepless child" rarely include the use of medication. Instead, I work with the family to set up new schedules, routines, and ways of handling their child. Sometimes the child's biological rhythms may need normalizing or he may have to learn new conditions to associate with falling asleep. The family may have to learn how to set appropriate limits on the child's behavior, and the child may need an incentive to cooperate. I always negotiate the specifics of the plan with the family. It is important that they agree with the approach and feel confident that they will be able to follow through consistently. If the child is old enough, we include him in the negotiating. Thus we use a consistent, firm, but fair technique, tailored to the child, the family, and the particular sleep disorder. This *works*, time after time.

Usually the sleep problem has nothing to do with poor parenting. Nor are the episodes (with a few exceptions) part of a "normal phase" that must be waited (and waited and waited) out. And finally there is usually nothing physically or mentally wrong with the child himself. Most parents are immensely reassured to know that sleep disorders are common in all types of families and social environments, and that most children with such disorders respond well to treatment.

In certain cases, such as in sleep apnea, or less often in bedwetting, medical factors may be involved and our intervention may include medication or surgery. In other instances, such as the sleepiness of depression, recurrent nightmares, adolescent sleep terrors, and extreme nighttime fears, emotional factors may play a role. Here the source of these feelings must be identified and satisfactorily dealt with before the sleep problems will resolve. Sometimes professional counseling may be recommended.

The case studies in this book are based on my experience at the Sleep Center. The discussions of these cases, along with descriptions of the underlying sleep disorders and explanations of the methods of solving them, will help you to identify, understand, and deal with your own child's sleep problem.

Can a Child Just Be a "Poor Sleeper"?

If your child is a restless sleeper or can't seem to settle down at night, you should be very cautious about assuming that he is just a poor sleeper or doesn't need as much sleep as other children of the same age. Your own expectations can have a very strong influence on how your child's sleep pattern develops from the day you bring him home from the hospital. I have seen many families who were told by the nurse in the maternity ward, "Your baby hardly sleeps at all. You're in for trouble!" Because these parents were led to believe their child was just a poor sleeper and there wasn't anything they could do about it, they allowed their baby to develop poor sleep habits; they did not believe there was anything they could do to help him develop good ones. As a result the whole family suffered terribly. Yet I have found that almost all of these children are potentially fine sleepers and with just a little intervention can learn to sleep well.

It is true that children differ in their ability to sleep. Some children are excellent sleepers from birth. In the early weeks they may have to be waked for feedings. As they grow older, not only do they continue to sleep well, but it is difficult to wake them even when you want to. They sleep soundly at night in a variety of situations—bright or dark, quiet or noisy, calm or chaotic—they tolerate occasional disruption of their sleep schedules, and even sleep well during periods of emotional stress.

Other children seem inherently more susceptible to having their sleep patterns disrupted. Any change in bedtime routines, an illness, hospitalization, or guests in the house, may cause their sleep patterns to worsen. Even though these children may have always been considered "non-sleepers," we usually find that they too can sleep quite satisfactorily once we make appropriate changes in their routines, schedules, surroundings, or interactions with the family. Such children may still have occasional nights of poor sleep, but if the new routines continue to be followed consistently, the more normal patterns will return quickly.

There are, of course, children who sleep very poorly for reasons we have, as yet, been unable to identify. For these few, our treatment may help very little, or not at all. If your child is up a great deal in the night it may be tempting to assume that he is one of these poor sleepers. But this almost certainly is *not* the case. Such instances of truly poor sleep ability are quite rare among young children, and in all probability your child's sleep problem can be solved.

Virtually all children without major medical or neurological disorders have the ability to sleep well. They can go to bed at an appropriate time, fall asleep within minutes, and stay asleep until a reasonable hour in the morning. And while it is normal for each child (and adult) to have brief wakings during the night, these arousals should last only a few seconds or minutes and the child should go back to sleep easily on his own.

It is *very* probable that your child, regardless of his present patterns, is just such a child, with a normal inherent ability to fall asleep and remain asleep. This is true even if he has a sleep disturbance such as sleepwalking or bedwetting. These events occur during sleep or partial waking, and children with these symptoms still have a basically normal ability to fall asleep and stay asleep. Sleepwalking and bedwetting are actually a bit more difficult to treat than sleeplessness, but nevertheless they too usually improve, and are often resolved, with the appropriate intervention.

How to Tell Whether Your Child Has a Sleep Problem

When your child's sleep patterns cause a definite problem for you or for him, then he has a sleep problem. This is true, for example, if he complains of inability to fall asleep, or if you find you must be up with him repeatedly during the night. Sleep problems such as sleep terrors, sleepwalking, or bedwetting are also readily apparent and quite easy to identify as sleep disorders. But others may be less obvious. You may not recognize that your child even has a problem, or you may not realize that the problem he does have should be considered a disorder that can and should be treated. You may not be aware that loud snoring every night, besides keeping you awake, may be a warning that your child is not breathing satisfactorily while asleep. Other symptoms of possible sleep abnormalities which should be identified and treated are: frequent difficulty falling asleep at bedtime, waking during the night with inability to go right back to sleep alone, waking too early or too late in the morning, falling asleep too early or too late in the evening, or being irritable or sleepy during the day.

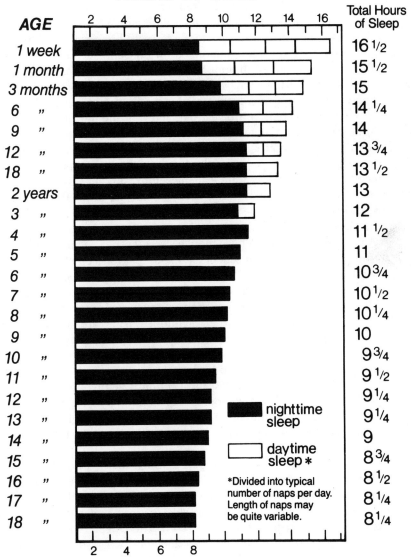

FIGURE 1 Typical Sleep Requirements in Childhood

One of the least obvious of sleep problems is that of insufficient sleep. There is no absolute way of measuring whether the amount of sleep your child gets per day is appropriate. Figure 1 on page 19 shows the average amount of sleep children get at various ages during the night and at naptime. But each child is different. We can watch each child's behavior during the day closely to see if he seems excessively sleepy or cranky. But the symptoms of insufficient sleep in a young child can be very subtle. If your two-year-old sleeps only eight hours at night but seems to be happy and functioning well during the day, it is tempting to assume he doesn't need more sleep. But eight hours is rarely enough sleep for a two-year-old, and with the proper intervention he can learn to increase his amount of sleep time considerably. You may begin to notice an improvement in his general behavior and only then will you be aware of the more subtle symptoms of inadequate sleep that actually were evident before you adjusted his sleep schedule. Now your child will probably be happier in the daytime, a bit less irritable, more able to concentrate at play, and less inclined to have tantrums, accidents, and arguments.

Adolescents often do not get enough sleep. Teenagers are not likely to wake spontaneously on school days and tend to sleep at least one hour longer on weekends. When adolescents have the opportunity to sleep as much as they like, they will average about nine hours per night, and this is probably closer to the optimal level for their age.

It is also difficult to decide when nighttime wakings are "abnormal." A young child from six months to three years may be getting adequate amounts of sleep at night, even though he wakes several times during the night and has to be helped back to sleep. Parents will say to me, "Tell me if this is normal. If it is, I will continue getting up; but if it is not, then we would like to *do* something about it!" I assure them that most healthy full-term infants are sleeping through the night by three or four months of age. Certainly by six months all healthy babies can do so.

If your baby does not start sleeping through the night on his own by six months at the latest, or if he begins waking again after weeks or months of sleeping well, then something is interfering with the continuity of his sleep. He should be able to sleep better, and in all likelihood his sleep disruption can be corrected. Chapters 5 through 9 will help you to identify his problem and show what you can do to remedy it.

How well your child sleeps from the early months affects not only his behavior during the day but also your feelings about him. I have often heard a parent say, "He is such a *good* baby. I even have to wake him for feedings." Although the parent is saying the baby is a good *sleeper*, the words imply that the baby is "good" in the moral sense. It is easy to see that this distinction will influence how you relate to your child.

If your child does not sleep well, he may well be making your life miserable. It isn't hard to think of such a bad sleeper as a "bad" baby. You will probably feel enormously frustrated, helpless, worried, and angry if you have to listen to crying every night, get up repeatedly, and lose a great deal of your own much-needed sleep. If your child's sleep disturbance is severe enough, your frustration and fatigue will carry over into your daytime activities and you are bound to feel increasingly tense with your child, your spouse, family, and friends. If this is the case in your home, you will be pleased to learn that your child is almost certainly capable of sleeping much better than he is now, and you should be able to get a good night's sleep yourself. To do this, you will need to learn how to identify exactly what your child's problem is, and then you can begin to solve it.

First, I want to explain briefly what we know about sleep itself. Although it is not necessary for you to be conversant with all the scientific research on sleep, it will be helpful for you to have some understanding of what sleep really is, how normal sleep patterns develop during childhood, and what can go wrong. Then you will be better able to recognize abnormal patterns as they begin to develop, to correct problems that have become established, and to prevent others from occurring.

Although the information on sleep in Chapter 2 is not overly technical, you may be eager to read the chapters that follow it to learn about the actual sleep disorders and their treatments. If that is the case, I suggest you scan the material on sleep in the next chapter and then come back to read it more closely when you have identified your own child's sleep problem. The information is very interesting to almost everyone, and especially important to parents who want to help a child sleep better at night.

ಃ⁄ *Chapter 2* ⅍

What We Know About Sleep

You may be surprised to learn that we still don't fully understand why people need to sleep and what purpose sleep serves. Obviously, without it we feel sleepy, and this feeling is only relieved by sleep. We know that sleep does serve some restorative function for our bodies and perhaps for our minds, and it is certainly necessary for normal functioning during the day.

Doctors and other researchers had thought until recently that sleep was a single state distinguished from waking. However, we now know that sleep itself is divided into two distinctly different states: REM (pronounced *rem*), or rapid-eye-movement sleep, and non-REM sleep. The non-REM stage is probably the closest to what we usually think of as "sleep," and most of the restorative function of sleep occurs in that state. During non-REM sleep, you lie quietly, with regular heart rate and breathing pattern. There is very little dreaming, if any, although thoughtlike processes may continue. In REM sleep there is much more activation of body systems, and it is in this state that we do our dreaming.

Non-REM Sleep

After the earliest months of life, non-REM sleep divides into four stages of its own. These stages represent progressive levels of sleep from drowsiness to very deep sleep, and each can be identified by monitoring brain waves, eye movements, and muscle tone on a machine called a polygraph.

As you begin to fall asleep, you enter Stage I, the state of drowsiness. Although you are unaware of it, your eyes move slowly about underneath your closed eyelids. Your awareness of the external world begins to diminish as well. You are perhaps familiar with the experience of becoming drowsy in a lecture or meeting. As you nod off, you miss some of the speaker's comments, yet you will wake instantly, often with a start, when your name is called or when your head is bent far enough forward that you are at risk of falling off the chair. You might think you had not been asleep, but your lapse of awareness would prove you wrong. On waking from the drowsy state, you might remember some thoughts of the kind usually referred to as "daydreams." Some people will report seeing or hearing things that seem more like true dreams. This "hypnagogic" (that is, in the act of falling asleep) imagery is similar to regular dreams that occur later, during REM sleep, except for being less well formed, shorter, and less strange.

As you continue your transition through drowsiness toward deeper sleep, you may notice a sudden jerk of your whole body which will actually wake you briefly and interrupt your sleep descent. This "hypnagogic startle" is quite normal, although it does not happen every time we fall asleep.

Drowsiness really represents a transition into the more fully established stages of non-REM sleep, but we can only identify the arrival of Stage II for certain if we monitor the brain waves. Short bursts of very rapid activity called sleep spindles, and large, slow waves called K-complexes, begin to appear (see Figure 2 on page 24). You can be waked easily from this stage, but on waking you may not believe that you had been asleep, depending on how long you had been in Stage II, how deeply into this stage you were at the time of waking, and, as always, on individual differences. After such a waking you would not likely report any odd dream images, but you might possibly describe some ongoing "thoughts."

As you fall more deeply asleep, you enter Stage III and finally Stage IV. The smaller and faster brain waves of light sleep and waking disappear and your brain waves now show predominantly large, very slow "delta" waves. Your breathing and heart rate become very stable, you may sweat profusely, and you will be very difficult to wake. Simply calling your name will probably rouse you out of Stage II, but you could well be oblivious to this stimulus in Stage IV.

However, if the stimulus is important enough, you would be likely to wake. Therefore it seems that even in the deepest Stage IV sleep our minds can still process some outside information.

Thus, although it may be difficult to wake you when it is your turn to get up and feed the baby, shouts of "Fire!" or a child's screams of

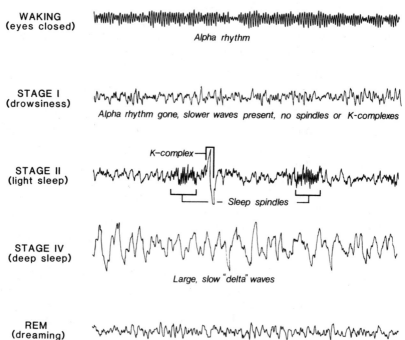

FIGURE 2 Brain Wave Patterns in Waking and in Sleep

pain will rouse you promptly. Even in these emergencies, however, you will find yourself awake but *confused*. You know that you must act quickly, but you have trouble thinking clearly, sorting out just what it is you should do, and "clearing the cobwebs" from your head. This difficulty in making the transition from Stage IV non-REM sleep to alert waking is very significant in several sleep disorders in children, as you will see when we discuss sleep terrors, extended periods of confused thrashing, and sleepwalking (Chapter 10).

In non-REM sleep your muscles are more relaxed than when you are awake. You still have the ability to move, since the connections of the nerves to the muscles they control are all working. However, you lie still because your brain is not sending messages to your muscles to move. Disorders such as sleepwalking and sleep-associated headbanging are exceptions to this rule and will be discussed at length later.

REM Sleep

After one or two cycles in non-REM sleep, you will enter REM sleep, a different state entirely. Both breathing and heart rate become irregular. Your reflexes, kidney function, and patterns of hormone release change. Temperature regulation is impaired, and so you will not sweat or shiver. Males will have penile erections in this state and females will have clitoral engorgement and increase in blood flow to the vagina, though the significance of these genital changes is not known.

REM sleep is an active state. Your body uses more oxygen, a sign that you are expending more energy. There is more blood flow to the brain, its temperature increases, and your brain waves will become quite busy again, resembling a mixture of waking and drowsy patterns. The mind now "wakes," but the wakefulness of the dream state is quite different from that of true waking. You respond mainly to signals originating within your own body instead of from the world about you, and you accept without question the bizarre nature of your dreams.

During this state you have very poor muscle tone, especially in the head and neck, where you become profoundly relaxed. Nerve impulses that otherwise would pass down the spinal cord and out to the muscles are blocked within the spinal cord, so that your muscles are not only relaxed but much of your body is effectively paralyzed. Signals to move may still be sent out from your brain, but they do not get through to your muscles. The only muscles spared are those controlling eye movements, respiration, and hearing. Because this blockade is not complete, some of the stronger signals will get through to the muscles, leading to frequent small twitches of the hands, legs, or face. So although REM sleep is very active in terms of metabolic and brain function, and although your brain does send out signals to move, you will remain fairly still.

Perhaps the most striking features of REM sleep are the bursts of rapid eye movements. During these bursts the heart rate, blood pressure, respiratory rate, and blood flow to the brain all increase and show other irregularities. Furthermore, if you are waked after you have been in the REM state for some minutes and have been having frequent eye movements, you will almost certainly report that you were having a dream. And the length of the dream you describe will correspond roughly to the time you had been in the REM state. Children as young as two have described dreams after such wakings.

We cannot say for sure whether the pattern of eye movements always indicates you were actually "watching" your dream occur. But we suspect that this is partly true and that at least some of the muscle twitching is in accordance with the action taking place in the dream. Fortunately, because only a few of the signals to move actually reach your muscles, you will only twitch a little now and then and not get up and move about, dangerously acting out a dream. Thus you would be wrong to assume that sleepwalking or sleep terrors result from pleasant dreams or nightmares, because such complex body movements cannot occur during REM sleep.

Some researchers believe that REM sleep has certain psychological functions. They suggest that REM dreaming allows us to process daytime emotional experiences and transfer recent memories into longer-term storage. But such theories remain unproven. Certainly dreams do have emotional significance, but their ultimate importance to the dreamer remains a mystery. It seems that REM sleep must be important, since we all dream every night (even those of us who think we don't), and if we are deprived of REM sleep for several nights we will compensate by getting more REM sleep the subsequent night. Yet when people have been deprived of REM sleep for long periods of time (on some medications, for example), they do not seem to show any major ill effects.

Sometimes you can be waked easily from REM sleep and at other times it is very difficult, possibly depending on how important the waking stimulus is to you and how involved you are in your dream. So the clock radio may not wake you immediately from a really interesting dream, and you may even incorporate something you hear on the radio into your dream. On the other hand, a very meaningful stimulus will wake you easily. Unlike the arousal from Stage IV sleep, you will become alert quickly.

Thus we seem to live in three distinct states. In the waking state we are rational and our thoughts can be carried out into actions so that we may maintain the necessary activity for survival. In non-REM sleep the body rests and restoration occurs. Mental processes are minimal in this state, although there may be some thoughtlike activity. And in REM sleep the mind is again active, although clearly not rational, but it is "disconnected" from the body; therefore major body movements do not take place despite the fact that the brain does send out signals to move.

One theory suggests that, over the course of evolution, REM sleep was an intermediate state between non-REM and waking in which the mind would "wake up" before being "connected" to the body. This would allow an animal to go to sleep and obtain the restorative value of non-REM sleep. In this state, with no movement and regular breathing, it would be safe from predators. A sudden waking from non-REM, however, would leave the animal confused and subject to attack. By switching first into REM sleep the animal's brain could become more alert but still disconnected from the muscles to prevent any movement that might alert a predator. Once the animal was sufficiently alert, it would wake fully, the muscle paralysis would disappear, and it could react appropriately to the danger.

This checking for danger may still be relevant in humans. We all tend to wake up briefly after an episode of dreaming. At this time, we will notice if something seems amiss in our environment: the smell of smoke, footsteps downstairs, or quiet sobbing from the next room. If all seems well, we simply return to sleep and usually do not remember this waking in the morning. Many young children, however, fail to return to sleep quickly after these normal arousals because something seems "wrong" to them. Perhaps when they wake, it feels wrong to be alone in their crib and not in a parent's arms. This is a common problem which will be discussed in detail in Chapter 5.

Now that you have a little background information on sleep stages, let's take a look at how infants develop normal sleep patterns.

How Sleep Stages Develop in Children

We have evidence that sleep patterns begin to develop in babies even before birth. REM sleep appears in the fetus at about six or seven months' gestation, and non-REM sleep between seven and eight months. In the fetus and infant, REM sleep is referred to as "Active Sleep," and non-REM as "Quiet Sleep." By the end of the eighth month of gestation, both these states are well established.

In the newborn, REM sleep is easy to identify because the baby twitches, breathes irregularly, and you can see his or her eyes dart about under the thin eyelids. Sometimes you may also see her smile briefly. In Quiet Sleep she will breathe deeply and lie very still. Occasionally you may see her make fast sucking motions and now and then a sudden body jerk or "startle."

Although the Quiet Sleep stage is well formed, it is still somewhat different from the non-REM sleep of older children and adults. The brain waves during this stage show large slow waves occurring in bursts rather than in a continuous flow. Also, the infant's non-REM sleep has not yet divided into four stages. During the first month of life the non-REM brain waves become continuous and startles disappear. By one month of age sleep spindles begin to appear, and over the next month we can begin to identify a sequence of non-REM sleep stages. We do not see the K-complex waves until a baby is about six months of age.

REM sleep is the earliest stage to form. Premature babies spend 80 percent of their sleep time in this state and full-term infants 50 percent. We do not fully understand the reasons for the preponderance of REM sleep in the early stage of development. We do know that Quiet Sleep requires a certain degree of brain maturation, and so we do not expect to see as much of this stage in newborns. We believe the large amounts of REM sleep early on may be important to the ongoing development of the fetus and newborn. In REM sleep, the higher centers of the brain receive stimulation from deeper, more primitive areas. Impulses come up the same sensory pathways that are used for sights, sounds, and perhaps touch, smell, and taste. Later on, such stimuli are probably incorporated by the brain into dream imagery. While we can know nothing of infants' "dreams," this state might allow the baby's developing brain to receive sensory input (that is to "see," to "hear") even before birth. This input might be important to the development of the higher brain centers.

We also know that the baby in the uterus makes no breathing motions in non-REM sleep. If respiratory movements were never practiced, the child would be born with no experience at all in using these muscles so vital to survival. However, respiratory motions are practiced in REM sleep, and it is conceivable that the baby is also practicing sending out signals that control other motor activity. In the fetus these impulses are not as completely blocked as they are in children and adults, so there is some actual ability to practice body movements in REM sleep. It is perhaps fortunate for the mother that there is some blockage of motor impulses during REM sleep, or the baby might never be still!

It may be, then, that REM sleep is most important in the early months as the fetus and baby develops, and progressively less so with increasing age. In fact, although at birth a full-term baby will have 50 percent of its sleep in the REM state, only 33 percent of sleep will be REM by age three, and the adult level of 25 percent will be reached by later childhood or adolescence.

Children's Sleep Cycles

It is important for you to have some knowledge of sleep cycles so that you may better understand the specifics of the various disorders children have.

Once non-REM sleep has developed four distinct stages, and most of the baby's sleep time is consolidated into a single nighttime sleep period, the patterns of sleep stage cycling take on a form that remains fairly constant throughout life. There are, however, changes in the length of sleep cycles and the amount of REM and deep non-REM sleep children and adults of various ages seem to require. The sleep cycle length, or the time between two consecutive appearances of the same sleep state, increases from about fifty minutes in a full-term baby to the adult level of ninety minutes by adolescence. The total amount and percentage of REM sleep decreases throughout childhood and levels out in adolescence. The total amount of Stage IV non-REM sleep also decreases throughout childhood and adolescence as total sleep decreases, but it continues to account for about 25 percent of the child's total sleep.

Although a newborn enters REM sleep immediately after falling asleep, by about three months of age she will enter non-REM first, a pattern that will continue for the rest of her life. A young child will plunge rapidly through drowsiness and the lighter stages of non-REM sleep into Stage IV usually within ten minutes (see Figure 3). In the youngster this is an extremely deep sleep, and waking a child from Stage IV sleep may be almost impossible. For example, if your child falls into Stage IV sleep at night in the car, you can probably carry her into the house, change her into her pajamas, and put her in bed with only the slightest sign of movement or arousal. A child who is rocked to sleep at bedtime and who keeps waking if put down before sleep is sufficiently deep will not wake when put into the crib once this stage has been reached. And if you wake your child from Stage IV sleep to urinate, she may do so in a semi-awake state and then return to sleep instantly without any recollection of the arousal in the morning. The arousal is only partial in this case, and is very similar to those we see in disorders of sleepwalking or sleep terrors.

A child will remain in Stage IV for about an hour, then will have a brief arousal. At that time she will probably move suddenly. The brain waves will also change abruptly, showing a mixture of patterns from deep sleep, light sleep, drowsiness, and even waking. The child will perhaps rub her face, chew, turn over, cry a little, or speak unintelligibly. She may even open her eyes for a moment with a blank stare or sit up briefly before returning to sleep.

There is actually a spectrum of behaviors that may occur during these arousals. The mild ones just described are quite normal. More prominent behaviors may also occur at these times. They are not so normal. These include sleepwalking, sleep terrors, confused thrashing, and perhaps bedwetting. These events all occur during partial waking from deep non-REM sleep with the child showing features of both sleeping and waking at the same time. These disorders will be discussed at length in later chapters, but for now remember that they are *not* stimulated by a dream. As you know, dreams, including nightmares, occur only during the REM state.

The partial waking may last for only a few seconds or up to several minutes. Occasionally the child may briefly wake fully before the progression of sleep stages continues. Although Stage IV will sometimes merge almost imperceptibly with REM sleep with no arousal, this happens infrequently.

Following this arousal the child will have a period of a few minutes resembling drowsiness or perhaps a beginning attempt to form REM sleep. There may actually be a short REM episode at this point, especially in adolescents and adults. The first REM episode, whenever it appears, tends to be relatively short, lasting only five to ten minutes, and is usually not very intense. There will not be many eye movements, and the breathing and heart patterns will remain fairly stable. After this episode of REM or "almost REM" the child will return to another cycle of non-REM sleep. In young children, the descent back into Stage IV sleep will probably be quite rapid, although not as rapid as the initial one.

After forty to fifty minutes she will have another arousal, followed almost certainly by a REM episode lasting five to twenty minutes. This REM state may be interrupted by several brief wakings and a rapid return to sleep. The REM state will end with a brief arousal, and the

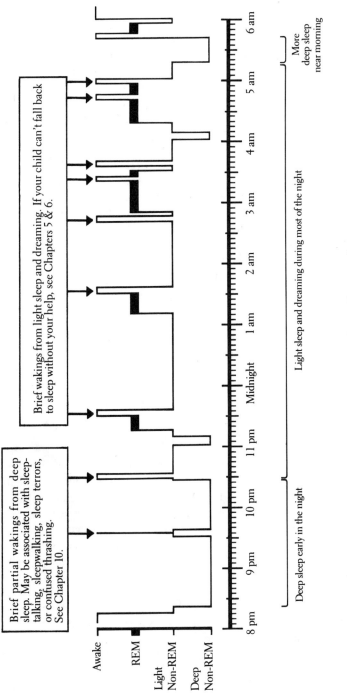

Brief partial wakings from deep sleep. May be associated with sleep-talking, sleepwalking, sleep terrors, or confused thrashing. See Chapter 10.

Brief wakings from light sleep and dreaming. If your child can't fall back to sleep without your help, see Chapters 5 & 6.

Awake

REM

Light Non-REM

Deep Non-REM

8 pm 9 pm 10 pm 11 pm Midnight 1 am 2 am 3 am 4 am 5 am 6 am

Deep sleep early in the night

Light sleep and dreaming during most of the night

More deep sleep near morning

FIGURE 3 Typical Sleep Stage Progression

31

child will move about, adjust her covers, check to see that everything is normal, then go back to sleep. This waking thus has several functions. The child needs to change position for the health of skin surfaces, muscles, and joints; and she may check to see that things are the same as when she went to sleep. It is important that you are aware that these wakings occur in all children and adults and are quite normal. Often parents perceive them as abnormal, most frequently when the child cannot return to sleep after the arousals because the conditions associated with falling asleep, such as being rocked, are no longer present. This will be discussed more fully in Chapter 5.

After this REM period the child will have another period of non-REM sleep. There will be another slower descent back into Stage III or perhaps Stage IV sleep, then another arousal and a longer and more intense REM episode. The rest of the night is spent alternating between REM and Stage II. Young children will often descend once more into Stage III or IV prior to the final waking in the morning, although this is less common in older children and adults.

This overview will give you an idea of what is actually happening to your child during the different stages of sleep during the night. It will also help you decide what state your child is in, based on when she fell asleep and what her sleep behavior is like at a given time. These observations will be a great help to you as you try to determine what sort of sleep disorder your child has, and how to deal with it.

Sleep and Waking Patterns

A newborn baby sleeps about sixteen or seventeen hours a day, but is unable to sleep for more than a few hours at a time and will have about seven sleeping and waking periods fairly evenly distributed throughout the day and night. The episodes, which will vary from twenty minutes to five or six hours in length, will begin with a period of REM sleep and, depending on the length of the sleep time, show several REM/non-REM cycles. Even when your baby sleeps well for a few hours, you can usually observe brief arousals. By the age of three or four months your baby will sleep about fifteen hours a day and her sleep pattern will have consolidated into about four or five sleep periods with two-thirds of her sleep occurring at night. At this age most infants have "settled," that is they are now sleeping through most of the night—at least from a late-night feeding to one in the early morning.

By six months almost all infants will have settled, and the continuous nighttime sleep has increased. A typical baby of this age will sleep about twelve hours at night with only occasional brief wakings. In addition she will take two one- to two-hour naps each day: one in mid-morning and a second in the afternoon. The pattern of settling varies with each child of course, and your baby may decrease the nighttime wakings very gradually, or she may settle quickly, as if the 2:00 A.M. feeding had suddenly been forgotten. Some babies settle in a very erratic fashion. In any case, at some point between three and six months, your baby should be sleeping well at night.

Most children by one year of age still sleep about fourteen hours a day altogether. If they still have a morning nap they will almost certainly give it up at some point during the second year. By age two, your child should sleep about eleven to twelve hours at night with a one- to two-hour nap after lunch. She will probably continue her afternoon nap until at least age three, and some children still nap up to age five.

From age three to adolescence, children need gradually less and less sleep. After the toddler period, napping is rare and nighttime sleep slowly decreases from about twelve hours in the preschooler to about ten hours in the pre-adolescent. During the four years of puberty rapid changes occur. Children aged fourteen to seventeen sleep only about seven or eight hours, although we believe this amount of sleep is culturally imposed and probably inadequate.

I must stress that these figures are only approximate and we cannot say precisely how much sleep your child needs. Sleep requirements vary among children. However, if your child is getting several hours more or less sleep than shown for her age in Figure 1 (page 19), you should at least be suspicious that she might have a sleep problem and you would do well to try to identify and correct it.

The Importance of Biological Rhythms

To understand certain childhood sleep problems, it is first necessary for you to know something about the circadian cycles that underlie sleep patterns. Circadian rhythms refer to biological cycles that repeat about every twenty-four hours. All of us have many such rhythms. They include patterns of sleeping and waking, activity and rest, hunger and eating, and fluctuations in body temperature and hormone release. It is important that these cycles be in harmony if we are to have a sense of well-being during the day. Our ability to fall asleep and to stay asleep is closely tied to the timing of these cycles. Typically we fall asleep as our body temperature is falling toward a daily minimum and we wake up as it starts rising toward a peak. The level of the hormone cortisol, which is secreted by the adrenal gland, also drops off early in the night, then progressively rises to high levels prior to our spontaneous waking in the morning. If we have to wake up when our temperature and cortisol levels are still low, we do so only with great difficulty. Similarly, we may have trouble falling asleep when our body temperature is at a peak.

It is important to know that the inherent length of these cycles in all of us is actually somewhat longer that twenty-four hours—closer to twenty-five hours. We reset the cycles each day by using various cues such as mealtime, bedtime, and especially the time of waking. In fact if we do not use these signals to guide us, our cycles will "free run" at their inherent rate and we will operate on a twenty-five-hour day. Adults placed in a cave or laboratory away from windows and clocks begin to go to sleep about one hour later each day and get up one hour later in the morning. They begin to operate on a twenty-five- instead of a twenty-four-hour day. Many of us follow this same tendency on weekends or vacation. We go to bed later, get up later, then have great difficulty adjusting to the earlier schedule when we must return to work.

Although it is not difficult for us to stay on a twenty-four-hour schedule, problems do arise when our routines are irregular or when we try to sleep, or ask our children to, at times that do not match the underlying sleep-wake rhythms. Shift workers are particularly prone to having sleep problems, and people who travel across time zones suffer the malaise, sleep difficulties, and lack of well-being commonly referred to as jet lag.

It is the same with children whose sleep cycles have been disrupted or shifted. They may sleep poorly at night and be sleepy or behave poorly during the day. It is important that you understand this, because the treatment of problems related to shifts in sleep-wake patterns is different than for other disorders. I will discuss this in more detail in Chapters 8 and 9. For now it will be helpful for you to know that normal circadian rhythms are necessary for normal sleep and optimal daytime function and that many abnormalities having to do with circadian rhythm shifts are quite simple to identify and correct.

Helping Your Child Develop
Good Sleep Patterns

We all have different ways of interacting with our children at sleep times and different means of shaping their sleep habits. These differences may occur within families, among ethnic groups, and between different cultures. The sleeping child may be swaddled, lightly clothed, or naked; he or she may sleep in his or her own room, share a room with one or more brothers and sisters, or the entire family may sleep in a single room—even in the same bed. The child may go to sleep on his stomach, side, or back in a room that is dark, dimly lit, or brightly illuminated. It may be quiet or there may be constant sounds from a humidifier or air conditioner; intermittent sounds from a radio, television, or traffic outside; or occasional noises from airplanes, sirens, and other children. He may fall asleep while nursing at the breast, sucking on a bottle or pacifier, rocking in a chair, or alone in bed. He may say goodnight downstairs and go to bed alone, or fall asleep only after having a story read to him, saying his prayers, playing a quiet game, or discussing the day's events. A child may go to bed at different times every night with no set routine, or he may follow exactly the same routine each night.

The Importance of Your Child's Bedtime Routines

Although I do believe some bedtime rituals are better than others, there are few absolute rules regarding sleep behavior. If your routine is working, if you and your child are happy with it, if he falls asleep easily and night wakings are infrequent, if he is getting enough sleep, and if his daytime behavior is appropriate, then it's likely that whatever is being done is fine.

However, it is important to keep in mind that some routines and approaches are more likely to help your child develop good sleep patterns now and avoid problems as he gets older. For example, if you are in the habit of rocking your child to sleep for twenty to thirty minutes each night and getting up once or twice to rock him back to sleep in the middle of the night, you actually may be interfering with his sleep and postponing the start of his sleeping through the night. Even if you "don't mind" getting up, I suspect you would be happier if you could simply put him down at bedtime without rocking and have him sleep through the night as well. Whether this is true or not, you should still be aware that it is in your child's best interests to have uninterrupted sleep.

Similarly, even if you and your child seem happy about his sharing your bed at night, and even if he seems to sleep well there, in the long run this habit will probably not be good for either of you, and you should consider making some changes in the nighttime routines.

By bedtime rituals or routines, I mean of course all the activities that take place as your child prepares for bed and while he falls asleep. If he is an infant, you probably change his diaper and then hold him until he falls asleep. Perhaps you rock and nurse him until sleep comes. Then you move him to his cradle or crib. Or your infant may still be awake when you put him down, so that he falls asleep on his own. Generally any of these patterns are fine in the first few months when you do not expect your baby to sleep through the night anyway. But by about three months of age most full-term healthy infants are, or could be, sleeping through the majority of the night. If your baby hasn't settled by five or six months, then you should take a close look at his bedtime routines. If your child is always nursed or rocked to sleep he may have difficulty going back to sleep alone after normal nighttime arousals. To help him sleep better at night you may have to change his bedtime routines. Thus, it is very important for some children to be put down awake so that they can learn to settle themselves and fall asleep alone both at bedtime and after nighttime wakings (see Chapter 5).

As your child gets older, the routines at bedtime continue to be important. If bedtime is a pleasant time, your child will look forward to this part of the day instead of becoming fussy when it is time for sleep. Bedtime rituals differ, of course, and you should choose a routine that suits your family, but make sure you always allow enough time to spend with your child each night. Follow the routine as consistently as you can. Your child should know when he has to change into his pajamas, brush his teeth, and go to bed. He should know what bedtime activities are planned and how much time will be spent on them, or how many stories will be read.

Bedtime means separation, which is difficult for children, especially very young ones. Simply sending a toddler or young child off to bed alone is not fair and may be scary for him. And it means you will miss what can be one of the best times of the day. So set aside ten to thirty minutes to do something special with your child before bed. Avoid teasing, scary stories, or anything that will excite your child at this time. Save the wrestling and tussling for other times of the day. You might both enjoy a discussion, quiet play, or story reading. But let your child know that your special time together will not extend beyond the time you and he have agreed upon, then don't go beyond those limits. It is a good idea to tell your child when the time is almost up or when you have only two or three more pages to read, and don't give in for an extra story. Your child will learn the rules only if you enforce them. If both you and he know just what is going to happen, there won't be the arguments and tension that arise when there is uncertainty.

Paul, for example, is a four-year-old boy. His father leaves for work early in the morning and doesn't see Paul until dinnertime at night. He likes to be the one to put his son to bed. If Paul's father did not handle the bedtime, the two would not have time together until the weekend. So the period from 7:00 to 8:00 each night is special for both of them.

At 7:00 they play together for about twenty-five minutes—with Paul's train or his Lego set—or in the warm weather they may play outside. Paul's father tells him when it is about 7:25 and then the bedtime routine begins. Paul has a bath and his father helps him put on his pajamas. Lately they have been reading a non-scary children's novel, one chapter each night. Both Paul and his father look forward to the night's reading, and the bedtime routine is one that Paul enjoys rather than resists. Paul's father tells him when only a few pages remain in the chapter. When the reading is over for that evening, the light is turned off, the night-light turned on, and the two lie quietly together for one minute. Paul then kisses his father goodnight, holds on to his stuffed monkey, lets his father leave the room, and goes to sleep.

In later years, your child will still appreciate having some time with you before he goes to sleep. He needs close, warm, and personal time. Simply watching television together will not provide this. Even if the shows are not exciting or scary (which is unlikely), and even if you are sitting next to him, the lack of direct personal interaction makes this bedtime routine a poor one. Instead, use this time to discuss school events, plans for the weekend, Little League, chorus, or music lessons. It might also be helpful to talk over any worries your child may have so he will be less likely to brood over them in bed. As your child gets older the bedtime ritual does not have to be the same each night. Some nights you may enjoy a walk outside, a trip for ice cream, a board game, Ping-Pong, or helping with homework.

A ten- or twelve-year-old will probably want privacy as he readies for bed, but do stop in to say goodnight and chat for a while. A final routine before bed will still be important, although he can now handle everything himself. He may want to read, listen to music, or busy himself with a hobby before he turns out the light.

Phyllis, eleven, has a good bedtime routine. After dinner she finishes her homework, practices piano, and may call one of her friends on the telephone. She and her mother, a single parent, then spend some time together. They like to build things—a bird house or a picture frame—and they are currently working on a giant jigsaw puzzle. While they work, they get a chance to talk. Then at about 9:00 Phyllis changes for bed and begins to read with the radio on. Her mother stops in for a few minutes to discuss plans for the next day, and at 9:30 Phyllis turns off the radio and light and goes to sleep.

Of course not every night in Paul's and Phyllis's homes is quiet and pleasant, but most are, and major disruptions at bedtime are rare. If such is not the case in your home and bedtimes usually are unpleasant and a time of struggle, the solution may be to establish more pleasant and consistent bedtime routines. At first it may not seem easy for you to do this, and initially your child may resist. But if you persist, both you and your child should grow to enjoy the bedtime routines, and the struggles will be over. It is certainly worth the effort.

Should Your Child Sleep in Your Bed?

Many parents give in to their children's desires or demands to share their beds in order to avoid arguments at bedtime and to decrease nighttime disturbances. Some parents feel this is in their children's best interests. Others simply prefer to have their children in bed with them. Although taking your child into bed with you for a night or two may be reasonable if he is ill or very upset about something, for the most part this is not a good idea. We know for a fact that people sleep better alone in bed. Studies have shown that the movements and arousals of one person during the night stimulate others in the same bed to have more frequent wakings and sleep state changes, so they do not sleep as well. But there are even better reasons for your child to sleep in his own bed. Sleeping alone is an important part of his learning to be able to separate from you without anxiety and to see himself as an independent individual. This process is important to his early psychological development. In addition, sleeping in your bed can make your child feel confused and anxious rather than relaxed and reassured. Even a young toddler may find this repeated experience overly stimulating. If you allow him to crawl in between you and your spouse, in a sense separating the two of you, he may feel too powerful and become worried. He wants the reassurance of knowing you are in control and that you will do what is best for him regardless of his demands. If you show you cannot do this and let him act out his impulses, he may become frightened.

These feelings may be heightened if only one parent is in the bed— if you are a single parent or if one of you is out of town, at work, or in another bedroom. If you take the easy way out and allow your child into your bed while one of you moves into his, your child will certainly not be reassured. Now he is literally replacing one of you in your bed as the other's partner. He may begin to worry that he will cause the two of you to separate, and if you ever do he may feel responsible. Often children of divorced or separated parents feel they caused the family upheaval, and they will feel even more confused and unhappy if they had been, or are now, sleeping in their parents' bed. And if as a single parent you begin a new relationship, your child will certainly resent being displaced in your bed by this "intruder."

Most children do not have serious ongoing problems sleeping alone. If your child is "too afraid" to do so, and you deal with his fear by letting him into your bed, you are not really solving the problem. There must be a reason why he is so fearful. You will help your child most if you work with him to find and solve the underlying cause of the fear and do not simply let him sleep with you to assure a quiet night. This may require considerable patience, understanding, and firmness on your part; and you may need outside help and support (see Chapter 4).

If you find that you actually prefer to have your child in your bed, you should examine your own feelings very carefully. Some parents who would otherwise be alone at night (single parents or people whose spouse works nights or travels frequently) find they enjoy the company, feel less lonely, and possibly are less afraid if their child is with them. If there is tension between parents, then taking a child into their bed may help them avoid confrontation and sexual intimacy. If any of this is true for you, then instead of helping your child you are using him to avoid facing and solving your own problems. As such a pattern continues, your child, and your whole family, will suffer. You need to understand and deal with your own needs and feelings and to resolve the tension between you and your spouse. If these problems cannot be simply settled, then professional counseling may be required.

Finally, if your child always sleeps with you, you may have great difficulty leaving him with a sitter. Your own social life may be affected and you may find that you begin to harbor angry feelings toward your child for this infringement. And as he gets to the age where you feel he should be sleeping alone, you may find you have real problems moving him into his own bed.

There are situations in which your child may have to sleep in your room nightly for an extended period of time, when living conditions do not permit otherwise. You may have only one bedroom or two bedrooms but several children. Grandparents may be living with you and need a room for themselves. You may be living in someone else's home and have only a single room. These are all difficult situations, but there are solutions. If your child must share your bedroom, try to give him his own place to sleep—perhaps a cot or even a mattress on the floor. Make that corner of the room his. Try to have space for some of his things and even a place on the wall for his decorations. Perhaps that area can be closed off with a curtain. But as soon as you are able, move him to a new room, either alone or with brothers and sisters.

The Special Toy or Favorite Blanket

Better than lying with your toddler or young child until he falls asleep at night is for him to fall asleep with a "transitional object"—a stuffed animal, a doll, a toy, a special blanket. The toy will often help him accept the nighttime separation from you and can be a source of reassurance and comfort when he is alone. It will give him a feeling of having a little control over his world because he may have the toy or blanket with him whenever he wants, which he cannot expect from you. His toy will not get up and leave after he falls asleep and it will still be there whenever he wakes.

A child will often choose such a special object early in the toddler years and may continue to use it (or new ones) until perhaps age six or eight. If your child does not have a special toy it is reasonable to offer him ones which you think might take on this role. However, he will always make the final choice, and you cannot make him attach to a toy because you think it will be appropriate. But if you always allow yourself to be used in the manner of such an object—to lie with him, to nurse or rock him, to be held, cuddled, or caressed by him, or let him twirl your hair whenever he tries to fall asleep—he will never take on a transitional object, because he won't need to.

If your child begins to favor a particular stuffed toy or doll, include it in the bedtime rituals. Have him tuck it in and let it "listen to" the story, or make sure he has his special blanket. It will make the final goodnight that much easier.

Developing Good Patterns

As you know from Chapter 2, newborn infants do not have regular sleep patterns, and it usually takes six to ten weeks for them to develop a good twenty-four-hour schedule, with the longest period of sleep at night. Your baby's sleep pattern during the first few days after birth should not be considered an indicator of things to come. Whether he sleeps well or quite fitfully in the hospital, and regardless of a nurse's reassurance that your baby is "extremely good" or her warning that she has never seen a baby who "sleeps so little," things may change considerably once you get home. If "problems" develop when you get home, you may assume your inexperience as a parent is to blame. If you do, you almost certainly would be wrong. And if you believe a nurse's warning about problems ahead, it may become a self-fulfilling prophecy.

Most babies show a sleep pattern emerging over the first two weeks, with many naps, some brief, some longer, distributed across the day and night. But some infants do seem to sleep unusually well from the beginning, even having to be waked for some feedings, but this is the exception rather than the rule. Try not to feel frustrated if your child takes a little time to fall into a reasonable and easy schedule.

Occasionally a baby will have his longest sleep period during the day and his longest period of waking at night. He seems to have his "days and nights reversed." This too will change. It is actually impressive that a child so young can show such a consistent (although inverted) pattern, since he has had little opportunity to form regular twenty-four-hour rhythms and even less chance to learn to distinguish day from night. This night-day reversal is less a problem than an indication that the child is inherently a good sleeper, and it will be easy to readjust his schedule if he doesn't do so on his own (see below and Chapters 8 and 9).

Although most infants will develop a good twenty-four-hour sleep schedule despite us, there is no question that parents can assist their babies considerably in developing good sleep patterns. You can do this by using approaches that properly take into account your baby's schedules, habits, learned associations, and nutritional and emotional needs while avoiding approaches that could interfere with the development of normal rhythms.

Feeding patterns are an important part of an infant's daily schedule. Fortunately, most pediatricians no longer urge parents to put their babies on a precise four-hourly feeding schedule from the beginning. Instead, they now recommend that you try to follow your infant's cues. You will soon learn to recognize when his cries mean that he is hungry. Only if your baby was premature or has medical problems or feeding difficulties will you have to follow a rigid feeding schedule.

A newborn baby usually needs to be fed every two to six hours. But there are two problems to watch for in a feeding-on-demand schedule. First, not all cries are hunger cries, and it will take you a little time to discern which sounds mean your child is hungry. Second, you should follow your baby's cues, but within certain limits. Naturally if a newborn seems to cry for feedings only every twelve hours, something is wrong. He simply has to be fed more often. But what may be less apparent is that a full-term healthy infant does not need hourly feedings, even if he seems hungry at these times and nurses when you offer the breast or bottle. Hourly feeding is exhausting for the mother, painful if you are breast feeding, unnecessary for the baby, and interferes with his developing more normal and healthy sleep-wake and feeding patterns.

Of course you want to show your baby that he has been born into a good and caring world, and for this reason you respond to his cries and try to do whatever is necessary to soothe him. Helping him develop good sleep schedules is also an important part of his care. But to do this you may have to tolerate some crying or find ways to calm him other than nursing. Babies will often stop crying if they are walked, rocked, or stroked for a while, and sometimes go off to sleep without feeding.

If your baby has been feeding every hour, begin to increase the time between feedings by an amount you feel comfortable with—perhaps fifteen minutes per day—until he is being fed every two hours, then every two and a half or three hours. He will adapt to the better schedule, the hourly crying will cease, and he will begin to develop the good sleeping and eating rhythms which should be forming over the first three months.

If your baby is sleeping six hours at a time during the day but is awake much of the night and if this pattern persists beyond the early weeks, then begin waking him earlier and earlier from the long sleep period so that he will start to treat this as a nap and move the longer sleep segment into the nighttime hours. Thus, although you are following your child's cues up to a point, you can still help structure his sleep-wake schedule.

Over the first three months most infants begin to adjust on their own to the external cues of darkness, quiet, and lack of activity at night, and light, noise, and activity during the day by developing a fairly well formed twenty-four-hour rhythm. By three or four months they will get most of their sleep at night, usually in a continuous episode of five to nine hours. Babies will continue to nap at three or four fairly predictable times during the day, and will have one period of more prolonged waking. At this point you should begin working with your baby to stabilize and further develop his schedule. You will be doing both your baby and yourself a favor, because as your baby settles you will be able to make better use of your own time and enjoy him more when he is awake.

As you begin to observe your baby's periods of waking, activity, feeding, and sleep, you will be able to anticipate his needs and know when to play with him, feed him, or put him down to sleep. Even if your baby is not crying for a feeding, he may be ready to eat at the expected time and will nurse quite eagerly. Similarly, he may be ready for his nap before he starts to yawn and become fussy. Although you can't tie your child's feedings, play, and sleep precisely to the clock, if you are aware of his emerging schedule you can encourage him to eat and sleep at reasonable and consistent times during the day. This will help him to further stabilize his developing twenty-four-hour cycles. In the early weeks you are for the most part following your child's cues, but by three months it becomes more important for you to provide increasingly consistent structure. If you keep to reasonable schedules as much as possible, then it is likely that your child will continue to develop and maintain good rhythms. And the more regular your baby's schedule is, the easier it is for you to keep your own schedule well adjusted.

Once your baby has developed a fairly predictable twenty-four-hour pattern, do your very best to provide him with a consistent routine from day to day so that he can maintain these rhythms. If the times of his feedings, play, bath, and other activities are constantly changing, chances are that his sleep rhythms will become irregular as well. It is very important once your child has achieved a good twenty-four-hour pattern, that you do not simply follow his cues without providing any structure for him. Remember from Chapter 2 that people will tend to "free run" on a twenty-five-hour circadian rhythm, and if you don't supervise your child's sleep you might soon see a pattern emerge that wouldn't surprise a sleep scientist, but might be surprising to you.

I have seen families with this problem. They were surprised to find that their child was operating on a regular pattern but one cycling at twenty-five or twenty-six hours instead of twenty-four. As a result, they were actually following the child around the clock, allowing him to stay up later and later at night and getting up with him one to two hours later each morning. At times they had to get their own sleep during the day. Of course, the child was just operating on the normal circadian rhythm: a rhythm that must be reset to twenty-four hours each day by our external schedule.

It is just as important to help our children maintain consistent schedules through infancy, childhood, and adolescence. In fact all of us, regardless of age, function best when we keep regular schedules. Studies in adults have shown that irregular sleep-wake patterns lead to significant alterations in our moods and sense of well-being, and undermine our ability to sleep at the desired times. The same is true of young children, although many parents don't seem to appreciate this fact. So *don't* let your two- or three-year-old decide what time he should go to bed. It would usually be only when he was so sleepy he could not stay awake any longer. Before long his schedule would be quite haphazard. He would fall asleep early one night and late the next; he might nap some days and not others; and when he did nap it might be in the morning, in the afternoon, or in the early evening. If his schedule were even more disrupted, his mealtimes would also fluctuate. He might have breakfast anywhere from 7:00 to 10:00 A.M. He would then want lunch and dinner at odd hours and might skip meals altogether. Such children can develop major sleep problems. Behavior problems may follow, though these can be subtle at first.

So do your best to help your baby establish a reasonable daytime schedule in his first three months and maintain it as much as possible throughout childhood. Your child cannot be expected to keep to a schedule on his own; you will have to set a reasonable one for him and then be willing to enforce it. Of course you should show some degree of flexibility. Some children need more sleep than others and some seem better able to tolerate variations in their day-to-day routines. You will have to learn from experience with your child what schedule is best and how rigidly it needs to be kept.

Consistent schedules also play a major role in treating sleep disorders. If your child is having a sleep problem, regardless of his age or the cause of the disorder, a schedule will help the treatment approach to succeed and at times may be a cure in and of itself. So if you are about to work with your child to correct a sleep disorder, it is important to set up and maintain a very regular schedule and to continue it rigorously for several weeks after your child has begun sleeping well again. At that point you will be able to alter the daytime routine a little. For example, you can eliminate naps occasionally for a special outing or take your child with you in the afternoon even though he may fall asleep in the car at a time different from his naptime.

Once a baby has settled into a good sleep-wake pattern it is still subject to disruption. Teething, an illness, a trip, or an upset in the family may interfere with his sleep pattern. The disruption can continue for months unless you intervene. You may need to restabilize your child's schedule, help him get rid of some bad habits, deal with his anxieties, or be firmer yourself in setting limits. We will discuss all of these approaches in detail throughout this book.

æ& *Chapter 4* №з

Nighttime Fears

If your child is like most children, he or she will occasionally feel frightened at night. These fears will depend on her age and her stage of emotional and physical development. As your child grows, she will have to face all kinds of new challenges. She must learn to tolerate separation from you when you are out of the room or when she is left with a sitter, at day-care, nursery school, or kindergarten. And, she must learn to accept separation from you each night when she falls asleep. She must learn to control her behavior, her bowels, and her bladder. She will know that her feelings of anger, jealousy, and aggression must not get out of hand, and she will also have to learn the give and take of interacting with her family and friends. She will learn, wonder, and worry about death, God, heaven, and hell. She will find pleasure in genital stimulation but may worry about masturbation. She will know her parents have certain expectations for her and wonder if she can live up to them. She will question her ability to perform as well as her peers.

The Child Who Is Anxious

At any stage of your child's development, specific events may intensify certain anxieties. For example, when she begins nursery school, her concerns about separation may increase for a while. She may be reluctant to leave your side during the daytime, and she may not want you to leave her at bedtime. If you become sick, your child may feel guilty, believing her angry words or thoughts may actually have caused the illness.

During toilet training there are other concerns. Your child may worry about her ability to control herself. She may be unsure that she wants to be trained and may even be tempted to soil. Yet, at the same time, she wants to please you and may fear incurring your displeasure. For many toddlers these worries may be heightened at night. To go to sleep means to relax control. How can they avoid soiling or wetting when asleep?

A scary movie may be particularly frightening for an older child. Your five- or six-year-old may be very upset by scenes of kidnapping or of a child showing aggression toward a parent. Such a movie can be very real to her. All children have aggressive fantasies and most feel a bit guilty about them, but seeing these thoughts acted out on the screen can become a source of great anxiety. And significant social stresses of any kind, over which the child has little control—illness, parental fighting, separation, divorce, alcoholism, death—may lead to a great deal of worry, guilt, anxiety, and fear at any age. At night, when a child must give up the little control she has over her world, and when she is unable to continually check in on her environment, fantasies stimulated by these strong feelings are most likely to emerge and be quite frightening. Bedtime difficulties and fears are to be expected.

Adolescents too have major worries as they undergo the rapid physical and emotional changes of puberty while they mature from children to adults. They start to worry about the future—college, jobs, money. Teenagers' sexual feelings are very intense. Moral issues become more relevant, and adolescents face constant dilemmas as they try to make many new and important decisions. They must weigh peer pressures, personal desires, and family standards against issues such as academic performance, sexual habits, and drug and alcohol use. They may try new value systems and abandon old ones. They may believe their parents no longer trust or support them, or they may reject their parents' help entirely.

During the day it is much easier to keep worries under control. Most children keep pretty busy and don't have time to brood over their problems. But at night as your child gets into bed, turns out the light, and prepares for sleep, she may begin to worry. If she lies quietly in bed, there is little to do but think, and her fantasies may run free. As your child gets sleepy, her ability to avoid certain thoughts diminishes. She has less control over her feelings, urges, and fears. In this state she begins to feel, and may even act, more childish. In this "regressed" state at night, a four- or five-year-old may need the same reassurance that a two- or three-year-old needs during the day. A five-year-old who has no difficulty leaving you for school in the daytime may have much trouble leaving you to go to sleep at night. It is not helpful to scold her and tell her she is being a baby. It would be better to try and understand why she is feeling insecure. Even if your child feels fairly confident that she can take care of herself in the daytime, she may feel less sure of herself at night when her thoughts seem to run out of control. At such times she may need you to be more involved in her care.

Thus, the period of transition from evening activity to bedtime is difficult for many children and it is not surprising that they are reluctant to go to sleep. Most families experience bedtime struggles at one time or another. Children will stall with requests for extra water, stories, or television, and requests to have the light on, the room checked for "monsters," or to sleep in your bed. Children often choose bedtime to initiate fights with brothers and sisters. Once in bed, your child may appear restless, rolling all over the bed or getting in and out of bed as she attempts to avoid worrisome thoughts through physical activity.

If your child begins to have difficulty going to sleep because she is worried or fearful at bedtime, it is important that you talk it over with her during the day. Try to be empathetic, reassuring, and supportive. I do not recommend, however, that you make any substantial changes in her bedtime routine. Rub her back for a few minutes perhaps, or sit in the room with her a little longer than usual, but keep her on her normal schedule as much as possible.

The Child Who Is Afraid of "Monsters"

Your child may also have trouble sleeping from time to time because of anxieties that do not seem realistic to you. She may think that there is a monster in the closet, a goblin under the bed, or a robber outside the window. Although she will be genuinely frightened at these times, she will not usually show overwhelming panic. Simply reassure her firmly and matter-of-factly that she is safe and that you will take care of her; then put her to bed with her usual story or quiet talk. Your child will be more reassured in the long run if you show her that you can take care of her than if you give in to these "fears."

Although it may be helpful to show her briefly that the shadows in the closet are in fact shadows and not monsters, it is generally not helpful to get into extended searches of the room or rearranging the furniture during the night. Remember, the "monsters" are not real, but your child's feelings, her urges, worries, and fears, are. She does not understand that it is these feelings that are making her anxious. She must use her imagination to come up with an explanation for these feelings; she must find something she can believe to be a cause of her fears—hence the monsters. So, your child does not need protection from monsters, she needs a better understanding of her own feelings and urges. She needs to know that nothing bad will happen if she soils, has a temper tantrum, or feels anger toward her brother or sister. At these times, she can be most reassured if she knows that you are in complete control of yourself and of her and that you can and will protect her and keep her safe. If you can convince her that you will do this, then she will be able to relax. Your calm, firm, and loving assurance will do more to dispel the goblins than will searches under the bed.

The Child Who Is Afraid of the Dark

The majority of children do not like to sleep in total darkness or with the door closed, and I see no reason why they should. There is no advantage in trying to train your child to sleep completely in the dark. It will be helpful if the bedroom is dimly lit by a night-light, a hall light, or even streetlights, so that when your child wakes up at night, especially after a dream, she can reorient herself within the room, reestablish a sense of reality, and put the dream in its proper perspective. And with the door open, she may feel less isolated and alone. So if your child has some anxieties at bedtime or after nighttime wakings, she may get some reassurance from being able to see about her room. With the door open, she will not feel shut off from everyone else in the house.

For some children, the fear of "shadows" is the same as that of monsters. Again, you may try to alter the lighting pattern in the room, but once you find a reasonable one, stick to it. Turning lights on and off or moving them around the room each night will do little to allay your child's fears. If she falls asleep with a particular light on at bedtime but becomes frightened on waking during the night and finding that light off, you should leave it on all night.

Bad Dreams

All children have nightmares now and then, but they are not a common cause of *frequent* nighttime disturbances. What many families consider to be frequent nightmares are really sleep terrors or other similar partial wakings (see Chapters 10 and 11). When your child does wake frightened from a scary dream, she should not have to stay alone, but you certainly want to avoid having to sit with her on a nightly basis. It may be helpful to discuss the dream matter-of-factly, either at the time or in the morning. This will help her to orient herself and to realize that she is not in any real danger. There are a number of good books for children about dreams and nightmares (see Appendix A). You may want to read one or two of them with her. If your child has frequent nightmares, however, they should be handled differently. (This and other aspects of dreams and nightmares are discussed in Chapter 11.)

How to Cope with Nighttime Fears

When your child complains of fears, try to determine how frightened she really is. Most children say they are more terrified than they actually are. Sometimes they are not afraid at all but say so because they have learned this will always get you to come in. If your child says she is afraid but shows no sign of real panic (and I do find most parents can make this distinction), you must be firm. Stick with the bedtime routine, say goodnight, and leave. Do not return repeatedly. If you need more guidelines for being firm, setting limits, or getting your child to cooperate, see Chapter 5.

There are occasions, however, when children do become extremely frightened at night, truly panicky, and irrational. Their emotional conflicts have gotten out of hand. In such cases being firm will not work and may make matters worse.

Recently I saw Tammy, a seven-year-old girl who was generally very cooperative and well behaved, and she was doing well in school. She apparently had many friends and, to all outward appearances, was busy and happy during the day. She seemed to get along well with her parents and an older brother, and the family did not seem to have any major problems. It was not apparent that she had strong fears until bedtime. Then she seemed to change completely.

She pleaded in an almost irrational manner to stay up. She would beg to be allowed to sleep in her parents' room and would do anything, including accepting punishment, to be allowed to do so. She was willing to sleep on their floor in a sleeping bag, and if they tried to carry her to her own room she would hang on to their legs, sobbing.

The struggle became so intense that her parents finally gave in and let her sleep on their floor most nights. Although this helped, Tammy still refused to go up to the bedroom ahead of her parents. In the end, she became reluctant even to be on the second floor alone during the day.

Tammy did have tremendous anxiety, which became overwhelming at bedtime. In the quiet darkness of the night while just lying in bed, scary fantasies which she seemed unable to control began to fill her mind. At this point, firmness would not have helped and would only have intensified the problem. If her parents had tried to put her in her room and close the door, Tammy would not have settled down or felt reassured, she would have become hysterical. Tammy needed sympathy and attention while her parents tried to help relieve her of the intense anxiety.

In situations like Tammy's, the nighttime fear is not a problem in and of itself. It is only a symptom of an emotional upset which needs to be treated first. Tammy and her parents began seeing a child psychologist. I suggested that during the first weeks of therapy Tammy should be allowed to continue to sleep on the floor in her parents' room and that one of the parents be upstairs at her bedtime to make it easier for her to go to sleep.

After several months in therapy, Tammy and her parents understood the cause of her fears. Some changes were made and gradually the fears resolved. Everyone was happier. And before long the nighttime problem took care of itself. Tammy redecorated her room a little, she began spending more time there during the day, and then she decided by herself to sleep in her own bed at night.

Psychotherapy, however, is not always necessary. If your child's fear is recent, even if it seems pronounced, it will likely disappear within a few weeks—with your support. You may have to find out what is causing your child to feel anxious during the day and help her overcome it. If she seems afraid to be in her room alone at night, it may be helpful to spend time there with her during the day, reading, talking, or playing a game. Gradually you can encourage her to spend more time there without you, first in the day, then in the evening, to help her feel comfortable again being there alone. At first you should be more lenient with her when she goes to bed. Sit with her if it is necessary. But as the intensity of her fear decreases, you will have to be firmer to re-establish normal routines and to prevent temporary adjustments from becoming permanent.

However, if your child is still extremely fearful and shows no sign of improvement in a month or so, if her nighttime fears are accompanied by a sense of real panic, and if your being firm leads to hysteria, not just angry crying, then, like Tammy's family, you may need outside help. This can be a difficult decision but you do not have to make it alone. Discuss the problem with your pediatrician or consult with a therapist for an initial evaluation to help you decide on a course of action. Many factors, usually relating to your child's age, stage of development, and the particular circumstances of her life, can contribute to such intense fears. If you begin seeing a counselor or therapist trained to work with children, he or she will work with you and your child to help you identify and then deal satisfactorily with these factors. Once this is done, the nighttime fears should disappear, as they did with Tammy.

Part Two

THE SLEEPLESS CHILD

Chapter 5

What Your Child Associates with Falling Asleep—the Key Problem

Your infant or toddler may be one of the many children who suffer from a severe sleep disturbance: he or she can't seem to settle himself or herself alone at night. Instead, he needs your help—you may have to hold and rock him, rub his back, or talk to him—until he falls asleep. Even then the problems are not over. During the night he wakes several times crying or calling out, and each time you must go in and help him go back to sleep again. In all likelihood you are tired and frustrated and probably angry at your child because your own sleep is so disrupted. At the same time you may feel guilty about your anger because you realize your child is not waking on purpose to spite you, and you feel that if he needs you it is your job to be there. You want to do what is best for your child, and if this means less sleep for you, then you believe you must learn to accept it. Furthermore, you may have been told that this behavior is part of a "normal" phase for some children and that there is nothing to do but wait until he outgrows it. Still, you wonder: "Is it really normal? Do I really have to wait, and if so, for how long?"

If you have such questions, you will be interested to learn that this behavior is not normal and that you do not have to wait for it to change. Although ongoing sleep problems are very common in young children, they are not an inherent and necessary part of growing up (unlike *occasional* problems, which may be). You can almost always identify correctable causes of these sleep disturbances and treat them successfully. If your child is at least five or six months old, you can begin to take the steps necessary to solve his sleep problems. If you wait and do nothing, his sleep will eventually improve on its own, but it could take many months or even years. However, if you find out why your child is sleeping poorly and make the necessary changes, he should be sleeping well in a few days to two weeks.

Betsy was a ten-month-old baby who was causing her parents much distress. Although she began to sleep through the night when she was three months old, at four months she started to wake repeatedly. When I saw her she was still difficult to put down, and she continued to wake up several times each night. In the evening Betsy's mother or father had to rock her and rub her back until she fell asleep, which usually took twenty minutes. They said that Betsy seemed to be trying to stay awake instead of letting herself fall asleep. She would begin to doze off then would suddenly open her eyes and look around before starting to nod off again. Her parents could not move her into the crib until she had been solidly asleep for fifteen minutes, or she would wake and start crying again. It was difficult to decide when her sleep was deep enough for her to be moved successfully. If her mother or father moved too soon from the rocker, she might wake and they would have to start all over.

Occasionally when Betsy started to wake as she was placed in the crib it was possible to rub her back and get her to sleep again. But here too, if her parents stopped rubbing her back and began to leave the room too soon, she would wake and cry again. Once Betsy was so deeply asleep that she could be left or placed in her crib without waking, she would remain asleep for several hours.

Between midnight and about 4:00 A.M., however, Betsy would wake several times. Each time she would cry vigorously and would not settle on her own. At these times she did not seem to be in pain, and in fact when her mother or father went in, picked her up and began to rock her, she would quiet promptly and return to sleep quickly. Again, she had to be deeply asleep before being put down in the crib, but this was usually easier during the night than at bedtime and rarely took longer than five minutes. From 4:00 to 7:00 A.M. Betsy slept well, but she usually woke crying in the morning.

Betsy had two naps, one in the morning and one in the afternoon, and she had to be rocked to sleep for both of these just as at bedtime.

Betsy's parents had let her cry several times for fifteen or twenty minutes before rocking her to sleep. This did not help. On one occasion, at the doctor's suggestion, they planned to let her cry until she fell asleep on her own. Betsy just cried harder and harder, and after an hour and a half her parents decided they were being cruel and couldn't stand to listen to any more crying, so they went in to comfort and rock her. Finally they asked the doctor for medication for Betsy. He prescribed an antihistamine, which Betsy took for one week. During that time she fell asleep a bit more quickly at bedtime, but night-time wakings and trouble at naptimes remained the same.

Although a problem like Betsy's is an extremely common one, it can be quite frustrating for you as parents. Yet once you understand the nature of the problem, it is usually fairly easy to correct.

What most parents don't realize is that what they view as abnormal wakings in the night are actually quite normal. And what they do to try to treat the "abnormal" wakings—namely going in to help their child go back to sleep—is actually *causing* the disturbance.

All children learn to associate certain conditions with falling asleep. For most children this means being in a particular bedroom, lying in a certain crib or bed, and holding a favorite stuffed animal or a special blanket. Such conditions are still present when these children wake normally at night between sleep cycles, and because they are, the children return to sleep rapidly. The conditions that Betsy and children like her have come to associate with falling asleep, however, are ones that are not present all night. The conditions are changed after these children fall asleep. This means these children cannot simply fall back asleep quickly after waking normally at night. For Betsy these conditions were being held, rocked, and having her back rubbed. When Betsy had normal nighttime arousals, however, she was lying in her crib alone, so she could not simply go back to sleep. She did not know how to do this by herself; she needed someone to come in.

Children like Betsy cannot fall asleep or return to sleep unless the "right" conditions are present. During the night these children have the usual nighttime wakings, but instead of these arousals being brief, they are prolonged because the children have not learned how to return to sleep on their own. The conditions they have learned to associate with falling asleep—rocking, back rubs, pacifier—are no longer present. Things are different from when the child fell asleep; something is "wrong." Instead of going back to sleep, the child wakes more fully and begins to cry. Thus the problem is *not one of abnormal wakings* but one of *difficulty in falling back asleep*. And the difficulty arises because of the child's particular associations with falling asleep. It will be easier to understand these problems in children if we are more aware of the types of sleep associations we all have.

Sleep Associations in Adults

As adults, we probably take our own associations with falling asleep for granted, but they are very important to us. We all learn to fall asleep under a certain set of conditions. For example, we usually go to sleep on a certain side of the bed, with a hard or soft pillow, with a heavy or light blanket, or after watching the news, listening to the radio, or reading. If the routine varies we may have some difficulty falling asleep. Some of us are more able than others to tolerate such changes, but all of us will feel the change to some extent.

As you will remember from Chapter 2, we spend most of the first few hours of the night in deep non-dreaming (Stage IV non-REM) sleep and the rest of the night we alternate between lighter non-REM (Stage II) sleep and dreaming (REM). Children usually return to deep sleep near morning. We all have brief wakings, especially during the transitions between non-REM and REM sleep. During these arousals we change body position, which is important to our physical well-being, and briefly check our environment to make sure everything is as it should be. Typically we turn over, straighten the blanket, and reposition the pillow. If all is well we return to sleep rapidly, usually without memory of the waking. At these times, however, if there are strange noises or worrisome smells, we do not simply return to sleep but wake more fully to investigate. It is not just potential danger that would keep us from returning to sleep. If anything doesn't seem "right," or if something is not the same as when we went to sleep, we may alert fully.

Think for a moment what it would be like if you had a normal waking during the night, turned over, and found your pillow gone. It would feel "wrong," and rather than simply returning to sleep you would wake more completely and begin to look for your pillow. If it had simply fallen on the floor, you would pick it up and probably return to sleep quickly. But what if your pillow was really gone? What if someone took it as a prank? It's unlikely that you would simply go back to sleep. Instead, you would turn on the light, get out of bed, and begin looking for it. You might get angry, curse, and show the same type of frustration that a child shows when he cries.

Even if your pillow fell out of bed every night, you would be able to reach over and pick it up and return to sleep fairly quickly. But if you were handicapped and if someone else had to come into the room to give you the pillow each time, then your sleep would show a pattern of what might be seen as "abnormal" wakings. Yet your friend would learn that by giving you back your pillow he or she could help you get to sleep again quickly. I think you will begin to see the parallel here.

Let's take this a step further. What if someone were stealing your pillow every night? If that happened, even falling asleep at bedtime would be difficult because you would know that as soon as you were asleep you would run the risk of having the pillow taken. Each time you started to fall asleep, you might catch yourself and become alert in an effort to prevent this loss.

Wrong Sleep Associations

For Betsy, the act of falling asleep meant being held and rocked in a rocking chair. This felt "right," and anything else felt "wrong." She could fall asleep fairly easily in this setting and probably if she remained there all night her sleep would seem more continuous. The person holding her might note that she would occasionally stir during the night, move around, and fall back to sleep, but she would not cry. Betsy had learned that as soon as she fell asleep she would be put down, and she had to be on guard for this. This seemed to interfere with her initial descent into sleep. Either she self-alerted, checking to make sure that she was still being rocked, or she was slightly aroused by a change in the rhythm of rocking or by the movement of being transferred to her crib. Once she was so deeply asleep that she would not sense the move to the crib, she slept well until her first spontaneous waking. Then, instead of simply moving about and returning to sleep on her own, things again felt "wrong." So, like an adult who finds himself or herself without a pillow and is unable to return to sleep, Betsy became frustrated. And she showed her frustration by beginning to cry. One of her parents would come in and re-establish the conditions Betsy associated with falling asleep so that she could fall back asleep once again. The fact that she could fall asleep rapidly in her parents' arms was proof that she had no actual sleep impairment. There could be no inherent abnormality in her ability to sleep which would allow her to fall asleep quickly in her parents' arms but not alone in her crib. The inability to settle alone in her crib was due to her experience, her *sleep associations.*

This disorder occurs most often in infants and toddlers, because older children have more control of the conditions in which they sleep and are less likely to need your participation. It remains common up to about age four.

Recently I worked with Bill, a three-and-a-half-year-old who had always had problems settling at bedtime and then again after several wakings during the night. Six months ago he moved from a crib into a bed and the pattern changed somewhat. Instead of rocking him to sleep, his parents began to lie down on the bed with him. When they did this he would usually fall asleep fairly quickly, although occasionally he would wake up if they tried to leave his bed too soon. He would sleep for about four or five hours then wake up calling his parents. He might complain about being "scared" or "seeing monsters," but he never seemed truly frightened. If his mother or father did not come in he would become more demanding and would sometimes go to their room and refuse to return to his bed. The parents were concerned about Bill's "anxiety" at night, so one of them always took him back to his bed and lay down with him. They knew he would then fall back to sleep within five or ten minutes. The parent would then return to bed, although occasionally he or she might fall asleep in Bill's bed. Typically Bill would wake one or two more times during the night. If his parent had remained in his bed, he seemed to sleep through the night.

Once again, Bill's problem was not one of abnormal wakings, but one of his particular associations with falling asleep. Bill could not fall asleep unless one of his parents was with him. However, not all problems with sleep associations have to do with the need to have a parent close by while falling asleep.

Sammy, age two, is another child who always had trouble going to sleep and staying asleep. His parents found it easier to let Sammy fall asleep on the couch next to one of them while they watched television. With this routine, the bedtime struggles seemed to disappear. Sammy could then be moved into his bed at their convenience, and he usually did not wake at that time. However, he would wake up several hours later, call out, seem to be wide awake, and not want to go back to sleep. In fact, if anything, he seemed to want to play. It could be difficult to get him back to sleep, even if the parents lay down with him or took him into their bed. He would not seem to be afraid, and sometimes his parents would just turn on his light and let him play, which he might do for an hour or so before falling asleep on the floor. Most often, however, he would not go back to sleep on his own. His parents found it easier to simply accompany him back to the living room, turn on the television and lie down on the couch while Sammy continued to play. Eventually he would lie down on the other end of the couch, fall asleep, and usually sleep through until morning.

Sammy certainly had developed the wrong associations with falling asleep, although in his case the associations were more focused on the living room, the couch, and the television than the need to be close to one of his parents. Furthermore, even though he could fall asleep only with the lights and TV on, he never fell asleep rapidly, because the light and TV also tended to keep him awake.

Most of us know that falling asleep listening to a TV or radio is not a good idea. If there is anything of interest it will catch our attention, and even if there is not, the constant changes in speech and music do interfere with falling asleep and remaining asleep. And once we do fall asleep, we may wake abruptly when the TV or radio is turned off. It is much better to learn to associate falling asleep with a dark, quiet environment.

Some children may also have associations that interfere with falling asleep even if they always fall asleep in their own beds alone in a dark, quiet room. Martin, for example, was an eight-month-old baby who always fell asleep with a pacifier in his mouth. He usually fell asleep quickly at bedtime, although not always. He would get drowsy, stop sucking, then wake, as Betsy had if the rocking stopped too soon, and have to start sucking again. Unlike Betsy, who could let someone else handle the rhythmical motions associated with her falling asleep, Martin had to do the movements himself. He had to suck to fall asleep, and when he stopped as sleep approached, he would wake. Occasionally the pacifier would fall out too soon and he would cry until it was replaced. At night he would wake three or four times crying, until one of his parents went in and put the pacifier back in his mouth so that he could quiet and return to sleep.

Heather was very similar to Martin. At eighteen months of age she still fell asleep at bedtime sucking on a bottle. She too woke several times each night but always fell back to sleep when she was handed another bottle. Nobody had to be there to hold her. Since she took only one or two ounces each time and since she was not held during the feeding, her association with the bottle was the cause of her problem rather than drinking too much liquid at night (see Chapter 6) or associations with being held.

Even though Martin and Heather both fell asleep alone and in their own beds, on waking at night they could not, by themselves, re-establish the conditions they associated with falling asleep. Someone else had to get up, come in, and replace the pacifier or bottle.

If your pillow falls out of bed you can get it yourself and return to sleep normally. Similarly, a child who falls asleep sucking his thumb can put his thumb back in his mouth after waking at night. But if your child needs your help to re-establish sleep conditions, then you will have to get up during the night—often more than once.

Thus for your child to sleep well at night he must learn to fall asleep alone in his crib or bed *and* he must fall asleep under conditions that he can re-establish for himself after waking at night. These conditions should not be stimulating, like Sammy's TV, and they should not require ongoing activity, like sucking a bottle or pacifier. What is best for almost all children then, after the first few months of life, is to learn to fall asleep in a crib or bed alone in a room that is fairly dark and quiet. They should not be held, rocked, or nursed and will be better off if they are not soothed with a bottle or pacifier, or the radio or television.

How to Solve the Problem

If you have a child like Betsy who is still in a crib, treatment of improper sleep associations is fairly simple and the change will be quite rapid. A young baby's sleep will show marked improvement, usually within a few days but at least within a week or two. You will have to help your child learn a new set of sleep associations. As you do so, you will need to be understanding, patient, and consistent until he adapts to the new patterns. There is no way to treat this problem without having to listen to *some* crying, but you can keep it to a minimum.

Think again about having to sleep without your pillow. If it became necessary, say for orthopedic reasons, that you sleep without a pillow, you would most likely find it quite difficult in the beginning. You would probably be uncomfortable at bedtime and thrash around searching for a comfortable position. You would no doubt curse your bad back and your doctor vehemently, even though you understood fully the importance of sleeping without the pillow. Also, even after you finally fell asleep, *you would find it hard to return to sleep after nighttime arousals.* Still, the only way that you could learn to fall asleep without your pillow would be to actually practice doing so. Each time you fell asleep without a pillow it would be easier, until it began to feel "right." At this point nighttime "wakings" would also cease to be a problem. And so it is with the children I treat.

The program I used with Betsy's family usually works quite well. I explained to them that Betsy was completely normal and that the nature of her sleep problem was her inability to fall asleep except while being held, rocked, and having her back rubbed. She had fallen asleep this way all her life and had never learned to fall asleep alone. I told them that Betsy would have to learn to fall asleep at bedtime under the same conditions that would be present when she woke spontaneously during the night, namely *alone and in her own crib.*

I used a progressive approach which is very effective and which I'll explain in detail here. The chart on page 78 (Figure 5) will help you to understand this method.

Once Betsy's parents understood the nature of her problem, we were ready to begin treatment. I asked them how long they felt they could listen to Betsy cry before feeling they had to do something.

Although they thought they could probably tolerate up to fifteen minutes of crying, we decided to start at five. I find that five minutes is usually a good place to begin, but if that seems too long you can even start at one minute!

Each night, at bedtime and after nighttime wakings, Betsy's parents were to be sure she fell asleep alone, without their being in her room. They were to allow her to cry for gradually longer periods of time before returning to her *briefly*, but they were always to leave while she was still awake. This was to continue until she finally fell asleep. The times of waiting before responding to her would then increase progressively on successive nights.

In Betsy's case, her parents got her ready for bed, had a little quiet play and talked to her, then put her in her crib *awake*. They were not to rock her or rub her back. They then left the room for *five* minutes and returned if she was still crying vigorously. They would stay in the room for two or three minutes, but were not to pick Betsy up or begin rocking her. Their return was to reassure Betsy that she was not being abandoned and that her parents were still there to care for her. It also helped to reassure the parents that even though Betsy was crying she was still all right and that they were not doing anything terrible to her. They were *not* going back in the room to help her fall asleep; in fact, Betsy had to fall asleep when her parents were out of the room. The parents agreed to speak to Betsy briefly and perhaps pat her back once or twice to help her quiet down, but within a few minutes they were to leave again, whether or not she was still crying and even if her crying intensified when they left.

If Betsy continued to cry vigorously for *ten* minutes, her parents were to return for the same brief intervention. And if she was still crying in *fifteen* more minutes they would return again. Fifteen minutes would be the maximum for the first night, and they would continue waiting for fifteen-minute intervals with brief return visits until Betsy finally fell asleep during one of the fifteen-minute periods that they were out of her room. If the crying had stopped, or if it was only mild whimpering, they were not to go back in. If Betsy woke up later in the night and began crying hard, they would begin the same type of program that they had used at bedtime, namely waiting for five minutes and working up to fifteen minutes. Since her usual waking time was 7:00 A.M., the parents were to continue this routine at all wakings until at least 6:30 A.M. If she woke after that, or if she was still awake then after waking earlier, they were to get her up for the morning.

They were to use the same routine at naptimes. However, if an hour had passed and Betsy was either still crying or awake after a short sleep, they would end the nap for that period. If she was still tired and later fell asleep on the floor or in the playpen, that would be all right. At least she was falling asleep alone. As long as the time in her crib was enforced each day, she would eventually start to nap there—once she began to associate lying alone in her crib with falling asleep.

On the second day of the program, Betsy's parents were to wait ten minutes before going into her room for the first time, moving up to a maximum of twenty minutes. This five-minute increase of all times would continue on each successive night.

The response Betsy's family had was quite typical. They braced themselves for the worst and found that things went much better than they had expected.

Their first night was difficult, although Betsy did fall asleep during the third fifteen-minute episode of crying. She had three wakings during the night, but she seemed to go to sleep more rapidly after each of them. On the second night, Betsy fell asleep after the first intervention in her second period of crying and fell back asleep on her own after waking during the night. On the third night, Betsy fell asleep on her own before any interventions were necessary and went back to sleep after spontaneous wakings during the night. By the second week hardly any nighttime wakings were still apparent. Her naps improved even more quickly. There were difficulties the first two days—the first naptime she didn't sleep at all—but by day three she was doing fine (see Figure 4).

Her parents reported several facts that are quite typical. As things were getting better they found that even though the nighttime wakings persisted at first, they heard shorter and shorter episodes of whimpering, after which Betsy would return to sleep on her own. Eventually she did not cry at all during these wakings. Of course her natural arousals continued, but her return to sleep was so rapid and uneventful that we would only be aware of them if she was actually observed closely or monitored all night. Many parents report the whimpering and then spontaneous return to sleep during the period in which the child is learning the new associations.

Because the parents were allowed to go in during Betsy's crying, as opposed to having to leave her all night, they could see that she was not really suffering, and that made it much easier for them to follow through on the program. By the end of the first week Betsy was sleeping quite well. Throughout the second week her sleep patterns were essentially normal. It has been many months since Betsy's parents first decided to help her sleep better, and her sleep has remained excellent.

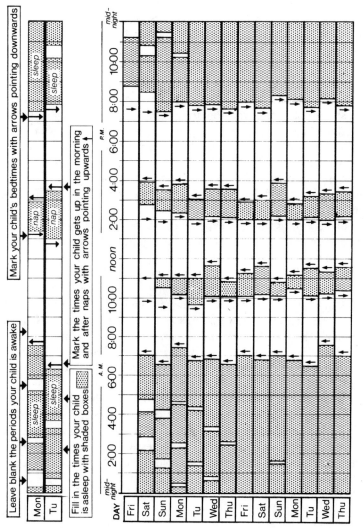

FIGURE 4 Betsy's Sleep Chart

65

This gradual approach is better for the child and easier for you to do than a "cold turkey" routine. Although putting your child in the crib at bedtime, shutting the door, letting him cry, and not returning until morning probably will work eventually if you never give in, there are good reasons to avoid this. Such an approach would be painful for you, it is difficult for your child, and you will be very tempted to quit in the middle. If, like Betsy, your child has always fallen asleep in your arms and if you have always gone to him quickly when he wakes, then to suddenly put him down awake one night and not respond to his cries until morning would be going from one extreme to the other. Such an abrupt change may be quite confusing to your child. He has learned to expect your prompt appearance when he cries. What is he to think if you don't come in? Where are you? What has happened? Are you ever coming back?

I believe it is better to use a more gradual approach. Your child has to learn some new rules, but he won't understand them at first. He should know that you are still nearby and taking care of him. And he can only learn this through experience. If you let him cry alone each night and do not return at all until morning, he will still learn that you always do come back eventually and that you are not really abandoning him, but the learning may be unnecessarily difficult. If you wait only a short period of time before going in, and then increase the waiting time progressively, the learning is much easier. Your child will begin to see after only a few minutes what you have planned. He finds out quickly that you are still around and responsive to him. There is much less uncertainty. And as you gradually increase the waiting times, he learns to expect this also. Eventually he will learn it is no longer worth it to cry for fifteen or twenty minutes just to have you come in briefly. He knows you will come, but there is little else to gain —no rocking, holding, or nursing. At the same time, he is learning how to fall asleep alone and in bed. This is the main goal. Because you are helping your child learn by progressive teaching, the amount of crying is kept to a minimum. A "cold turkey" approach, however, is more likely to keep the crying near maximum.

Although I don't recommend it, I did say that simply "letting him cry" could work. But parents often say to me, "If you're going to suggest I let my baby cry, forget it; we already tried it and it didn't work." What they tried was "cold turkey." If you have tried this approach unsuccessfully, you might be interested to learn why it failed. Perhaps you simply found, quite understandably, that you could not or would not listen to two or three hours of crying night after night. Although a child under one year of age may surprise you and fall asleep on even the first night after only a short period of crying, an older child will likely continue to cry constantly or intermittently for at least one or more hours. And the longer he cries, the more likely it is you will change your plans and decide to go in. Also, you may not have understood fully how this approach was supposed to work. Since you may have been told that you were "spoiling" your child and that you should simply let him cry, the message was that the *crying* would lead to better sleep. But the crying does not help at all. Better sleep comes only when the child learns how to fall asleep, and return to sleep, alone. And this happens only when he gets practice doing just this. So when a family tells me, "We tried letting him cry for several nights," it usually turns out that this is all they did—they *let him cry* but did not *let him fall asleep.* For example, they might have let their child cry on waking at night, but after twenty or thirty minutes they would go in and rock him. And at bedtime they may have continued to rock him to sleep without letting him cry at all. Or they may have let him cry for up to three hours at bedtime several nights in a row, but always went in eventually to help him go to sleep. In effect then, all that crying was for nothing, because it is not the crying that helps but the practice of falling asleep under new conditions.

If the final transitions to sleep still occur under the old conditions, things will not improve no matter how much crying there is. You cannot learn how to fall asleep without a pillow if every night you go to sleep with a pillow but have someone take it away after you are sleeping soundly. To learn to fall asleep without a pillow it is best to be without one each and every time you fall asleep. Similarly, for a child to learn to fall asleep without being held or rocked, without the TV on, and without a pacifier, none of these "sleep aids" should be present at any of the times he goes to sleep—at bedtime, at naptime, or after nighttime wakings.

I believe you will understand, then, why crying does not help in developing appropriate sleep associations and why we try to keep crying to a minimum. Initially, as your child tries to learn to fall asleep a new way, he will be unhappy, but he should not have to feel abandoned or deserted. If you come in regularly to comfort him, he will feel less deserted, and the very long periods of crying we see with a cold turkey approach do not usually occur.

For Martin and Heather we used the same routine as with Betsy, except they were put down without a bottle or pacifier. I told the parents that it was better if they did not initially stay with their child while he or she learned to fall asleep without the bottle or pacifier, since this would only lead to new associations which would have to be broken as a second step. Most families, like Martin's and Heather's, choose to correct the associations in a single step. Martin and Heather were typical of children who already know how to fall asleep in bed alone but need a bottle or pacifier. Once they had a few opportunities to practice falling asleep without them, these children quickly learned to sleep very well.

It is not necessary to wean your child in order to break the association of nursing with falling asleep. It is only necessary to dissociate the two. Thus, instead of nursing at bedtime you may nurse earlier in the evening, and daytime nursing need not be at naptime. If your child starts to fall asleep at the breast or with a bottle, stop and place him in the crib or bed—let him continue to fall asleep in that setting.

If your child is taking a lot of fluid at night, whether from bottle or breast, his sleep may be disturbed in several ways other than just by the effects of the sleep associations. At the same time, however, suddenly stopping the nursing at night would be hard on your child and difficult for you. For this reason it is a better idea to reduce gradually the number and frequency of feedings. The problems of excessive feedings and their solutions are discussed in the next chapter.

If your child uses the pacifier only when he is going to sleep, then once he learns how to fall asleep without it, he will no longer use it at all. But if he has it in his mouth most of the day, then it is going to be more difficult to simply eliminate it at night. In this case I suggest you work first to decrease the amount of time your child has his pacifier during the day. You can be with him then to give him extra attention and provide diversions so that he will get used to having it less often. Still, you may have to listen to some crying during the day as he learns to feel comfortable without the pacifier, just as you do when he learns new associations at night.

Decide on certain periods in the morning and afternoon when your child should not use the pacifier, then increase the time periods gradually each day. Once he is using the pacifier mainly at sleep or rest times, you can eliminate it and begin the progressive program we used for Betsy. By now he will be quite used to being without the pacifier and will only have to learn how to fall asleep without it.

The treatments for Bill and Sammy were based on the same progressive approach used for Betsy, although the procedures were a little different because they were older and able to get out of bed on their own. For older children, intervention sometimes has to proceed a bit more slowly, but should be just as successful. Still, the child must learn to fall asleep with the same set of conditions that will be present at the time of normal nighttime wakings, namely alone and in bed.

If your child is used to having you with him when he falls asleep and no longer sleeps in a crib, you can break the association in one of several ways.

Explain to your child, if he is old enough, that you can no longer lie down with him while he falls asleep. Make sure you have an appropriate and pleasant bedtime ritual, however (see Chapter 3). When you finish the story, quiet talk, or game, tuck your child in, then leave the room, but leave the door open. Some children will only keep calling out or crying; others will get out of bed. If your child simply calls out he can be handled in exactly the same way we treated Betsy. Simply increase progressively the amount of time between your brief responses to him. Go back into the room but do *not* lie on his bed, and always make sure he falls asleep when you are *out* of the room.

If your child gets out of bed, then you will need to employ a different approach. When you are certain your child has gotten out of bed, go back into the room and put him back in bed and tell him that he must stay in bed or you will have to close the door. If he gets out of bed again, put him back in again and close the door for a very brief period, about one minute. Don't lock the door, but hold it closed if he tries to pull it open. Locking a child in his room is very scary for him and will not help this new learning process. Simple door closing is a much more controlled pattern of enforcement than, for example, trying to hold your child in bed, spanking him, or locking the door and leaving. You want to show him that having the door open is under *his* control. If he stays in bed, the door stays open; if he gets out of bed, the door stays closed. It is as simple as that. If you prefer you may use a gate instead of a closed door, as long as your child is unable to open it. In this case just be sure that you are out of his view during the periods of gate closure.

Do *not* spank or threaten your child. It will only make matters worse. It is important that he know you understand he is having a tough time and you want to help him through this period. Please offer support, not punishment.

You may continue to talk to your child in a reassuring manner through the closed door, or from another room if you are using a gate, so that he will know you are still nearby. Tell him if he gets back in bed you will be able to leave the door open after the minute is up. If he does not get back into bed, go in yourself, put him down, close the door, and wait two minutes. If he continues to get out of bed, increase the door closure to three minutes and then to five minutes (see the chart in Figure 6 on page 79). Five minutes should be the maximum for the first night. When your child finally does stay in bed or goes back to bed on his own, open the door after the time is up, give him a word of encouragement, then leave without going into the room. If he starts getting out of bed again later, perhaps after nighttime wakings, follow the same routine you used at bedtime, starting again at one minute. On the second night begin with two minutes and increase this each subsequent night as shown in the chart. If he wakes and cries but does not get out of bed, switch to the routine of waiting longer before you respond briefly (Figure 5). Naptimes too will have to be controlled with the door-closing technique, but if your child has not fallen asleep after one hour, or if he is awake again after a period of sleep, declare the nap over for that day.

The first few nights will not be easy, and children will vary in how much they are willing to struggle. Some will learn quickly that they would prefer to stay in bed and have the door open than get out of bed and have the door closed even briefly. Other children continue getting out of bed a number of times, being willing to accept longer periods of door closure before giving in. This method will likely take longer than with a child confined to a crib, but it works. If you persevere, things should still be much better within one or two weeks at the most. But you should follow the schedule consistently. Your child must learn exactly what to expect. If you are lenient sometimes and firm others, your child will always assume that this may be one of the times you are going to give in.

If your child is old enough, usually three or three and a half, you may want to try a reward system to help the initial phase of relearning go much faster. This can be done before, or in association with, the door-closing technique. You can set up a star chart like the one described in Chapter 12, so that he will earn stars or stickers and occasional small prizes for going to sleep without getting out of bed. The star chart will help to motivate him to try to go to sleep without your presence, and it will allow him to feel that you and he are working together to solve this problem. When the novelty of the star chart wears off he may begin to make more demands at bedtime again. If so, you will have to be especially careful not to give in or the old problems could reappear. However, now that your child has learned how to fall asleep on his own, it is no longer a matter of teaching him how to do it, but simply of enforcing the rules. If you are firm, and start or restart the door-closing routine if necessary, the good sleep patterns will return quickly.

If the sudden change from having you with him when he falls asleep to having to do so alone seems too large a step for your child to take all at once, then you can proceed in more gradual steps. But this will take longer, and your child may have to go through a period of re-learning each step of the way. If you want to try a more gradual approach, you should still institute a pleasant bedtime ritual. Tell your child that you cannot lie in bed with him when he falls asleep. But instead of actually leaving the room, agree to sit on a chair near his bed until he falls alseep. If he accepts this, fine. But if he tries to get out of bed or tries to get you into his bed, then begin the door-closing routine. However, on opening the door, return to the chair. Thus your child will learn that, by his own behavior, he can control having you either in the room near him or out of the room and the door closed. Your being in bed with him is not an option, and he will quickly learn that he prefers to have you nearby than outside. Once he has accomplished this, you have helped him with the major part of the relearning. He is now falling asleep in his bed alone, although you are still in the room.

The next steps may be taken at one- to two-week intervals. The first step is to move your chair farther away from your child's bed. Next move your chair just outside his bedroom door. Finally you should simply leave his bedtime area altogether after saying goodnight. Each of these steps should be enforced with the same door-closing routine as necessary. There may be struggles with each step, but the first—your getting out of his bed—will probably be the hardest. Usually the second most difficult step is removing yourself from his room alto-gether.

If your child seems to be very anxious, this gradual approach may be necessary. But in general I prefer the one-step method because it is less protracted and allows a good sleep pattern to emerge much more rapidly, with only one difficult period of relearning. Further-more, in the more gradual approach, the time it takes your child to fall asleep may be extended, since he knows that you will leave once he falls asleep, and he may begin to fight sleep, alerting each time he enters the drowsy state, much as Betsy did.

Bill had always fallen asleep in physical contact with a parent, ini-tially in the rocking chair, but more recently in his bed; and being alone in bed felt "wrong" to him. His parents opted for the first ap-proach. They did in fact face major struggles over the first few days. They got little sleep and began to wonder if the plan would work. But they persevered and by the end of the first week Bill was beginning to sleep much better. By the end of the second week his protests when his parents left the room were very mild, and now he sleeps continu-ously through the night.

For Sammy, falling asleep meant not only being near a parent but being in a room other than his own with the television on. Not many of us are faced with such difficulties. Imagine how you might react to waking at night and finding yourself in a room other than the one in which you went to sleep. This would certainly tend to rouse you rather than allow you to return to sleep. This is what was happening to Sammy. Unfortunately for him, the existing associations for falling asleep did not even include his own bedroom.

Sammy had had no formal bedtime ritual at all, and when he woke in the night the only way he could recreate the conditions he associated with falling asleep was to go to the living room and play while the television was on. Sammy's parents chose a program similar to Bill's. They began a pleasant bedtime ritual, which Sammy quite enjoyed, although he was less enthused at first about being put into bed and told to stay there. As with Bill, Sammy struggled valiantly over the first week to maintain the status quo, but by the second week he too was sleeping quite normally.

As you have seen, consistent, progressive learning of new routines can be very difficult to initiate, but it works remarkably well in a variety of situations. If your child's problem is similar to those of the children described in this chapter, your program can be very similar. The younger the child the easier it usually is to make changes, but children of all ages with this problem will respond well to the program if parents are willing to stick to it.

General Observations

There are some general points that are useful to keep in mind when you try to determine the cause of your child's sleep problem and correct it.

1. If after he wakes crying at night your child quiets rapidly and returns to sleep promptly as soon as you re-establish the conditions that were present at bedtime—such as rocking him in your arms— then you can be quite certain that his problem is only that he has learned to associate the wrong conditions with falling asleep. There is no inherent abnormality in his ability to sleep. The body systems controlling sleep in a child cannot function in such a way as to physically prevent that child from sleeping well unless he is being held or rocked. If these systems were not working properly, your child would not sleep well under *any* condition. Thus you can be sure that the cause of his sleep disturbance is not a neurologic abnormality, a dietary imbalance or food sensitivity, or significant discomfort. A child

who wakes because of pain may be soothed by being held, but he will not return to sleep almost immediately.

Does this mean that your child must have some physical problem if you are unable to get him back to sleep promptly? No it does not. He may stay awake because he is frightened. Or he may become so agitated if you do not respond to him instantly that it takes him a while to calm regardless of the conditions. Or, as we saw with Sammy, if he is accustomed to falling asleep in a stimulating environment (with the television on and people about), then he may have difficulty falling back asleep after waking at night, whether he is in a new non-stimulating environment (wrong conditions—too quiet and dark) or back in the stimulating one (because the television keeps him awake as much as it allows him to sleep).

There are a few situations, however, when physical problems can be responsible for sleep difficulties. These are discussed in Chapter 7.

2. You may have found that your child's sleep associations at bedtime do not always affect what happens later in the night. For example, he may sleep through the night without waking even though you always rock him to sleep at bedtime. Or he may fall asleep alone at bed- or naptime but needs to be rocked after nighttime wakings. This only means that your child has learned to associate different conditions with falling asleep at different times. He is no more or less normal than other children who seem to need the same conditions present each time they fall asleep. Therefore it is not necessarily wrong, or even sure to cause trouble, if you rock your child to sleep. If he falls asleep rapidly, is easy to move to his crib, and sleeps through the night, and if you are happy with this routine, then there is really no problem. Your only motivation to change would be the knowledge that if you teach him how to fall asleep on his own when he is young you can avoid having to go through the relearning process later when it may be more difficult, and your child will be more likely to continue sleeping through the night as he grows. But if the bedtime routine is prolonged, as it was with Betsy, you should certainly consider changing it. And if your child has wakings most nights that require your presence, then you definitely should alter the routines. It will be in your child's (and your) best interests to have continuous sleep at night.

3. Occasionally, when you are increasing the time before you respond to your child, he may cry so hard that he actually throws up. If you hear this happen you should go in even though the "time isn't up" yet. Clean him up and change the sheets and pajamas as needed. But do so quickly and matter-of-factly and then leave again. If you reward him for throwing up by staying with him, he will only learn

that this is a good way for him to get what he wants. Vomiting does not hurt your child, and you do not have to feel guilty that it happened. This, like the crying, will soon stop.

4. Even a child who wakes frequently at night may sleep well for several hours before his first nighttime waking and again after his last. For example, he may sleep from 7:00–10:00 P.M. and from 4:00–7:00 A.M. but be restless with frequent wakings between 10:00 P.M. and 4:00 A.M. This is only a reflection of the child's underlying normal pattern of sleep state cycling. As you learned in Chapter 2, the child spends the first few hours of the night in deep sleep and often returns to this same state near morning. The period of lighter sleep in between is more subject to wakings.

5. Once your child has learned how to fall asleep by himself with the proper associations, he will probably continue to sleep well. But there may be occasional disruptions. If you are visiting friends or relatives your child may have to share your room and you may want to respond to his whimpering quickly to be extra sure that he doesn't cry and disturb your hosts. Or your child may be sick with a high fever, perhaps in pain with an ear infection, so you sit with him or take him into your bed. Then when you get back home or when the illness passes, he wants to continue going to sleep under the "new" conditions. If you give in here, your child may well develop an on-going sleep disturbance. This happens commonly, especially during the second half-year of life. Temporary changes on a trip or during an illness are necessary and reasonable. But if your child's sleep remains disrupted after everything else has returned to normal, then you simply have to go back to the progressive program described in this chapter for several days to re-establish the previous patterns.

6. Parents often ask me, when they realize they will have to let their child do some crying, "Won't this cause permanent psychological harm?" They want their child to feel safe and cared for and are afraid that even several minutes of crying in a room alone will be traumatic.

Although this concern is common, I have learned that it always turns out to be only a temporary one. Allowing some crying while you help your child learn to improve his sleep will never lead to psychological harm. It will be harder on you than on your baby. Even the most concerned parents with whom I have worked have told me afterwards that they found the relearning process very helpful and not harmful for their child.

You want to do what is best for your child, and helping him form good sleep patterns is part of that. Your child cannot yet understand what is best for him and will cry if he doesn't get what he wants. You have to be the judge of what he can and cannot have and do. If what he wants is bad for him or dangerous, you won't give it to him no matter how hard he cries, and you won't feel guilty or be worried about possible psychological consequences. A poor sleep pattern is also bad for your child and it is your job to correct it. Therefore, there is no need to be overly concerned if he cries somewhat during the initial stages.

Of course if your child does not get enough love and attention during the day, then he may well develop psychological problems. But if you show your love and provide warmth and care during his early months and continue to show your affection during the day as he grows, then a little extra crying for a week or so—no matter how mournful or angry-sounding—will not hurt him in the least. Even when a child becomes more clingy for a day or two, as sometimes happens, the rapidity with which everything improves convinces parents that they have done the right thing. In fact, in terms of possible psychological effects, things can only improve. With better sleep at night, your child will feel better and be less irritable during the day. Since he will be more fun, and because you yourself will be more rested and less angry, you will be able to enjoy your child more and interact with him in a more positive and nurturing manner.

7. Once you decide on a schedule, follow it closely. Know ahead of time how long you are supposed to wait, and use a watch or clock. Your judgment in the middle of the night may not be very good, and ten minutes may seem like an hour. Sometimes, however, it may be better not to go in to your crying child even when the "time is up." If you notice that your baby is beginning to calm, going in and leaving again may only interrupt this and exacerbate things. If you sense that waiting a bit longer will actually be easier on your child, then do so. See if he will continue to calm on his own or if the crying starts to increase. You can always decide to go in if he becomes more upset.

8. If your child falls asleep by himself at naptime but needs you at night, then you can expect the relearning to go very quickly. He already knows how to fall asleep on his own; he simply has to learn to associate that behavior with nighttime as well.

9. If you have been going in to your child during the night to help him fall back asleep, you may have been told that you were spoiling him. That is not what is happening. You "spoil" a child if you give in to every request, never say no, and abdicate your responsibility to decide for him what is best. If you are going in at night it is more likely because you feel that is the right thing to do for him, not because you cannot say no or are incapable of discipline. In the daytime it may be

easier to distinguish your child's *wants* from his *needs*, and you will of course deny him any inappropriate requests without difficulty, even if he cries. But if he wakes and cries at night and only settles when nursed or rocked, you may decide he is hungry and needs to be fed or is in pain or has some basic need to be held. You may also think he has some inherent problem that makes it impossible for him to go back to sleep without the gentle rocking you can provide. Just as you know it is right to walk a colicky baby of two months, you may feel it is right to walk a sleepless crying child of six, twelve, twenty-four or thirty-six months. The problem is not that you are spoiling him but that you did not know enough about sleep and sleep associations to help you distinguish your child's *wants* from his *needs*.

Once you understand that your child's need is simply to learn a new way to fall asleep (whether it is what he wants or not) it is easier for you to see that this need is met.

10. When you are considering a program that will involve some crying or screaming at night, you may feel that it would be fine if you lived in the middle of the Sahara Desert or had only one child. But if you live in an apartment building you may be concerned about reactions from your neighbors and the landlord. If you have other children, and especially if they are young, you may be worried that they will be kept awake. And if you are going to use the door-closing technique, it is certainly more difficult with another child in the room.

Some of these problems are easier to solve than others. Explain to your neighbors what you are doing and tell them the problem should only last a few nights. Start the program on the weekend if they prefer. If they are still intolerant, you may want to wait until they will be away for a few days. Or you may have to use a very gradual approach, in which you stay in the room initially in an attempt to keep crying to a minimum.

As for your other children, you probably don't need to worry too much. Even if their sleep is disturbed for a few nights it will return to normal quickly. If another child shares the room with the one who will be doing the relearning, the other child may have to sleep in another room for a few nights, especially if you have to use the door-closing technique. Generally the child with the sleep problem wants his brother or sister back and that is further motivation for him to cooperate.

11. Since it is important that you follow through on your program consistently, you should wait for a convenient time to begin. Do not start at a time when you cannot afford to lose some sleep yourself—before an important meeting or a job interview, for example, or when

someone is coming for a visit. Even if the timing is otherwise all right, you may want to wait until a Friday night to begin so that you have the weekend to catch up on any missed sleep.

12. Many parents ask whether the same adult should handle all bedtimes and wakings during a period of relearning. Actually it is better if both parents take turns. Your child should feel comfortable with either parent at bedtime and after wakings. You do not have to alternate strictly—just pick a schedule that suits you best. One parent may find it easier to get up in the first half of the night and the other parent may prefer the second. Or, work demands may mean that one parent must do more on the weekends and the other on weekdays. If one parent has handled all the bedtimes and wakings till now, the other parent may have better luck breaking the old associations, since he or she isn't part of them. It is probably best that whichever parent is handling a particular waking, he or she should continue the responses until the child falls asleep, so that the child does not sense that by crying enough he can control who will come in.

For similar reasons it is good advice not to let your child insist that "I want Mommy" or "I want Daddy." You should decide who will handle each bedtime or waking and stick to it. You do more to convince your child of your love by staying than by giving in to his demands. Once he learns that you really mean that you want to be the one to care for him at that time, he will look forward to it, if that is part of the usual bedtime ritual, and in any case he will be more reassured.

During the actual relearning it is probably better not to use a sitter. But if this becomes necessary for a night or two you may let the sitter put your child to bed in the easiest manner. It is not fair to ask the sitter to follow through on your program, and the fact that he or she does it differently will not really affect what your child is coming to expect from you. So, if you have to be out one night, the program can be interrupted for that evening. Nothing will be lost in the long run. Just be sure to restart the program the next day. Once the new routines are well established, however, you might ask your sitter to try them.

If your child is left with a sitter most days, the sitter will know your child well, and he or she could be involved in the relearning program for naptimes. If this is not possible, or if you feel that it is inadvisable, then you may have to institute the program just at night. This should work anyway. When a sitter (or day-care provider) handles naptimes differently from the way you handle bedtimes, there are usually fewer problems than when you handle both bed- and naptimes yourself but do so in an inconsistent manner.

FIGURE 5 Helping Your Child Learn to Fall Asleep with the Proper Associations—The Progressive Approach

NUMBER OF MINUTES TO WAIT BEFORE GOING IN TO YOUR CHILD BRIEFLY

Day	At First Wait	If Your Child is Still Crying		
		Second Wait	Third Wait	Subsequent Waits
1	5	10	15	15
2	10	15	20	20
3	15	20	25	25
4	20	25	30	30
5	25	30	35	35
6	30	35	40	40
7	35	40	45	45

1. This chart shows the number of minutes to wait before going in if your child is crying at bedtime or after nighttime wakings.

2. Each time you go in to your child, spend only 2 to 3 minutes. Remember, you are going in briefly to reassure him and yourself, not necessarily to help him stop crying and certainly not to help him fall asleep. The goal is for him to learn to fall asleep alone, without being held, rocked, nursed, or using a bottle or pacifier.

3. When you get to the maximum number of minutes to wait for that night, continue leaving for that amount of time until your child finally falls asleep during one of the periods you are out of the room.

4. If he wakes during the night, begin the waiting schedule at the minimum waiting time for that day and again work up to the maximum.

5. Continue this routine after all wakings until reaching a time in the morning (usually 5:30 to 7:30 A.M.) you have previously decided to be reasonable to start the day. If he wakes after that time, or if he is still awake then after waking earlier, get him up and begin the morning routines.

6. Use the same schedule for naps, but if your child has not fallen asleep after one hour, or if he is awake again and crying vigorously after getting some sleep, end that naptime period.

7. The number of minutes listed to wait are ones that most families find workable. If they seem too long for you, use the times shown on the chart in Figure 6 on page 79 (though without closing the door). In fact, any schedule will work as long as the times increase progressively.

8. Be sure to follow your schedule carefully and chart your child's sleep patterns daily (Figure 8, page 105) so you can monitor his progress accurately.

9. By day 7 your child will most likely be sleeping very well, but if further work is necessary, just continue to add 5 minutes to each time on successive days.

FIGURE 6 Helping Your Child Learn to Stay in Bed

NUMBER OF MINUTES TO CLOSE THE DOOR IF YOUR CHILD WILL NOT STAY IN BED

		If Your Child Continues to Get Out of Bed			
Day	First Closing	Second Closing	Third Closing	Fourth Closing	Subsequent Closings
1	1	2	3	5	5
2	2	4	6	8	8
3	3	5	7	10	10
4	5	7	10	15	15
5	7	10	15	20	20
6	10	15	20	25	25
7	15	20	25	30	30

1. This chart shows the number of minutes to close your child's door if he will not stay in bed at bedtime or after nighttime wakings.

2. When you get to the maximum number of minutes for that night, continue closing the door for that amount of time until he finally stays in bed.

3. Keep the door closed for the number of minutes listed, even if your child goes back to bed sooner. However, you may talk to him through the door and tell him how much time remains.

4. When you open the door, speak to him briefly if he is in bed, offer encouragement, and leave. If he is still out of bed, restate the rules, put him back in bed (if it can be done easily), and shut the door for the next amount of time listed. If he lets you put him back easily and you are convinced he will stay there, you may try leaving the door open, but if you are wrong, do not keep making the same mistake.

5. If your child wakes during the night and won't stay in bed, begin the door-closing schedule at the minimum time for that day and again work up to the maximum.

6. Continue this routine as necessary after all wakings until reaching a time in the morning (usually 5:30 to 7:00 A.M.) previously decided to be reasonable to start the day.

7. Use the same routine at naptimes, but if your child has not fallen asleep after one hour, or if he is awake again and out of bed after getting some sleep, end that naptime period.

8. If he wakes and calls or cries but does not get out of bed, switch to the progressive routine described in the chart in Figure 5 on page 78.

9. The number of minutes listed to close the door are ones that most families find workable. However, you may change the schedule as you think best as long as the times increase progressively.

10. Be sure to follow your schedule carefully and chart your child's sleep patterns daily (Figure 8, page 105) so you can monitor his progress accurately.

11. Remember, your goal is to help your child learn to sleep alone. You are using the door as a controlled way of enforcing this, not to scare or punish him. So reassure him by talking through the door; do not threaten or scream. By progressively increasing the time of door closure, starting with short periods, your child does not have to be shut behind a closed door unsure of when it will be opened. He will learn that having the door open is entirely under his control.

12. By day 7 your child will most likely be staying in bed, but if further work is necessary, just continue to add 5 minutes to each time on successive days.

13. If you prefer you may use a gate instead of a closed door as long as your child can't open or climb over it. In this case you must be out of his view during the periods of gate closure, but you can still talk to him reassuringly from another room.

Feedings During the Night— Another Major Cause of Trouble

It may seem hard to imagine that your child's nighttime feeding can be the cause of a major sleep disturbance, but in fact that is very often the case. Once your baby is about three months old, he or she no longer needs to be fed at bedtime and again several more times during the night. Yet you may find that having your child fall asleep as you feed her at night is very rewarding for you and satisfying for her. And there is nothing wrong with continuing to nurse your child to sleep during her first year as long as you are happy doing so and as long as she sleeps through the night. But if she wakes repeatedly and has to be fed to go back to sleep, then she is developing a sleep problem, and the feedings are the cause.

Certainly a baby with this problem has learned to associate nursing with falling asleep, as we discussed in the last chapter; but when your child has large amounts of milk or juice at night, her sleep will be disturbed for other reasons as well. If she drinks a lot at night, her diapers may be soaked and the discomfort could certainly wake her. Also, some of her body rhythms can become irregular and interfere with a good night's sleep. For example, the extra fluid and calories your child ingests at night will stimulate her digestive system, which should be "shut down" for the night. The additional nutrients may also alter her release of various hormones.

Even the timing of her feelings of hunger may be affected. We all feel hungry at times of the day or night when we are accustomed to eating. So if your child gets used to being fed often during the night, she may wake feeling hungry, then nurse or take her bottle eagerly, even though she has simply *learned* to eat on this schedule and does *not* have a nutritional need for food at those times. This learned hunger then becomes a trigger of abnormal wakings.

Finally, it appears that a child's underlying sleep-wake and eating patterns may be disrupted by the repeated wakings as much as by the feedings. If your child becomes accustomed to being fed throughout the night, her system will begin to regard the nighttime sleep periods as only naps between feedings. You don't expect your baby to sleep for twelve hours when you put her down for her afternoon nap, and by the same token, because she is used to waking and being fed every few hours at night, she won't sleep twelve hours then either.

Sleep disruption caused by too much fluid at night usually occurs in children who are still breast feeding or using a bottle—in the first year or two. Cory, for example, was only eight months old when I first saw her. Her parents said that she fell asleep easily at bedtime while nursing at the breast. Once asleep, she could be moved into the crib without difficulty. She slept for two and a half hours, but then woke crying. Her father was unable to comfort her, and only her mother seemed able to put her back to sleep. When she picked Cory up and nursed her again, Cory would stop crying and go back to sleep within ten minutes. But she would continue to wake up every one or two hours during much of the night and the same process had to be repeated. Cory woke five or six times most nights and often had to be changed before nursing. Since her mother was always the one to take care of Cory in the night, she had become exhausted and frustrated. Occasionally she was so tired that she just wanted to let Cory cry, but her husband insisted that she go in. Not surprisingly, she was angry with both her husband and Cory, and there was a great deal of tension in the family.

You will probably recognize by now that Cory had associated falling asleep with being held and nursed. But when such associations are the only problem, a child usually has only a few full wakings at night. Only some of the normal partial wakings that occur during the night are followed by more complete waking with difficulty going back to sleep. Cory, however, woke much more often—sometimes hourly. I knew that something was either waking her frequently or was causing her to become fully awake after practically *every* partial arousal during the night.

Sandy, another child I saw with this problem, was two and had never slept through the night! She was no longer held or rocked to sleep but was handed a bottle when she was put down in her crib. She always finished all eight ounces (sometimes as much as twelve), turned over, and fell asleep. After about three hours, she woke crying and would not stop unless she was given another five to eight ounces. Again she fell asleep quickly. But she would wake four to six more times during the night and need a bottle to go back to sleep each time. Thus Sandy would drink over a quart of milk each night.

Often when she woke she was soaking wet despite the fact that she was in double or triple diapers. At each waking her mother or father would go in, change her if necessary, hand her another bottle, and leave. When Sandy's parents went to bed they would prepare four or five bottles and leave them in the refrigerator or on Sandy's window ledge. Since either parent could go in, the entire burden did not fall on Sandy's mother as it had on Cory's, and since they did not have to hold their child the parents could go right back to sleep themselves. Still, after two years, they too were tired and frustrated and they usually went to bed early in the evening just to be sure they got enough sleep.

Sandy, like Cory, did have associations that interfered with falling asleep—in this case sucking on a bottle. Sandy did not need the bottle to actually fall asleep, however, because she usually did not fall asleep with the bottle in her mouth. She would finish it, toss it aside, roll over, and then go to sleep. Clearly her disturbance was more closely related to the large amount of milk she took during the night.

Originally Cory's and Sandy's wakings were probably the normal arousals of an infant who is just beginning to develop good sleep habits. But because their parents tried to "treat" the wakings with the extra feedings, the wakings did in fact become abnormal. The "cure" in this case was the cause of the disorder.

How to Tell If Your Child Has This Problem

If your child, like Sandy, is at least three months old and still requires a bottle at bedtime and several more during the night, add up the number of ounces she takes from the time she goes to bed until she wakes in the morning. If she drinks only six to eight ounces, then her problem is more likely one of associations with sucking rather than of too much fluid. But if your baby has more than eight ounces, then the extra liquid may be an added cause of the problem. If you are breast feeding her and have to nurse more than one or two times during the night, you should also be suspicious that your child is getting too much milk, especially if each nursing lasts more than two or three minutes.

If your baby's diapers are usually soaked when she wakes during the night, then it seems likely that she is drinking too much. She certainly can't be thirsty or not getting enough fluids if she is wetting that much. If a medical problem such as diabetes were causing her to drink and wet so much at night, then it would cause the same problem in the daytime. If you are at all concerned, you should consult your doctor. But in all likelihood your child is probably just drinking too much fluid at night because this has become a habitual pattern. And the amount of fluid may be considerable. If your child takes four full eight-ounce bottles during the night, she is drinking one full quart—a great deal even for an adult. Is it so surprising then that your child, like Sandy or Cory, is not sleeping well?

How We Solve the Problem

Once you decide that too much fluid at night is disrupting your child's sleep patterns, you can take the steps necessary to correct the problem. In fact although this is one of the most severe disorders in terms of actual nighttime disruption, it is also one of the easiest to treat. You simply decrease gradually, and eventually eliminate, the feedings at bedtime, naptime, and after nighttime wakings.

If your child has this problem, you will have to begin by progressively decreasing the amount of milk or juice she takes when she falls asleep. It is not reasonable to stop suddenly. Your child would not suffer because of lack of nourishment at night, though at first she might feel hungry because she has learned to expect feedings then. Nevertheless, since she has become so accustomed to going to sleep while being fed and since she may feel hungry, a program designed to allow new patterns to develop gradually will be easier for her and probably for you.

You really have two jobs to do. One is to eliminate the feedings during the night to avoid the various disrupting effects these feedings have on sleep and to help your child learn to be hungry only at reasonable times during the day. The other is to teach your child new sleep associations so that she can fall asleep alone in her crib or bed without you or her bottle. If you find that decreasing both the feedings and the speed with which you respond to her crying is too much to do at the same time, then you may continue to go in to comfort her as soon as she cries at the times when she would previously have been fed. Once the feedings have been stopped you can correct your child's associations to your presence as a second step.

Use the chart on page 85 (Figure 7) as a guide for following the steps to solve this sleep problem. If your child uses a bottle, you know how much she usually takes. So begin by putting one ounce less in each bottle at naptime and nighttime feedings. If you are breast feeding, you know how long your child usually nurses. You can start by shortening the time of nursing at night by a few minutes. If your child is nursing, or if you hold her while she takes the bottle, put her back into the crib or bed when the feeding is complete whether or not she is asleep. If she cries when the feeding is over, or on waking before two hours have passed since the last feeding, do not feed her again. Stick to the schedule. The baby may still be feeling hungry but she does not *need* nourishment; remember that you are helping her to change her feeding schedule so that she will feel hungry only during the day. If more than two hours have gone by since the last feeding, you may nurse her again or give her a bottle. This waiting period will be increased over the coming days. When she is awake and crying before the time for the next feeding, you may choose to go in to rub her back or otherwise try to comfort her. But do this only if you find it to be helpful. She may become even more upset if you are there but

FIGURE 7 **Eliminating Extra Feedings at Sleep Times**

Day	Ounces in Each Bottle or Minutes Nursing	Minimum Hours Between Feedings
1	7	2.0
2	6	2.5
3	5	3.0
4	4	3.5
5	3	4.0
6	2	4.5
7	1	5.0
8	No More Bottles or Nursing at Sleep Times	

- The ounces and times in this chart are general guidelines. You will want to alter them to fit your own routines.
- If your child takes less than 8 ounces in the bottle, start with 1 ounce less than she usually takes and continue reducing from there.
- If you are breast feeding, use the time spent nursing as an approximation of volume. Begin by nursing 1 or 2 minutes less than you usually nurse and continue decreasing the times from that point.
- If you prefer you may follow this chart but decrease every other day instead of every day. It will just take a little longer.

not feeding her, and she may calm more quickly with you out of the room. If you stay, try not to hold her. Soothe her or talk to her as she lies in her crib or bed. The purpose here is only to comfort her and help her fall asleep while she is learning not to expect a feeding. Of course, once the nighttime feedings are stopped entirely, you may have to break these other associations, but this can be done quickly and easily.

Each day, or every other day if you prefer, decrease the amount of fluid in each nighttime bottle by another ounce, or shorten the time of nursing by one minute, and increase the minimum time between feedings by thirty minutes. You handle naptimes like bedtime, except that if your child does not fall asleep within one hour, you end that nap for that day.

By the end of the first or second week there should be no more feedings at sleep times. Many families tell me, however, that they actually stopped the nighttime feedings sooner. After they decreased the volume of liquid to two or three ounces, or shortened the length of nursing sufficiently, they felt it best to simply stop the bottle or nursing at sleep times altogether rather than continue the gradual changes further. They did so because they found that the very short feedings seemed more upsetting than calming. Also, they had already seen such a marked decrease in the number of wakings that they became convinced that eliminating the nighttime fluids was indeed the correct approach. The response is usually so dramatic that children are often sleeping quite normally by the end of the first week.

Once your child is falling asleep without nursing or taking a bottle, then you have solved the problem of excessive fluids, and she no longer has the association of falling asleep with the bottle or breast. If your baby still needs you to rub her back or rock her in order to go to sleep, then you can begin to correct those associations as described in Chapter 5. Once the excessive fluids are no longer complicating the picture, this relearning usually happens quickly.

If you are a mother who is breast feeding and are following the program to eliminate frequent nighttime feedings, it may be helpful, often, to have your husband go in when your child is crying at a time that is too soon for you to nurse. If you go in you may have a "letdown" response, your child will smell the milk, and in any case if you are there she will expect to nurse. If your husband goes in, your child may still seem a bit frustrated, but at least the immediate temptation of the breast is not there. This will help your child learn not to expect you and the nursing during the night.

If you have been bottle or breast feeding your child only at bed- and naptime—that is, if she drinks from a cup the rest of the day—you may want to wean her altogether. If so, you will accomplish this when you discontinue the sleep-time nursings. If you do not want to wean your child yet, you must still eliminate the nighttime feedings. But you can continue to nurse or bottle-feed her at times other than bedtime—earlier in the evening or during the day (except at naptime of course). If she starts to fall asleep when you nurse her at these times, stop and put her in her crib or bed so that she will remain accustomed to falling asleep without nursing or sucking on her bottle. If she cries it will be because she is still associating nursing with falling asleep. You can change this association the same way you change other sleep associations—by letting her cry for a little longer each day until she falls asleep without nursing and without much fussing (see Chapter 5).

If your child nurses or takes a bottle during the day as well as at sleep times, then decreasing the nighttime feedings will generally not affect her daytime feedings. If your baby has been getting most of her nourishment at night, however, you will eventually notice some increase in the amount she takes during the day (though this may take several weeks).

Bottle or breast feeding at appropriate intervals during the day will not interfere with your child's sleep at night or during naps. However, if your child walks around all day with a bottle or is put to your breast repeatedly whenever she so desires or each time she seems the least bit upset, then her nighttime sleep may be affected. In these cases the bottle or breast becomes as important as the pacifier does to a child who has it in her mouth all the time (see Chapter 5). Now your child associates the breast or bottle not only with drowsiness and falling asleep but with a feeling of well-being when she is awake too. If your child has never learned to feel comfortable without the breast or bottle always immediately available to her, then you may have difficulty eliminating extra feedings only at night. Still, if you are consistent, you should be successful.

If you find that you are unable to follow through, or that the difficulty at night is more than you want to face, then you may consider trying to decrease the nursing in the daytime first. Your goal is to help your child learn ways to calm herself other than by sucking on the breast or bottle, and you will be trying to limit the feedings to times she actually needs to be fed. This way she can begin to associate breast or bottle primarily with hunger and feedings. Once you do this and see that you were able to help your child accept these changes without bad effect—in fact, she probably will seem happier in the daytime—

you should be able to work on the nighttime changes with a new confidence.

There is one other approach that some families find helpful when eliminating the unnecessary bottles. They start by watering down the milk or juice in the bottle to half strength, then quarter strength, until the baby is just getting water. Even those children who seem to know instantly when their drinks have been diluted and protest loudly, usually will prefer it to no bottle at all. If your child will accept this, the wakings and feedings may progressively decrease on their own and it will be easier to finally eliminate the bottle at sleep times. If you want to try this approach, you should be aware that it may only be a first step. You still may have to progressively decrease the amount in each bottle and increase the time between feedings. But once your baby is only taking water the effects of the *nutritional* intake are no longer important. She may still be wet at night but she probably won't be hungry.

We used the gradual methods described in this section with both Cory and Sandy, and both little girls are now sleeping soundly through the night. Cory's mother still nurses her twice a day, but never at night. She will occasionally nurse Cory to sleep at naptime, because she found that this did not seem to affect the good sleep that had become established at night and because she continued to find it a rewarding and pleasurable experience. Cory's father realized that he had been wrong to insist that his wife get up to nurse through the night, and the tensions between the parents eased.

Sandy gave up the bottle within a week after the treatment began. Her mother followed through on the plan of decreasing the amount of milk in Sandy's bottle by one ounce each night and was surprised at how quickly things improved. Sandy did cry a little when the night bottle was taken away altogether, but this happened on only two nights and only lasted five minutes. Her parents can now enjoy their time together in the evenings and have found out what it is like to sleep through the night again!

In summary, then, it is important that you realize how disruptive large amounts of milk or juice can be to your child's sleep patterns. If your child stops crying when she is given a bottle or nursed, you may have made the reasonable assumption that she is hungry and needs to be fed. If so, you were right—and wrong. Your child probably does feel hungry at these times, but she does not *need* to be fed. Because the timing of hunger is learned, she is actually hungry at those times because you have been feeding her then. A normal child of four to six months or more can certainly get enough calories during the day so that she will not need further nourishment at night. And if you allow the night feedings to continue, the problem may go on for a very long time—years even. On the other hand, when you begin to change the routine the resolution is usually very rapid. Quite likely your child—and you —will be sleeping well before the end of the first week.

es Chapter 7 ⅹ

Colic and Other Medical
Causes of Poor Sleep

Your child's sleep may be disturbed at night because of medical problems. Certainly any acute illness or condition, especially with fever or discomfort, can disrupt sleep patterns temporarily. If your child is ill, he or she may sleep fitfully at night and nap off and on during much of the day. Teething pain also can cause a young child to sleep poorly for several nights, but it does not cause sleep problems that go on week after week, as parents sometimes suppose. Such ongoing sleep disturbances in young children are not usually caused by medical factors. Still, you may have to consider a medical problem if you have investigated and ruled out the more common and obvious causes of sleep problems or if you know your child has a significant medical problem or condition.

Colic

Probably the most common cause of a significant sleep disturbance in the early months is colic. In the first weeks after birth some babies begin to have daily crying spells. The episodes usually occur in the late afternoon or evening and can go on for several hours. If your baby is colicky, he will be crying very hard and be difficult to calm. You may find it helpful to walk about with him for long periods of time or to place him over your legs while you rub his back. Often, however, nothing you do seems to help.

A baby who is colicky may have a distended stomach, his legs likely will be pulled up, and he may seem relieved by passing gas or having a bowel movement. For these reasons, colic is often considered to be caused by intestinal pain. If the colic is very severe, your pediatrician may even want to prescribe a medication to help relax the bowels and ease the discomfort. But the distention, the increased gas, and at least some of the apparent discomfort may actually be caused by the swallowing of air that takes place during long vigorous crying. The initial cause of the crying, and much of the reason that it continues so long, may be something very different.

Frequently it seems that the colicky infant is either overly sensitive to things going on about him or is exposed to excessive amounts of handling and other stimulation. What he experiences—sees, hears, and feels—may seem like an unpleasant and disorganized barrage. This "chaotic" input is difficult for the infant to handle and may lead to upset and a build-up of tension throughout the day to the point that his coping abilities may become overloaded. If so, he may need an opportunity to discharge this tension at the end of the day. This is what is meant by a "need to cry." So if your baby seems to have colic and cannot be easily comforted, allow him to cry alone in the crib for fifteen to thirty minutes. If he has not settled by then, you may try to console or feed him once again in a very calm, soft-spoken, and gentle manner. Avoid trying to quiet him by bouncing or similar vigorous stimulation. If your gentle attempts are still not helpful, you should allow him to cry for another fifteen- or thirty-minute period. By so doing you are responding to your child's needs, not ignoring them. If his need were to be held, nursed, rocked, or just to use a pacifier, then these interventions would calm him. It is often enough for your child to cry undisturbed in this manner during just two or three consecutive colicky periods. His crying spells will likely decrease in intensity and length within one or two days—and he will sleep better too. By allowing your infant to cry in this manner, you will be giving him a chance to release the built-up tension and he will be better able to "organize" himself and feel comfortable with the daily routines. This is probably why babies hospitalized for severe colic often seem "cured" just by being in the hospital—because the nurses there are more likely than the parents to allow the infants to cry by themselves if they do not accept comforting.

Colic is not, in and of itself, a sleep disorder. It is discussed in all books on baby care, and you should talk the matter over with your pediatrician. Fortunately, in almost all cases symptoms are completely gone by three months of age. However, colicky infants often do go on to develop long-standing sleep problems. These problems may seem to be the same as they had during the colicky months, but they are not.

What happens is that the habits that form when your child is colicky may well persist after the colic has disappeared. If your baby is colicky, you may spend a considerable amount of time walking, rocking, holding, and otherwise trying to comfort him to help him get to sleep. But once the colic is gone, you should no longer have to use these methods. However, your child may still want you to, not because he is in any true distress (despite his crying), but because he has come to expect to be held, rocked, walked about, or patted until he falls asleep at bedtime, and after nighttime arousals. If this happens, you will have to help him learn new, more appropriate associations with falling asleep, as we discussed in Chapter 5.

The difficult part is to decide when the colic is gone. This happens gradually, not overnight, so it may not seem obvious to you when the time has come to change your pattern of response. Keep in mind that colic is usually gone by age three months. It occurs during the day, not just during expected sleep hours. A colicky baby seems to be distressed, not just frustrated, angry, or hungry. And it is difficult to ease a colicky baby's distress by any simple intervention. So if your baby cries mainly when you put him down in the crib at bed- and naptimes or when he wakes during the night, if he does not seem in pain, if the crying stops promptly when you pat his back or pick him up and begin to rock him, give him a pacifier, or feed him, and if he quickly returns to sleep, then it is unlikely that colic is still causing the trouble. Once you realize this, you may go on to identify the real cause of the current sleep problem and take the steps necessary to correct it. If you do not, it may persist for months, even years.

Chronic Illness

Many chronic conditions may contribute to ongoing sleep disturbances. A child may be in pain or discomfort—possibly he has a skin irritation with annoying itching, migraines with nighttime headaches and nausea, scoliosis with the need to wear an uncomfortable orthopedic brace, asthma with difficulty catching his breath, or a severe burn requiring painful operations. His sleep may be disrupted by the direct consequences of a disease or disorder—perhaps he wakes feeling jittery or with the need to urinate because of poorly controlled diabetes, or his sleep may be broken by epileptic seizures. Your child may also be bothered by the indirect consequences of a medical disorder; for example, poor sleep is a side effect of particular medications, or it may result from anxieties a child may have about his illness.

If your child has such a chronic illness or condition, then you're probably well aware of it. The difficulty lies in sorting out which factors related to the illness are causing the sleep disruption. Is it because of the effects of the illness itself on sleep systems, or is it because of the pain, medication side effects, or simply the child's concern and anxiety? Several factors may be contributing simultaneously. Thus, this can be a very complex problem and may be difficult for you to solve alone. Ask your pediatrician or the specialist who is treating your child to help.

Several conditions do seem to merit special discussion here. These are chronic middle ear disease, the use of certain medications, and brain damage.

Middle Ear Disease

Unlike most chronic conditions associated with sleep disturbances, chronic middle ear disease often goes unrecognized, yet it is very amenable to treatment. In this condition, fluid collects in the middle ear cavity behind the eardrum and does not drain satisfactorily. This fluid may or may not become infected, but even without infection the fluid buildup can lead to a temporary decrease in hearing and, if persistent, eventually damage the bones of the middle ear cavity permanently. For this reason the condition should be treated.

During an acute infection the pressure in the middle ear cavity increases, the eardrum bulges, and your child is in real pain. But when the fluid does not become infected, children usually do not complain of discomfort. Nevertheless, their sleep may still be disrupted.

I recently treated Tanya, an eighteen-month-old girl with a long history of frequent wakings at night despite the fact that she went to bed easily. Upon waking she was usually crying. She calmed somewhat if lifted, but returning to sleep was difficult for her, regardless of what her parents did to help. Even when they walked with her or rocked her she usually whimpered for ten to fifteen minutes before finally going back to sleep. Nothing they did seemed to help at all.

Tanya's history did not suggest a cause for her sleep disturbance except that her parents did report that Tanya had had three or four ear infections over the past year. When I examined Tanya I found that much fluid was still present behind her eardrums.

It is not clear how fluid in the middle ear disrupts the sleep patterns of children like Tanya. Possibly when the child is lying down at night, middle ear drainage is even more inadequate than during the day, more fluid collects, pressure increases, and the child feels discomfort. In any case, I have seen many children with this problem who had significant sleep disturbances that did not seem to fit into any other category.

When I see a young child like Tanya, I always take a careful look at the eardrums before deciding on a diagnosis and plan of therapy. It is striking that when these children are treated medically or, if necessary, by having drainage tubes inserted through the eardrum, not only is their middle ear problem cured, but the sleep disturbance disappears as well.

Tanya's ears did not drain with medication. An ear, nose, and throat specialist then inserted drainage tubes, and her sleep problem resolved without further intervention. By recognizing the true cause of her problem we avoided a series of behavioral interventions that would have had no possibility of success.

Medication

In recent years the medical community has begun to appreciate that sleeping pills have *caused* far more sleep disorders in adults than they have ever *helped*. This is just as true with youngsters, and you may be surprised to know that sleep medication is misused in children *very* frequently. When a child is not sleeping well and supposedly everything has been tried, the family feels frustrated and hopeless and will often beg the doctor to help. Often he or she will prescribe some sort of sleep medication. The ones most commonly used are the antihistamines such as diphenhydramine (Benadryl—which has sleepiness as a side effect), a major sedative such as chloral hydrate or phenobarbital, or even a major tranquilizer such as diazepam (Valium). Yet such a medication will rarely solve the sleep problems of a child who is otherwise normal and healthy. Often there is a "paradoxical response" to the medication and your child becomes "hyper," unable to sit still and unable to sleep at all. Even if your child were to sleep well on the medication, he would be far better off if you could understand the cause of the disturbance and help him learn to sleep well without drugs. Sometimes medication will improve a child's sleep for several nights, possibly for a few weeks, but usually the old pattern returns. In addition, the stronger medications often affect your child's daytime mood and performance. He may become overactive or clingy, cranky, and babyish. In a very short time you would likely be feeling more upset than ever with your child. Only occasionally will short-term (one to two weeks) drug treatment serve to break the cycle of a poor sleep pattern and allow a good one to emerge so that normal sleep persists after the medication is stopped. If this is successful, the medication probably does no harm, but proper behavioral approaches would also have been successful. If you are able to correct your child's sleep without medicine, you will not be left with a nagging anxiety that he has an inherent sleep problem (that is, that there is something basically wrong with him), and you will feel more confident in dealing with any problems that may emerge in the future without feeling that you have to head immediately for the medicine cabinet.

Not long ago Terrence, a three-year-old whom people had always thought of as tense and irritable, was brought to my office. His parents said he had great difficulty sleeping at night and wasn't very happy during the day. Because of the boy's repeated nighttime wakings the parents had sought medical advice and Terrence was given one milligram of Valium at bedtime at least three or four times a week. He had been on this medication for the past nine months.

When I saw Terrence he was such an unhappy and irritable child that I was quite concerned. He interacted poorly and I felt he would likely need psychological evaluation as part of the treatment. But to get a clearer picture of the situation and to provide a basis for making further decisions, I first had the family stop the medication altogether. When I saw them several weeks later, they were vastly relieved. After a few difficult nights in the beginning, Terrence was now going to bed easily and sleeping through the night for the first time in a year. In addition, he was much happier in the daytime and the parents had begun to enjoy him again. When I saw him in my office, Terrence was smiling, obviously happy, and good-natured in our conversation. In short he was a delightfully normal three-year-old. His good sleep pattern and normal daytime behavior have continued, and there has been no need for further intervention.

I am sad to say that I see too many young children given a powerful medication such as diazepam in an attempt to improve a sleep disorder that could be corrected by other means. In many cases the medication only makes matters worse. Most of the time, whatever the child's problem is, medication will simply complicate matters at night. In some cases, such as sleep apnea (see Chapter 14), medication can be very dangerous. Also, the child's daytime behavior and ability to concentrate and learn may well be compromised.

A child receiving sleep medication regularly may react the same as an adult on sleeping pills: he cannot sleep without the medication, yet with the medication his sleep is disrupted. So I do not recommend medication for a child with a sleep disorder except on *very* rare occasions, and when I begin to treat a child who has been taking medication just to improve sleep, I start treatment by stopping the medication. You may want to speak with your doctor about doing the same.

There are many situations, of course, in which your child may have to take certain medications to treat particular medical conditions. Phenobarbital or other drugs with sedative properties may be required for the treatment of epilepsy. Theophylline (Slo-Phyllin), metaproterenol (Alupent), terbutaline (Bricanyl), or other similar medications may be necessary to treat asthma. Stimulant drugs such as the amphetamines, methylphenidate (Ritalin), or pemoline (Cylert) may be used to treat attentional-deficit disorders ("hyperactivity"). Your child may need certain antibiotics on an ongoing basis as protection against recurrent infections. These and many other medications may be associated with a sleep disturbance. Again the various effects of the underlying medical disorder, the medication, and other causes of sleep problems have to be sorted out—not always an easy task. The dilemma can be further complicated if your child has had many hospitalizations and has become fearful at night, or if you, understandably, find it hard to set firm limits on your child because he has a chronic illness or has suffered a great deal.

If it seems possible that the medication may be causing the sleep problem, you should discuss this with your doctor, since there are several approaches that may be helpful. The dosage or the time when you give your child the drug may be changed. Your doctor may try alternative drugs. Even if this is only done temporarily, it will help you decide if the original medicine was causing the sleep problem. Asthma medications taken by mouth may also be available in a form that is inhaled, with fewer side effects. Although it is unlikely that antibiotics themselves cause much of a sleep problem, the additives in the liquid preparations may. Switching to pills, or even to a different brand of liquid, may be helpful.

In any case, the changes will take time and require a certain amount of trial and error. But you should *not* make any changes before you talk to your child's specialist. With his or her help, it is quite possible that your child's sleep problem can be improved significantly.

Brain Damage and a True Inability to Sleep Well

Sometimes I do see children who apparently sleep poorly because of some impairment in the brain mechanisms that control the act of falling asleep or the ability to stay asleep. Most of these children will have an impairment significant enough to be quite obvious. Usually they are retarded, and often they also have seizures or are blind or deaf.

When such a neurological disorder is accompanied by a sleep disorder, we have to consider all the factors very carefully. For example, the child could have any of the sleep problems described in this book *apart* from his illness, and the problem could be solved in much the same way as for any other child. Of course it may be more difficult for you to be firm at night if your child has a neurological disorder or sensory impairment. You may ask, "How can I leave my child, who is blind, alone in a room crying?" But very often the only way to solve his sleep problem is to be willing to listen to some crying as you help him learn new associations with falling asleep (see Chapter 5). It is still in your child's best interest that you do so. You may just have to proceed much more slowly than you would otherwise. Instead of setting an initial goal of being out of the room while he falls asleep, you might simply work on helping him learn to fall asleep when you are out of his bed, even if initially you remain in the same room. Other steps, such as correcting an inappropriate sleep schedule, are easier to carry out and are quite important, especially in sensory handicapped children who may have a poor sense of daily schedules (see Chapters 8 and 9).

Of course, any medications your child is taking for his disorder could also be the source of his sleep problem. Finally, it may be that your child's brain damage is directly responsible for his inability to sleep—that is, the brain systems that control sleep may not be working properly. Unfortunately, this is very difficult to test.

When I treat a child who is neurologically impaired I first try to identify and treat factors apart from the brain damage, such as medication or a separate sleep problem. I have been successful on a number of occasions, and the child's sleep problem was resolved despite the neurological illness. Only after all other factors are eliminated do I decide that the child is sleeping poorly as a direct result of the brain damage. This is thus a diagnosis of exclusion.

In a number of children the brain damage is in itself the cause of the sleep problem. I saw Reggie, a four-year-old boy who is moderately retarded following a birth injury. He had always been a poor sleeper and although he now falls asleep fairly easily it is not until 10:00 P.M., and he wakes at about 4:00 A.M. He will either stay awake for the rest of the night or not return to sleep for several hours. At the time of waking he calls out, throws toys around the room, and sits and bangs his head against the wall. The parents want very much to keep Reggie at home, but having to get up with him every night is a tremendous strain, and some of Reggie's behavior is dangerous to himself. During the day Reggie will sometimes nap for about thirty minutes, but rarely longer than that.

When I treated Reggie for the sleep disorder by changing some of the ways his parents handled the bedtime routines and his nighttime wakings, he showed only minimal improvement over several months. Finally I had to assume that behavioral intervention would not work and that he had a true inability to get the sleep he needed. The only other explanation, which seemed to be unlikely, was that he simply didn't need very much sleep, in which case there would be little I could do.

In children like Reggie, sedative medication may be useful. Generally I will recommend such drugs only when I know that brain function has been impaired and am convinced that this is responsible for the sleep disturbance. I have had moderate success with such children using a significant dose of a sedative such as chloral hydrate. While I'm not at all happy about having to use such a drug, these children have been able to go to sleep more easily and, more important, to maintain their sleep long enough to get sufficient rest.

Reggie began sleeping from 9:00 P.M. to 6:00 A.M. While this was still less sleep than "normal" for his age, it was a major improvement and made life much easier for his parents. In addition, in a manner typical for children with neurological impairment, Reggie did not seem to show any lingering drug effects in the morning, and the teachers at his special school said he seemed more alert.

Thus it does seem that children such as Reggie are not sleeping poorly because of any major decrease in sleep requirements. It has also been interesting to note that such children, even when they are on this medication for extended periods, continue to sleep well, whereas a normal child kept on such medication will usually show progressively less effect, then eventual worsening of sleep. Even when I use medication I continue to monitor children frequently and carefully and we will try drug-free periods at appropriate intervals to see if they still need the medication. These are prescription drugs and can only be managed under the care of a doctor. My experience shows that when neurologically impaired children require medication to help them sleep, they seem to need a fairly powerful one in substantial doses. If children show improvement on a mild medication such as an antihistamine, then I am convinced that these children can show the same improvement without drugs.

If your child is neurologically impaired and not sleeping well, you may consider discussing a trial of medication with your doctor. But before you decide to give your child a strong sleep medication, do try to identify other possible causes of a sleep disturbance and then to regulate his sleep patterns according to the methods outlined in this book. The program has been successful with a number of neurologically impaired children, and just might be all that is needed for your child.

Part Three

SLEEP RHYTHM
DISTURBANCES

Chapter 8

Daily Schedules and Their Effect on Sleep—Biological Rhythms Revisited

A major advance in understanding and treating sleep disorders came when researchers began to view sleep and waking as a rhythm that had to act in harmony with other body rhythms, including body temperature, eating, hormone release, and activity (see Chapter 2). If we are to sleep well and function at our best during the day, these biological rhythms have to be smoothly synchronized.

There are a number of ways in which our body rhythms become irregular and our sleep cycles adversely affected. Most of us are familiar with the condition of jet lag which occurs when you travel across the ocean to a new time zone but find that you do not feel alert when it is daytime there and that you can only sleep when it is nighttime back home. Shift workers experience the same difficulties—they must try to sleep when they feel awake and try to get up when they feel tired. If they change shifts too frequently, their sleep rhythms cannot stabilize and they may have ongoing sleep problems. They will probably have great difficulty sleeping at desired times and may never feel up to par while awake.

Children also have sleep disturbances caused by problems in their patterns of sleeping and waking and in their daily routines. Their schedules may be too irregular, they may be regular but inappropriate in certain ways, or the time of day your child is *able* to sleep may not be the time when you *want* him or her to sleep. If your child's daily patterns are inconsistent, then her sleep at night may be broken. If she naps or eats at unusual times, then she may wake too early in the morning or fall asleep too late at night. If she has become accustomed to sleeping at the "wrong" hours, then she may actually be unable to fall asleep as early or sleep as late as you wish.

Although alterations in daily schedules and biological rhythms may be the only factors affecting your child's sleep, these disturbances are often complicated by other problems. If your child is not tired when you want her to go to sleep, you may inadvertently teach her to associate being rocked or having a bottle with falling asleep as you try to help her settle down. Or if you have difficulty being firm at bedtime, your child may always stay up too late, and the time at which she is able to get to sleep may shift. As you can see then, the treatment may involve several factors. When a child has a sleep problem that includes a disturbance in her sleep rhythm, it will probably not be enough to simply correct her sleep associations or be firmer at bedtime. You will have to correct the schedule problems as well. But to do this, you must learn to recognize and understand your child's particular schedule disturbance so that you can best decide how to treat it.

Irregular Sleep-Wake Schedules

Many of the children I see have difficulty sleeping because their sleep-wake patterns are irregular. They fall asleep early one night, late the next, wake at odd hours, and never have their naps at the same time two days in a row. Mealtimes are just as varied.

Your child's daily pattern may be like this. If you are not sure, chart it (Figure 8, page 105) for one or two weeks. You may be quite surprised by what you find. If her schedule is very irregular, then in all probability her circadian rhythms (see Chapter 2) have become very disrupted. Her body temperature may be rising when she goes to bed and falling when she gets up, the opposite of what it should be. She may be hungry between meals or when she should be sleeping and not hungry at mealtimes. She may be active when she should be napping and sluggish when she should be playing. And your child may have difficulty falling asleep at bedtime—if there is one—and may wake during the night.

It is important that you realize, however, that her problem differs from those of the children with bedtime difficulties and nighttime wakings described in Chapters 5 and 6. For a period of time—hours even—your child *cannot* go to sleep, or back to sleep, no matter what you do. This is true even if you lie down with her, turn on a night-light, are firm, give her a bottle, or nurse or rock her. She *cannot* sleep because her sleep-wake rhythm is in the waking phase.

Children's daily rhythms can only become established and maintained in a regular twenty-four-hour pattern if they are set each day by events that always occur at the same times. The most important of

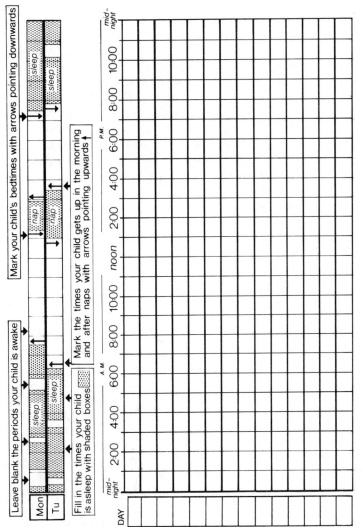

FIGURE 8 **Sleep Chart for Parents to Use**

105

these are waking in the morning, going to sleep at night, napping, eating, and exposure to light and dark. If your child does not have reasonable consistency in her daily routines, her system does not know when she should be asleep and when she should be awake.

If your child's circadian rhythms are disrupted, her sleep-wake patterns deteriorate. Her usual sleep pattern, which allows her to sleep for long periods at night and to nap during the day, begins to disappear. When she goes to bed at 6:00 or 7:00 P.M., for example, her body does not know if this is a late nap or an early bedtime. Should she wake up after one hour or ten? Her sleep patterns become disorganized into irregular fragments, none of which even approximates the ten or more continuous hours of sleep a young child should have at night. Instead of her nighttime sleep being interrupted by only brief arousals with rapid returns to sleep, she may have complete wakings for long periods. And some daytime naps may be unusually long.

Jimmy, for example, was a four-year-old boy who would wake in the middle of the night and not want to go back to sleep. He had no formal bedtime and no regular bedtime routines. He went to sleep any time from 7:00 P.M. to 11:00 P.M.—whenever he got sleepy, which depended somewhat on when he had napped that day. Sometimes he fell asleep in his own bed, but more often it was wherever he happened to be at the time.

When Jimmy woke during the night he seemed wide awake. He was not frightened or demanding, but he simply could not be made to go back to sleep quickly. Since he would stay awake even if he had to stay in bed, his parents allowed him to play until he grew tired and fell back to sleep—usually after one or two hours. He often woke a second time a few hours later. He got up in the morning anywhere from 6:30 A.M. to 10:00 A.M., depending on how much he had been up the night before. Jimmy's naps were also quite irregular. Some mornings, especially after little sleep the night before, he could nap as early as 9:00 A.M. On other days he would nap before lunch or skip a morning nap altogether. In the afternoon he might lie down at 1:00, 4:00, or sometimes as late as 6:00 P.M. His naps could be as short as thirty minutes or as long as four hours.

The loose structure in Jimmy's home was not due to family problems or to lack of caring. Rather it was a style typical in his family's community. Among Jimmy's family and their friends, irregular mealtimes and bedtimes were quite common and accepted. Jimmy's parents were not bothered by these irregularities—in the daytime—but they were concerned about his wakings at night. They did not realize there was a connection between the two.

When the family sought my help Jimmy did not have any appropriate associations with getting ready for bed and falling asleep. So, of course, it was important for the family to establish a pleasant bedtime ritual. But this alone, even if it were at a consistent time each night, would not have solved Jimmy's sleep problems. We needed to bring more order to his haphazard daily schedule as well.

Jimmy's fundamental problem with sleep was that his twenty-four-hour sleep-wake pattern had become badly disrupted. When he woke during the night, it was as though he had waked from an afternoon nap. He was happy, energetic, and ready to play, and it was simply *impossible* for him to return to sleep at that time. Although his problem seemed major, the solution was straightforward.

How to Solve the Problem of Irregular Sleep-Wake Schedules

Jimmy's parents agreed to set up a daily schedule for him so that he would have a regular bedtime, a constant time of morning waking, and a consistent naptime. In addition, they would give him his meals at the same times every day. And the parents decided upon an appropriate bedtime routine. Although these decisions were contrary to their customary less-structured lifestyle, they were quite willing to make the changes once they understood Jimmy would sleep better at night and probably feel better during the day.

Jimmy would go to bed at 8:00 P.M. after a story or quiet game, and they would wake him at 7:00 A.M. He would always sleep in his own room. When he woke during the night his parents were to go in; but they had to be firm and not allow middle-of-the-night play, which would only reinforce the wakings. They had to insist that he stay in bed at bedtime or after wakings even if he had difficulty at first falling asleep at these times. They could sit with him if necessary, but there was to be little discussion. Once his sleep rhythm was normalized, which I told them should occur within two weeks, and he could fall asleep or back to sleep quickly, they were no longer to stay with him. He would have to go to sleep alone. They agreed that if need be this would be enforced with the progressive waiting or door-closing techniques discussed in Chapter 5. But as I expected, since Jimmy was never demanding when he was awake, and since he never really associated his parents' presence with falling asleep, these were not necessary.

Naptime was to be at 1:00 P.M. and would be handled like bedtime. I told them that Jimmy should not be allowed to nap at other times. If he managed to fall asleep at the wrong time anyway, they were to wake him after ten or fifteen minutes. He should have at least one quiet hour in his bed at naptime whether he slept or not. After his nighttime sleep became normal, it would become clear if he needed a daytime nap at all. If he did, he would start napping; if not, he would stay awake all day.

Although Jimmy's problem was long-standing, the family was able to follow through because they now understood the reason for keeping a good daytime structure. They charted his sleep patterns for two months. I asked them to do so for several weeks, but they continued longer because it was so helpful to them. Like most parents, they found it much easier to be consistent when they could see the progress in black and white. Jimmy resisted during the first week, partly because he was used to his old ways and partly because he really couldn't sleep at the new, regular times. His parents were firm and supportive, though at first they were up more at night than they had been before they started to make these changes. Jimmy and his parents came to look forward to the period before bed; it allowed for a closeness they hadn't had before. By the end of the second week Jimmy was falling asleep easily at a regular bedtime and sleeping through the night. It soon became apparent that he did not need to nap, so they didn't try to put him down in the afternoon. The only reason he had been napping once or twice each day was that his sleep rhythms were so disordered and some of the sleep that should have been occurring at night was shifted into the daytime.

Whether the irregular schedule is the main problem, as it was with Jimmy, or is only one factor complicating other problems, setting up and sticking to a regular schedule is a necessary, if not sufficient, step toward resolving most sleep problems. For the first few weeks it makes sense to stick to a fairly strict schedule for going to sleep, waking, and eating. Once things are going well, it is all right to be more flexible within reason. But remember, if your child's days and nights have been fairly unstructured in the past, they will become irregular again if you are not careful.

Usually I have found that schedules become disrupted because the parents have not understood the importance of keeping consistent daily routines. But occasionally the disorganization and loss of structure occurs because of underlying family problems. When issues such as marital strife, medical or psychiatric illness, death, separation, or divorce are involved, parents may find they are unable or unwilling to maintain a normal schedule for the children. In these cases I always urge the family to see a counselor before or during the time we begin to set up schedules to solve their child's sleep problem.

Regular Schedules Can Cause Trouble Too

It is very apparent that children function better when their daily schedules are fairly consistent. However, regular routines can cause problems when they are poorly timed. For example, if you turn on your child's light and practice your tuba every night at 3:00 A.M., your child's sleep will be disturbed—even though the schedule is perfectly regular. But more subtle factors can also influence sleep and result in early-morning wakings, bedtime difficulties, or nighttime wakings.

1. Early-Morning Wakings

One of the most troublesome disturbances, and often one of the hardest to correct, is that of early-morning wakings. Emily, for example, was a thirteen-month-old girl who would wake too early each morning. She went to sleep at 7:30 at night with no fuss but woke at 5:00 every morning and refused to go back to sleep. This meant that her parents had to get out of bed two hours earlier than they would otherwise. Frequently Emily's mother retired early at night just to be able to wake up early enough in the morning to take care of her. Although this was workable, she would have preferred to stay up later and have the time with her husband. Emily's mother said that during the day Emily did well: she napped early in the morning at about 8:00, and again right after lunch.

Emily's problem appeared to be quite different from Jimmy's. She had a regular routine, went to bed easily, and did not wake during the night. Her early waking was really her parents' only complaint. In Emily's case, however, there was one very pertinent fact: her morning nap was unusually early. It seemed that she had to nap early because she woke very early in the morning and would be tired a couple of hours later.

I believed there were two possible explanations for Emily's early waking. One was that she needed less than ten hours of sleep at night and thus would wake up nine and a half hours after an established bedtime. If this were true, then delaying her bedtime to 9:00 P.M. would gradually lead to a later morning waking. However, most children of Emily's age can sleep more than ten hours at night, and so I considered the second alternative first. I believed the early-morning nap was actually the cause of the problem.

I proceeded on the assumption that Emily's final sleep cycle, which should have taken place from 5:00 until 6:30 or 7:00 A.M., had become separated from the rest of the night and appeared several hours later as an unusually early morning nap. Therefore, I asked the parents to keep her up progressively later each morning before allowing her to nap, aiming for a naptime of about 10:00 or 10:30 A.M. In addition they were not to go in to Emily as soon as she woke at 5:00. We agreed they would not go in before 5:15 for several days and then not until 5:30.

At first when Emily woke in the morning, she would cry. But within a few days after her parents started delaying the morning nap, she began falling back to sleep after a short while. After a week or so the early-morning crying became halfhearted. Emily would wake in the morning, perhaps whimper a bit or play in her crib, and then return to sleep for the final sleep cycle. By then she was waking between 6:30 and 7:00 in the morning and napping twice at more appropriate hours during the day. Thus Emily did not have a short sleep requirement. She could sleep eleven to eleven and a half hours at night and wake at an appropriate time in the morning—once her naptime had been adjusted.

Hillary was two years old and Rory was six. Their stories were very similar to Emily's in that they woke very early in the morning, but neither of them napped unusually early. However, Hillary was given a bottle of milk as soon as she woke at 5:00 A.M. and Rory would get up early and watch cartoons.

Hillary was not fed at bedtime or during the night, so her problem was not one of inappropriate associations or excessive feedings, but she had *learned* to be hungry at 5:00 A.M. If her hunger could be postponed until 6:30 or 7:00 A.M., then she could sleep later. You will find more discussion on the learned aspects of hunger in Chapter 6. By simply delaying the time she would be given the bottle by about ten minutes each day, regardless of when she woke, the parents found she started to go back to sleep after waking at 5:00 and would sleep another hour and a half to two hours.

Rory was simply getting up to watch cartoons. Like most people who are lucky enough to have something they want to do every morning, he learned to wake at the necessary hour. For Rory to learn to sleep later, his family had to insist that he no longer watch television in the morning. In exchange for giving up the cartoons, his family substituted other more appropriate rewards during the day, such as a magic show, a baseball game, and trips to a special playground. It took Rory longer than Hillary, but after about four weeks he too was sleeping later.

Early-morning wakings may also occur because of early-morning noise or light. By 5:00 in the morning your child will have completed most of her night's sleep—the drive to sleep is less strong than at bedtime or earlier in the night. Some children will wake at this hour if there is even a mild disturbance. Light entering the room, traffic sounds, or noise from an early-rising family member can wake them. These environmental disturbances (like the tuba) may directly cause early wakings. In the process, they affect the sleep-wake rhythms. If the morning disruptions are frequent enough, your child will begin to anticipate them and may wake spontaneously just before dawn, or before the family gets up.

These problems are best solved by reducing the disturbing factors. Light can be reduced by room-darkening shades and perhaps curtains. The curtains will also help to mute sounds from traffic outside, and you may have to shut the windows as well. Sometimes it is helpful for a child who wakes early to switch to a quieter bedroom, changing with a sister or brother who sleeps more soundly. Sources of constant noise, such as "white noise" machines or vaporizers, are sometimes useful. They may help block outside noise that is quite loud and intermittent—heavy traffic or the sound you hear if you live near train tracks or an airport. Generally, however, I believe you should avoid these devices, because your child needs to learn how to sleep under natural conditions and should not be dependent on such a machine. If she is, she will have trouble sleeping where it is quiet.

There are two other situations in which regular schedules are associated with early-morning wakings. One is caused by an early sleep phase, with your child both falling asleep and waking too early (see Chapter 9). The other happens when your child has a short sleep requirement—she actually needs less sleep than you think she does and wakes early for this reason. However, you should not be too quick to arrive at this conclusion. You may find that your child continues to wake early even if you make her bedtime later. Perhaps your child has learned to associate something with waking at that time—a little light at the window, an increase in traffic, and the fact that you come in to her at that hour (which is likely if you view 5:00 as "early morning" and not as "middle of the night"). So, before deciding that your child needs little sleep, try to see if she will sleep longer in the morning. Keep her room dark, then postpone your response to her a little more each day, thus giving her a chance to go back to sleep. Use the technique described in Chapter 5 for teaching new associations. Try the plan for a few weeks and you may find that she begins returning to sleep for a final sleep cycle. If you do this frequently enough it may start to become routine, as it did with Emily.

When the approaches described in this section are successful we have reason to be pleased. But be aware that early-morning wakings are a tricky business. I have also worked with children who were very early wakers and who continued to wake early despite our best efforts to change their sleep pattern a little. It is likely that these children are "larks"—they wake early feeling alert and active. The early morning is their best time and they tire in the evening. The same happens with some adults, but they are more bothered by difficulty staying up late than by their early wakings. If your child seems to wake too early and does not respond to any of the changes I have suggested here, you may just have to accept things as they are and look forward to the time when she is old enough to be up and about without waking you.

2. Bedtime Difficulties

We have already discussed several causes of bedtime difficulties, including irregular sleep-wake patterns. There are three other schedule-related causes of a true inability to sleep at bedtime, despite a regular schedule: a late sleep phase (discussed in Chapter 9), an inappropriately early bedtime (addressed later in this chapter), and problems related to the child's naps.

LATE AFTERNOON NAP   If your child naps from 4:00 to 6:00 P.M. each day, she may be unable to fall asleep before 9:00 or 10:00 at night. If you try to put her to bed earlier you will likely be met with real struggles. Most families will recognize this problem and will make the nap earlier. But, if your child is used to napping at 4:00 P.M. and you want to have her nap at 1:00, she will probably be unable to do so. Again, gradual change works better. Make her naptime and her bedtime ten to fifteen minutes earlier each day until she is sleeping at the desired times. If your child still has a morning nap, it may have to be moved earlier as well to allow for the afternoon nap. If your child has passed her first birthday, she may be able to give up the morning nap altogether.

Sometimes the afternoon nap may only be a little late, perhaps starting at 2:00, or last a bit too long—for three hours let's say—yet still be enough to affect your child's ability to go to sleep at bedtime. It will be relatively simple for you to find out by starting the nap a little earlier or by waking her after only two hours.

TOO MANY NAPS   By the second year of life most children have given up their morning nap and sleep in the daytime only in the early afternoon. If your child continues to nap twice a day, it may cut into her nighttime sleep. The amount of sleep she gets in a twenty-four-hour period will be unchanged, but more of it will be shifted to the daytime.

If the morning nap is very early, she may begin to have early-morning wakings. If the naps are later, however, your child may not get sleepy until the late evening. Shifting the naps will just shift the problem. You may have to try to eliminate the morning nap and move the afternoon nap earlier, to right after lunch. If this is difficult to do all at once, then do it gradually. Try delaying the morning nap, and shortening its length about ten minutes each day until it can be stopped completely. Some parents prefer to gradually postpone the morning nap into the early afternoon, while decreasing the length of the afternoon nap until it has been eliminated.

NOT ENOUGH NAPS We might assume that if too much napping will make it difficult for a child to fall asleep or lead to early-morning wakings, then decreasing or eliminating naps will always lead to easier bedtimes and better sleep. However, that is not the case.

Simply making a child sleepy will not always make her sleep better —in fact it may have the opposite effect. When your child is overtired she is stressed, she may become irritable and overactive, and her behavior may worsen. In this state she may find it difficult to relax at bedtime, she may struggle against going to sleep, and she may be awake longer than she should. Even if she does fall asleep promptly, the overtired child may also have increased wakings at night and is more likely to have sleep terrors and other partial arousals (see Chapter 10).

Helen was two and a half years old and refused to go to sleep until at least 10:00 P.M. Her parents said that she used to sleep several hours each day in the late afternoon, but they had cut out her nap, trying to improve her bedtime. When they did this, however, several new problems developed. Helen continued to be sleepy in the late afternoon and her parents had to work hard to keep her awake. She seemed quite unhappy at this time and wanted to sleep. If she happened to be in the car at that time she would always fall asleep and be difficult to wake. Dinner became unpleasant because Helen was so irritable. After dinner, when it was time for Helen to go to sleep, she got a "second wind." She seemed almost overcharged, and putting her to bed at 8:00 P.M. was impossible.

I told Helen's parents that she was overtired. She had to have an afternoon nap, but at an appropriate hour. We started with a late nap when Helen got tired and gradually made nap- and bedtimes earlier. She now is napping an hour and a half in the daytime after lunch and sleeping several hours more at night. Her problem was not that she didn't need much sleep, it was that she wasn't getting enough. With the extra sleep, she became much happier during the day and settled down easily at bedtime.

With younger children, you may have a similar problem if you eliminate the morning nap too soon, especially if your child's nighttime sleep does not increase proportionally. Older children who no longer need a nap may also have bedtime difficulties when they are overtired because their bedtimes are too late.

If you wait until your child seems very sleepy before you put her to bed you may be waiting too long. Try an earlier bedtime with a nice bedtime ritual and you will probably find she falls asleep quickly. She will get more sleep and her behavior in the daytime may improve.

If your child never seems tired at bedtime and if you have explored all the causes of bedtime difficulties and nothing seems to fit, it could be that your child is an "owl." She will be at her best late in the evening and always have trouble waking in the morning no matter how much sleep she gets. Even if she stays on a fairly regular schedule, she may have difficulty falling asleep at the proper bedtime. This pattern is common in adults, but happens less frequently in children. Children fall asleep much more easily than adults. If your child has this tendency to "wake up" near bedtime, you should still be able to avoid major problems, but you will have to keep her on a very regular schedule. You must be especially sure that she wakes at the same time every day. And you should plan her bedtime routines with care and assure that they are not rushed.

3. Nighttime Wakings

Regular schedules are not usually a *cause* of nighttime wakings, although a child who is not getting enough sleep may wake repeatedly during the night as well as, or instead of, having bedtime struggles. A more common way in which regular schedules can lead to nighttime wakings is through regular nighttime interruptions. Recurrent feedings at night are the most common cause of this (see Chapter 6). Sometimes a child may get other reinforcement for waking at night. If you make the nighttime waking time very pleasurable for your child —by going in and playing with her—then she will be motivated to continue waking. In this case you must eliminate the play if you want your child to learn that there is no point in waking during the night. Even if you scold or punish your child during the night wakings, the wakings may still be reinforced by the attention she gets. This is especially likely if your child gets too little attention during the day, and particularly if she spends too little time with you alone. If you think this might be the case, do your best to set aside special times for her in the daytime. When she feels less needy she will not demand attention at night. If you find that you are unable to provide extra time for her, or if she seems very needy even when you do, then you should consider seeing a counselor to help you decide what the problem is and how best to proceed.

Normal Sleep, Abnormal Expectations

You may be dissatisfied with your infant's or toddler's sleep patterns, but they may be completely normal. Perhaps you like the time after 7:00 in the evening for yourself and also like to sleep until 10:00 in the morning. If your child falls asleep at 7:00 P.M. and wakes at 6:30 A.M., or if she won't go off to sleep until 10:30 P.M. but sleeps until 10:00 A.M., you may be irritated with her. But be mindful of the fact that your child only needs a certain amount of sleep, and you will have to consider her schedule as well as your own. Most children simply cannot sleep for fifteen hours. If your child is sleeping ten to twelve hours at night she is quite normal; it is your expectations that need to be adjusted. You can't have it both ways: with your child going to bed early and waking late. But you can make her schedule more convenient for you. Observe how much sleep she gets, then adjust her present sleep period so that it best fits with your schedule (see Chapter 9). But you will have to make concessions: you will have to be up with her later at night or you will have to get up with her earlier in the morning than you might like.

This problem is not limited to young children. Gregg, for example, was twelve years old and his parents complained that he would not go to bed at bedtime. He would stall for two hours and his parents would get very angry. Gregg had any number of excuses—he was thirsty, he had to go to the bathroom, or he wasn't tired. The last of these was quite accurate. His parents expected him to go to bed at 8:00 P.M. and get up at 7:00 A.M. But eleven hours was much more sleep than Gregg needed at night. The 8:00 bedtime was unrealistically early. When the parents agreed to move the bedtime to 9:45 P.M., the problems disappeared and Gregg fell asleep quickly.

It may also be that bedtime is not a problem but your child has difficulty waking in the morning. Ten hours of sleep may seem reasonable, but perhaps your child needs twelve. She should have an earlier bedtime. If she is an adolescent and still needs twelve hours of sleep at night, however, you may have problems. Most teenagers wouldn't consider going to bed at 6:00 or 7:00 P.M. Your child may have to be somewhat sleep-deprived during the week and try to make up for it on the weekend. It is a compromise, but it may be the best solution.

The chart on page 19 is a guideline for how much sleep children need at each age. Each child is different, however, and estimating your child's sleep requirement is not always easy. You can usually get a good idea by watching her sleep patterns. Chart her sleep for one to two weeks and see how much sleep she now gets, especially when she does not have to be waked in the morning, and see if she seems tired or irritable in the daytime. If your child needs more or less sleep than the chart suggests, you may have to adjust your expectations accordingly.

এ✗ *Chapter 9* ✗ঌ

Normal Sleep at the Wrong Time— Sleep Phase Shifts

B y now you know that your child's ability to fall asleep and to be
awake varies throughout the day. This rhythm is closely synchronized with his or her other body rhythms, especially with the rise and
fall of body temperature. There are definite sleep and waking periods
in the daily circadian rhythm (see Chapter 2) which allow your child
to fall asleep easily and wake naturally. If you try to put him to bed in
the waking phase you may find he seems "unwilling" to go to sleep;
but the fact is he simply is not sleepy. And if you try to wake him up
in the sleep phase, you again may find he seems "unwilling," this time
because he really isn't ready to wake.

The same holds true for you. Let's say you usually sleep from 11:30
at night until 7:30 in the morning and that you fall asleep easily and
wake without an alarm, feeling rested. The sleep phase of your sleep-
wake cycle clearly runs from 11:30 P.M. to 7:30 A.M. Now think for a
moment what will happen if you try to change your bedtime or your
time of waking.

- *If you go to bed early*, let's say at 8:00 P.M., before the start of
  your sleep phase, *you will have difficulty falling asleep*—even if
  you do doze, you certainly won't sleep through the night.
- *If you try to wake early*, perhaps at 4:00 A.M., before your waking
  phase begins, *you will be very sleepy* and have much difficulty
  getting out of bed. You may feel terrible for several hours, but
  then near the hour you would normally wake, you will start to
  feel ready to face the day.
- *If you go to bed late* after your sleep phase begins, possibly at
  2:00 A.M., you will fall asleep easily but *you will wake "early,"*

that is, close to your normal waking time when your wake phase begins. Thus you will get less sleep than usual and you may feel tired during the day.

- *If you try to sleep late,* into your waking phase, perhaps until 10:00 A.M., *you probably will be unable to do so.* Or at best you will doze on and off for the last few hours.

As you recall from Chapter 2, our basic daily rhythms tend to cycle every twenty-five hours and we reset them to twenty-four hours by our daily routines. Because of this, we have a tendency to stay up a little later each night and get up a little later each morning. Thus, the third and fourth schedule changes described above—going to sleep later and waking later than usual—are easier to do than going to sleep early or waking early.

These examples describe what happens if you try to go to sleep or wake at times that do not coincide with the beginning and end of your sleep phase. The same is true for children. When their bedtimes or times of waking do not match their sleep-wake rhythms, they may have trouble going to sleep at night and difficulty getting up in the morning, or they may have problems staying awake until bedtime in the evening and then may wake too early in the morning. When this happens, it means that the sleep phase of your child's sleep-wake cycle is not where you want it to be—it has *shifted.* It may be too early—an *early* sleep phase—or it may be too late—a *late* sleep phase.

Early Sleep Phase

Your child has an early sleep phase if his natural sleep period—the time from when he falls asleep at night to when he wakes in the morning—occurs earlier in the twenty-four-hour day than you would like (see Figure 9).

Nina was eight months old and her parents were bothered by her sleep schedule. She went to sleep at 5:30 P.M., slept well, and woke at 5:30 A.M. Her two naps started at 8:30 A.M. and 12:30 P.M. She had her meals at 6:00 A.M., 11:00 A.M., and 4:00 P.M. Her parents' main concern was her 5:30 A.M. waking. They wanted her to sleep until 7:00 A.M. Yet when they tried keeping her up until 7:00 P.M., she became very fussy and she still woke at 5:30 A.M.

Although Nina was eating and napping early, she was getting twelve hours of sleep at night. The early feeding and nap were not causing the waking. In fact, Nina's whole schedule—sleeping, waking, and eating—was completely normal, except that it had shifted so that

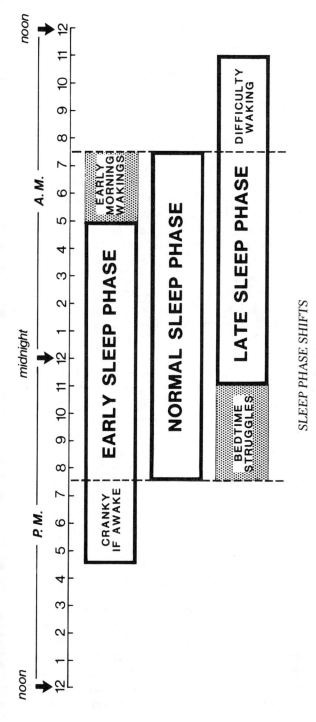

SLEEP PHASE SHIFTS

This chart shows where in the 24-hour day a young child's sleep phase may fall. Here a normal phase is assumed to run from 7:30 P.M. to 7:30 A.M. An early sleep phase occurs when the phase shifts to earlier hours, and a late sleep phase occurs when it shifts to later hours. Of course, the position of the "normal" phase depends on the particular schedule required by your child and your family. For an older child, the length of the normal phase will be shorter and will begin later.

everything happened about an hour and a half too early. Her sleep phase began and ended ninety minutes before her family wanted it to. So if we could delay the timing of her sleep phase by ninety minutes, everyone would be happy.

How to Adjust an Early Sleep Phase

Although it was only Nina's time of waking that annoyed her parents, they agreed it would be more convenient if her meals, naps, and bedtime could be adjusted to coincide better with their schedule. I told them that we would have to intervene gradually. Simply keeping Nina up late for one or two nights would not help, because that did not allow enough time for the sleep phase to shift to a new time. Furthermore, changing the bedtime and not changing the rest of the daytime schedule was not enough.

When Nina's parents understood what was happening, they agreed to change her complete schedule a little at a time. Nina's bedtime, meals, and naptimes would be moved ten minutes later each day. After nine days she would be going to bed at 7:00 P.M., napping at 10:00 A.M. and 2:00 P.M., and eating at 7:30 A.M., 12:30 P.M., and 5:30 P.M. Things went very well. As often happens, the changes in morning waking lagged behind the other changes, but after two and a half weeks this too had improved. Nina's overall schedule was now the same as before—but at a better time of day. The problem had been resolved and Nina's sleep phase was no longer early.

An early sleep phase is less common than a late sleep phase, because our natural tendency is to shift later, as you will recall in our discussion of the inherent twenty-five-hour cycle (see Chapter 2). But an early sleep phase occurs often enough—especially in very young children. Although toddlers are less likely than infants to try to fall asleep earlier than you think they should, some of them may, and if they are frequently allowed to do so, their sleep phases may shift in an early direction.

If your child has an early sleep phase, it will be fairly easy to recognize the problem and gradually correct it. Remember, it often takes at least two weeks to shift and fully stabilize sleep rhythms even by as little as one and a half to two hours. And don't forget to examine your child's entire daily schedule, not just his bedtime. You may have to alter nap- and mealtimes as well. And like Nina's parents, you may have to make a compromise. You will have to decide where you want the sleep phase to be, realizing that *a later waking means a later bedtime*. If your child is already getting the amount of sleep he needs, you can change the time of day he sleeps, but you cannot substantially increase the number of hours.

Late Sleep Phase

If your child's natural sleep period occurs later in the twenty-four-hour day than you would like, he has a late sleep phase (see Figure 9). This problem occurs in children of all ages and is very common.

I first saw Matthew just after his first birthday. His parents described problems with him both at his 7:30 P.M. "bedtime" and again in the middle of the night. At bedtime they tried to rock him to sleep, but he did not seem tired. He fussed and cried and did not settle. Generally his parents simply gave in, let him play for a while, and then tried again later to help him get to sleep. Most nights Matthew finally fell asleep at about 10:00 P.M. He slept fairly well at night except for one waking at about 3:00 A.M. Although he would be crying, he did not seem wide awake, as at bedtime, and he could always be rocked back to sleep quickly. In the morning, because Matthew had fallen asleep so late and his parents felt he should catch up on his sleep, they left him until he woke on his own, about 10:00 A.M. Also, his mother found that when she did have to wake him earlier, for example at 7:00 A.M. for errands or a trip, Matthew was difficult to wake and he remained cranky for several hours. Matthew napped twice a day, once at noon before a 1:00 P.M. lunch and again at 4:00 P.M. Matthew had a late sleep phase. His sleep phase ran from 10:00 P.M. to 10:00 A.M., but his parents wanted him to have one that started at 7:30 P.M.

Vanessa was seven years old. Although six years older than Matthew, she suffered from the same basic problem. Despite the fact that she behaved well during the day, her bedtime at 8:30 P.M. had become the source of major struggles and was quite unpleasant for the whole family. Vanessa resisted the bedtime routines, and tension would start to build by 7:30 P.M. Like many children, she had a variety of excuses for not wanting to stay in bed: She was thirsty, her stomach "hurt" (sometimes "so much" that she cried), and she didn't feel tired. Often she said she was frightened and wanted the light turned on, the shades pulled, and her closet door shut. She never fell asleep before 11:00 P.M.

Her parents were very upset, confused, and concerned about her behavior and had tried many ways to improve things. At first they thought they were being "too soft," so they refused to go along with her extra requests. Then they tried punishing her by taking away privileges and occasionally with spankings. All of this only seemed to make matters worse. They became concerned that Vanessa might really be suffering from a stomach ailment. Although the doctor reassured them that Vanessa was healthy and that stomach pains which occur only at bedtime are not a cause for alarm, they had lingering doubts. And they remained concerned about her nighttime fears. They talked to her at length about her problem getting to sleep and asked whether she was upset about something, but she claimed not to be. They spoke to her teachers. Everything in Vanessa's life seemed quite normal, except bedtime. Finally they came to believe that she did not have a significant emotional problem, but they remained mystified as to what might be keeping her from falling asleep. In the morning they always had to wake her for school and always with great difficulty. She was grumpy in the morning, slow to become fully alert, and did not feel like eating breakfast. Now and then she seemed so tired that they let her stay home rather than go to school.

At this point in our initial conversation I was already suspicious that Vanessa's main problem was a late sleep phase—that her "natural" times of falling asleep and waking were too late. After we talked a bit more, I was sure. On weekends or vacations Vanessa slept late, till about 10:30 A.M., unless there was a very important morning activity. On waking at that hour she would be in good spirits and want to eat breakfast. And I discovered that Vanessa always fell asleep between 11:00 and 12:00 P.M. no matter what time she was sent to bed. There was nothing her parents could do to make her fall asleep earlier. Even if they sat with her, she would be up for a few hours. But *when she got to stay up late*—perhaps to 11:30 P.M.—after a family outing, on a special occasion, or on vacation, *she went to bed without objections,* without stalling, without stomachaches, and without feeling afraid. And she fell asleep quickly. There was *no problem when she went to bed when she was ready to fall asleep.*

For Vanessa, and other youngsters like her, having to stay in bed unable to sleep for several hours is unpleasant. She would lie there, toss and turn, and *think.* It was hard for her not to have scary fantasies in bed, wide awake, alone, in a darkened room, without distractions. It is really not so surprising that Vanessa objected so vehemently to going to bed. She faced a dilemma each night. Either suffer alone in bed or get up and have her parents angry at her.

Both Matthew and Vanessa had a late sleep phase. And both of them had all of the main symptoms:

1. Bedtime struggles or difficulty falling asleep at the expected bedtime, regardless of bedtime rituals or punishment.

2. Difficulty waking at a "normal" hour.

3. Consistent (but late) time of falling asleep.

4. No bedtime struggles or sleep difficulty when bedtime is near or later than the usual time of falling asleep.

5. Amount of sleep is normal when morning wakings are allowed to occur spontaneously.

If your child suffers only from a late sleep phase, then he will not have nighttime wakings. Matthew, however, did wake at night because in his parents' efforts to get him to sleep they had inadvertently taught him to associate rocking with falling asleep. And in some ways Vanessa was like a child testing limits or with exaggerated fears. But these symptoms proved to be secondary to her inability to go to sleep early. They were not causing the problem.

How Late Sleep Phase Begins

Late sleep phase shifts occur for a number of reasons, but the most common underlying factor is the natural tendency of the sleep cycle to drift later unless held in check by an appropriate and regular schedule. For example, if your child doesn't have a regular schedule and is allowed to stay up late at night and to sleep late in the morning, his cycle will gradually drift on its own. If he goes through a period in which temporary fears, excitement, a trip, or an illness interfere with his falling asleep, and at the same time he is allowed to sleep late, his cycle may also shift. Then, even when conditions return to normal, he may have a problem falling asleep at the old bedtime.

Also, some people seem more prone to develop a late sleep phase than others. As discussed in the last chapter, so-called "owls" like to stay up late; they feel energetic and productive at night but have difficulty waking in the morning regardless of the amount of sleep they have had. At the slightest opportunity they allow their sleep-wake schedules to begin moving later and later. But "larks," as you remember, do not feel very alert in the evening; instead they wake early in the morning full of energy. Larks will be much less likely to let their sleep phase shift late, even on vacations.

We don't know at what age these differences develop in children or if they carry these early tendencies into adulthood. And we don't know if these differences are inborn or if they arise primarily from environmental influences, such as growing up on a farm or having parents who work at home and maintain late schedules themselves. But we do know that many children—infants, toddlers, school-aged children, and certainly adolescents—already show a preference for either early mornings or late evenings.

In any case, family patterns may be important in determining how a late phase develops. If you like to sleep late, are happy if your child sleeps late, and are not tempted to wake him regularly at an earlier hour, then his sleep phase may begin to drift. But if you are an early riser, like to get up and out, and are unwilling to sit around waiting for your child to wake on his own, it is less likely his sleep phase will become delayed.

You may be wondering how Vanessa's sleep phase had drifted when she had to get up early five days a week. It was really the weekends that were keeping Vanessa in trouble. Sleeping late even one or two mornings a week may be enough to allow a sleep phase to drift late or to prevent it from being pushed back earlier. It is not difficult to imagine how Vanessa must have felt. Many of us stay up late Friday and Saturday, sleep late Saturday and Sunday, and find that we have trouble going to sleep early Sunday night and can hardly get out of bed Monday morning.

How We Solve the Problem

Once you recognize that your child's problem is due to a late sleep phase, treatment is relatively straightforward. The easiest way to treat a delayed sleep phase is to begin with a schedule that fits his present times of falling asleep and waking, then gradually advance the sleep phase by making the bed- and waking times a little earlier each day.

If you are going to adjust your child's sleep schedule, allow him— for now—to stay up until about the time he normally falls asleep so that you can be assured he will fall asleep fairly easily. Thus you will eliminate the bedtime arguments. Bedtime can then become a pleasant period rather than one full of tension, bickering, anxiety, and frustration. If your child is old enough to understand, he will be relieved to learn you are no longer angry with him for not settling down earlier and that you agree that, at least for a while, he should be allowed to stay up much later.

Next you must decide when you want your child to sleep. If you and he do not have to be up and out at an early hour, then you have some choice. For example, I told Matthew's parents that he could sleep about twelve hours, starting any time between 7:00 P.M. and 10:00 P.M., but they would have to choose. Vanessa's family had less choice; Vanessa had to get up for school.

Now you can begin to adjust his schedule. To move his sleep phase earlier, you must begin in the morning. You cannot *make* a child fall asleep, but you can make him wake up. If your child does not have to be up and out of the house early because he is not yet in school or day-care or because he is on vacation, then you can begin with his natural time of waking. Every one or two days wake him about fifteen minutes earlier. For example, Matthew, who usually woke at 10:00 A.M. was awakened for two days at 9:45 A.M., two days at 9:30 A.M., and so on. After the waking has been moved up by thirty to sixty minutes, so that your child is mildly sleep-deprived each night, you can begin making his bedtime earlier too. For Matthew this meant going to bed at 9:45 P.M., then 9:30 P.M., then 9:15 P.M. and so forth. Once you have reached the desired morning waking time, you may have to continue to advance the evening bedtime somewhat because you started the morning changes first. At this point you may also have to make other small adjustments in sleep times and daily routines to insure a sleep pattern that is both satisfactory and convenient. If your child's nap- and mealtimes are late, as they were with Matthew, you will have to change these gradually as you advance bedtime and waking.

You may find that when you begin to advance your child's hour of waking in the morning he will be a little more tired during the day and will have a natural tendency to add fifteen to thirty minutes to his nap. Don't allow this to happen. If he has been napping for an hour and fifteen minutes, hold him to that schedule so that he will need to go to sleep a little earlier at night.

If, like Vanessa, your child is already getting up early for school five days a week, you will have to work with the bedtime schedule. You will not be able to let him sleep late and begin waking him progressively earlier. You should still start with a late bedtime but you must wake your child at the same early hour *every day*, including weekends. We did this with Vanessa. I knew at first this would leave her a bit tired each day, but as long as she didn't nap, it would be easier for her to fall asleep at the earlier hour once she started to advance her bedtime. I suggested to her parents that they allow Vanessa to have an 11:00 P.M. bedtime for two weeks to give them all a chance to enjoy peaceful bedtimes, an experience they had never had. Then they should move Vanessa's bedtime about fifteen minutes earlier every week. There was to be no rush about moving up the bedtime. We wanted to avoid having Vanessa lie awake in bed for long periods. If the family could keep the earlier morning waking consistent, then Vanessa would gradually be able to go to sleep earlier. It took about three months to get Vanessa's bedtime to 8:30 P.M. But they were three easy months. Bedtimes were pleasant. The main problem for the parents was having to get up early on Saturday and Sunday so that there wouldn't be any setbacks in Vanessa's progress, but they both agreed it was worth the inconvenience.

You will know that you've really solved your child's late sleep phase problem when he begins waking on his own at the right time in the mornings, especially during the week when the wakings are for school and not for cartoons. This is the most telling sign that his sleep phase is now appropriately positioned within his twenty-four-hour day.

In Matthew's case, advancing the sleep phase was complicated by his associations of being rocked with falling asleep, which also needed to be corrected. We had three choices: correct the sleep phase and the association at the same time; correct the association first and the sleep phase second; or advance the sleep phase, then stop the rocking. Any of these would work. I believed that since Matthew actually went to sleep fairly easily at 10:00 P.M. and only had to be rocked briefly once during the night, this association could be broken within a few days. The parents kept the 10:00 P.M. bedtime for the three days it took to break his association to rocking. Then they began waking him in the morning and putting him to bed at night ten minutes earlier every other day. In less than three weeks Matthew was sleeping well and at the appropriate times.

I must stress again how important it is for you to know exactly what is causing your child to sleep badly before you try to correct the problem. With Vanessa, for example, the ongoing bedtime battle would certainly have become worse if she had simply been made to stay in bed from 8:00 P.M. until she fell asleep, and her nighttime fears and physical complaints would only have increased. But by allowing her to start with a later bedtime, the nightly fights with her parents disappeared, and Vanessa fell asleep rapidly. Admittedly she did not enjoy having to wake early on weekend mornings, but this unpleasantness progressively lessened as her sleep phase moved earlier and, in any case, was minor compared to what the nighttimes had been like for her in the past. She cooperated fully, and she and her parents were delighted with the results.

Late Sleep Phase in Adolescents

Adolescents often have problems with a late sleep phase and they are more difficult to treat. On the weekends, teenagers frequently stay up late and then sleep until noon or later, and their sleep cycles can shift profoundly. As a result they may well be very sleep-deprived during the week when they most need to be alert.

Arthur, a fifteen-year-old high school junior, had trouble falling asleep early and difficulty waking for school for many years; but over the summer before he came to see me, the situation developed into a major problem. By the start of school he was going to bed at 11:30 P.M. on weeknights but was unable to fall asleep until 4:00 or even 5:00 A.M. He would listen to the radio and occasionally get up to get something to eat. Needless to say, he had great difficulty getting up for school at 6:30 in the morning and in fact had missed many days.

His parents were becoming angry with him and there were battles every morning when they had to try over and over again to wake him. On the weekends Arthur would often stay up very late watching television and not even bother getting into bed until 3:00 or 4:00 A.M. On weekend mornings and when he missed school, he would sleep until noon or 1:00 P.M.

Arthur's problem is a bit more complex than that of younger children with a late sleep phase because it is much more difficult for a parent to assume control over an adolescent's sleep cycle. Even if your teenager understands the importance of maintaining a regular sleep schedule, he may be unwilling to do so. Pressure from friends is very strong in these years and most adolescents love to stay up late watching television, talking on the phone, or listening to music.

Arthur was an average student. Although he didn't particularly like school, he did want to attend and graduate. He was quite upset about having so much trouble falling asleep at night and he hated getting up in the morning after only two hours sleep, feeling tired, listless, and in a fog. When he was in school he was so exhausted that he had a great deal of difficulty paying attention. He was happy when I told him that I understood what was wrong and that we could solve his sleep problem. He found it reassuring to learn that I sympathized with his difficulty waking in the morning, that I knew he was not just "lazy," and that I agreed that he *couldn't* fall asleep early, at least not yet.

Like Matthew and Vanessa, Arthur had a late sleep phase, but his was a *very* late sleep phase, with a delay of five or six hours. His sleep phase ran from about 4:30 A.M. to 12:30 P.M. Although theoretically Arthur could have changed his sleep phase by getting up early seven days a week and not napping, I knew that, in practice, such a five- or six-hour shift in a fifteen-year-old would be very difficult to achieve by that method. All the time he was shifting he would be getting much less sleep than he needed. He would be tired, his motivation would fail, and he might sleep late occasionally, especially on the weekends. If he could not stick to the planned time of waking every day, then the treatment would not work.

So for Arthur we needed a somewhat different approach. First of all it was important that he assume control over his bedtime and wakings. In particular he should be responsible for getting up in the morning. He was not to rely on his parents; he had to take over that job himself. He bought a clock radio, set it to a loud morning talk show, and had a second backup alarm clock across the room just in case. Also, he was to stop listening to the radio in bed when it was time to go to sleep. Although it is more pleasurable to listen to the radio than just to lie quietly, if you are interested in the radio show it is harder, not easier, to fall asleep.

To correct the timing of Arthur's sleep phase the quickest and easiest way possible, he had to go to bed later each night. Yes—*later.* Instead of struggling to make his sleep phase earlier, Arthur was to delay it further each night until he had gone around the clock to the times he wanted—for example, until he was going to sleep at 11:00 P.M. and waking at 6:30 A.M. At that point the morning waking time would become key. Once he was sleeping at more normal hours, he would be able to maintain his sleep phase by getting up at the same time every morning, even if he stayed up later on the weekends. I felt that Arthur would be more likely to follow through with the plan if he were allowed to stay up late some nights. And as long as he got up by 6:30, or perhaps 7:30 at the latest on the weekends, the occasional late bedtime would not cause his sleep phase to shift later again. He also agreed to chart his sleep patterns so that he and I could follow his progress.

Arthur was to go to sleep and get up three hours *later* each day until he reached the desired times for bed and waking (see Figure 10). For example, the first night he was to go to sleep at 7:00 A.M. and plan to wake by 3:00 P.M. The next day he would go to bed at 10:00 A.M. and get up at 6:00 P.M. He was to continue this pattern of progressive change until he arrived at an appropriate schedule. If he overslept while making the shift it would help to speed up the process, but once he began to near the correct times, he had to be sure that he did not sleep past 6:30 A.M.

If you have a teenager with a late sleep phase, you will find this adjustment is fairly easy to make; it means that during the period of change your child is falling asleep quickly, getting enough sleep each night, and not having difficulty waking. Because of this he will lose any unpleasant feelings he may have learned to associate with just being in bed. Also, this schedule goes in the same direction as the natural tendency of his circadian rhythms—a little later each day. Within a week he should be sleeping and waking at the desired times.

Then, as long as he keeps his morning wakings constant, his sleep cycle will remain regular and become progressively stable. During this program he may have to miss one or two days of school but this can be kept to a minimum by starting the program in the early hours of a Saturday morning. If this is done, he will be sleeping during the morning on Saturday, Sunday, and Monday, but by Tuesday or Wednesday he won't be going to sleep until after school (see Figure 10). And once his sleep schedule is adjusted, his attendance should be even better than it was before.

If your teenager's sleep phase is only one and a half to three hours late, however, it makes more sense first to try and correct the phase shift by starting with the late bedtime and then moving it progressively earlier while keeping the time of morning waking early every day and avoiding naps. You cannot do this for him. You can explain to him the "why" and "how," but *he* must want to change things and *he* must be willing to get himself up each morning.

A "Desired" Late Sleep Phase

There is one other form of late sleep phase that we see mainly in adolescents. Some teenagers actually want a late sleep phase, although they may not be willing to admit it. It is important that you be able to recognize this problem because it won't get better by the types of schedule changes described here.

Susan was fourteen years old and, like Arthur, she had a very late sleep phase, but with several important exceptions. Instead of her problem being worse in the summer, when she didn't have to get up for school, it improved. In fact in the summer she slept from 1:00 A.M. to 9:00 A.M. But during the school year, Susan usually fell asleep at 5:00 A.M. and woke at noon. The school made special allowances so that she could come in at 12:30 P.M. for a half-day, but shortly afterwards Susan became unable to fall asleep until 7:00 A.M. or wake before mid-afternoon. When I saw Susan she had missed most of the first semester. Her parents tried to get her up in the morning but they had to go to work, and Susan usually went back to sleep when they left. Although Susan's problem had only been severe since she started high school, she had always fought going to school and was absent frequently. Her family situation was tense, unhappy, and unsupportive; and Susan's feelings about school had never been resolved. She was depressed, she had no close friends, and she hated school. Because she was unable to fall asleep until morning and could not wake until the afternoon, she missed a great deal of school, and she had

	Bedtime	Waking
Sleep phase *BEFORE* *starting program*	4:30 am	12:30 pm
Saturday	7:00 am	3:00 pm
Sunday	10:00 am	6:00 pm
Monday	1:00 pm	9:00 pm
Tuesday	4:00 pm	midnight
Wednesday	7:00 pm	3:00 am
Thursday	10:00 pm	6:00 am
Friday	11:00 pm	6:30 am
Sleep phase *AFTER* *finishing program*	11:00 pm	6:30 am

FIGURE 10 A Sample Routine for Around-the-Clock Sleep Schedule Change to Correct a Late Sleep Phase

little opportunity to spend time with other children her age. But that was what she really wanted. Susan allowed her sleep phase to shift because it gave her an excuse to stay home, to miss school, and to avoid being with her peers. She convinced her family and herself that she "wanted" to have a more normal sleep schedule but just "couldn't." This was partially true. She *couldn't* fall asleep early once her sleep phase had shifted, but she also didn't *want* to.

Adjusting Susan's sleep phase, either by gradual advance or progressive around-the-clock delay, would not work, because she would never cooperate. We tried a progressive delay just to be sure, but she did not follow through at all. Although she had previously complained that she couldn't fall asleep before 7:00 A.M., she now said she was "unable" to stay up later than that, but she never really tried. Instead, before 7:00 A.M. ever arrived, she would get into bed and turn out the lights.

Susan was depressed and isolated with very little self-esteem. Most of all she hated going to school. If she did not have to go to school, her sleep problem would have largely corrected itself.

For Susan and other youngsters like her there can be no direct treatment of the "sleep problem" because the sleep isn't really the problem. The late sleep phase is only a symptom of an emotional problem and the proper treatment is psychotherapy. In situations like Susan's I always recommend psychological evaluation and counseling. Often family therapy is the best approach because the problems are usually long-standing and intimately tied to the child's relationships with other family members. Sometimes a child may even feel an obligation to stay home during the day to care for a parent who is feeling depressed and isolated. Here the parent is actually providing subtle encouragement for the child to maintain a late sleep phase. Since neither of them really wants anything changed, the recommendation for counseling is often turned down.

If the family does follow through and obtains the needed counseling, things will improve and the sleep problem will usually resolve on its own without carefully planned schedule changes. If it does not, the necessary adjustments can be made later.

Susan and her parents were initially quite reluctant to seek any form of counseling. But, after a few months they finally agreed to give it a try. At first they found it difficult to discuss matters openly. Very gradually, however, they began to understand many of the problems they previously denied even existed. Although many issues remain to be settled, the family has already made much progress. Susan still does not like school, but she is attending regularly. She is not outgoing, but she has made a few tentative efforts toward making friends and is clearly happier. Family relationships have improved. And though she still tends to stay up until about 1:00 A.M., her sleep phase is now much closer to normal than it was before. If Susan and her family continue to take advantage of the help they are receiving as they work out their problems, I am confident that things will continue to improve even further.

Part Four

INTERRUPTIONS
DURING SLEEP

Sleeptalking, Walking, Thrashing, and Terrors—a Spectrum of Sudden Partial Wakings

L isa, at eighteen months, was a happy baby, but every night, a few hours after falling asleep, she woke crying and rolling about in her crib and could not be comforted. Eldridge, at two and a half years, would wake two or three hours after falling asleep and thrash and yell in a bizarre manner for fifteen to twenty minutes. Marcy, at age four, would often moan, babble phrases that were difficult to understand, and move about her bed restlessly for a few minutes about two hours after falling asleep, but she always went back to sleep on her own. At age six, Christopher began to walk in his sleep, quietly and calmly, with a blank expression on his face. By the time he was eight he would sit up at night, scream out, and appear frightened. Shannon was a twelve-year-old girl who would jump out of bed and run about her room or even thrash on the floor frantically almost every night. David, seventeen, would suddenly leap out of bed after sleeping for two or three hours and run around so wildly in apparent terror that he actually injured himself.

You may wonder what all these youngsters have in common—a baby who wakes crying, a toddler who wakes thrashing bizarrely, a young child who talks in her sleep, an older child who sleepwalks and wakes apparently frightened as if from a bad dream, a pre-adolescent who runs or thrashes frantically at night, and an adolescent who runs about wildly in terror and sometimes injures himself. All of these children do have a similar sleep problem, however—an incomplete waking from deep *non-dreaming* sleep. The specific characteristics and the significance of these arousals vary depending upon the age of the child and upon certain physiologic and emotional factors.

While sleeptalking is so common that it can hardly be considered "abnormal" or even a "sleep problem," sleepwalking has always been one of the most curious sleep disorders, one that is well known, and one that has been worrisome to parents and fascinating to sleep specialists and poets. Sleep terrors are perhaps the most dramatic of all sleep disorders. They are certainly the most frightening, at least to the family members who observe them. However, most people know little about them and do not realize that many children have them. Less intense but more long-lasting periods of confused thrashing can be equally if not more frightening to parents. Doctors and parents often misinterpret these episodes as bad dreams, from which the child should be waked, or as epileptic seizures needing medical treatment.

What Happens During These Partial Wakings

As you recall from Chapter 2, the onset of sleep is followed by a rapid descent into Stage IV, the deepest stage of non-REM sleep. In this state, the system seems to be on "autopilot," with very stable regulation of heart rate, respiration, and other functions. At the end of the first sleep cycle, usually sixty to ninety minutes after falling asleep, there is a brief arousal to a lighter stage of sleep and perhaps even a brief waking. In children this is usually followed by another fairly rapid descent back into Stage IV sleep for the second sleep cycle, though adults may have a brief nondescript dream at this time. The second sleep cycle ends similarly to the first, and most of the rest of the night is spent alternating between lighter non-REM sleep and REM. Just before morning, children often descend once again into Stage III or Stage IV sleep before their final waking, but this is not as deep as the Stage IV early in the night. The REM periods that appear toward morning tend to be longer, more intense, and are associated with more interesting and exciting dreams, occasionally even scary ones (true nightmares, see Chapter 11).

We know that the episodes described in this chapter could not possibly occur during the dream stage, since the near-paralysis which occurs during REM sleep effectively prevents us from acting out our dreams. You cannot sit up, you cannot thrash about, you cannot walk, you cannot scream, you cannot run. But during non-REM sleep you can move, and you usually do, at least during the transitions between sleep cycles. Most often these movements are minor and brief. But minor or major, basically the same thing is occurring. You will see that even thrashing, sleepwalking, or screaming are really quite similar to the quieter behavior that happens normally at the end of a period of deep sleep. They just may be more sudden, intense, complex, long-lasting, and dramatic.

The events I am describing here happen most frequently about one to four hours after falling asleep, at the end of the first or second sleep cycle during a partial waking from Stage IV non-REM sleep. The end of a period in Stage IV usually occurs suddenly. Even when we monitor a child in the laboratory, we find nothing to tell us that a change in state is about to occur. Suddenly and without warning, the child moves. He or she may turn over in bed and will often briefly open and close his or her eyes before descending again into deeper sleep and beginning the next sleep cycle. This arousal is only partial. Full waking does not occur. The brain waves show a mixture of patterns, including those from deep sleep, those seen during transitions toward waking, and some patterns from the drowsy and waking states themselves.

Sometimes, however, your child may not make this transition rapidly. Instead, she may moan, speak in a mumbling and incomprehensible manner (here, not during dreams, is where most sleeptalking occurs), and move about restlessly for several minutes, as Marcy did each night. She may lift her head, grind her teeth, and even sit up briefly and look about in a confused manner before returning to sleep.

What we are seeing is apparently the simultaneous functioning of both the child's waking and deep sleep systems. Both processes seem to be going on together and, in fact, your child shows evidence of being awake *and* asleep. She may appear to be "awake" since her eyes are open, she may speak, and she may move about, but she can't manage complex actions requiring higher levels of mental functioning such as reading a book or even forming memories. She may behave oddly, seem distressed, confused, and disoriented; and she may not recognize you or her surroundings.

If her arousal is a bit more intense (see Figure 11, page 138) your child may begin to crawl about the bed in a somewhat confused manner as though she were looking for something, or she may even get out of bed and walk around. Although her eyes are open and she can make her way about the room or house, she has little awareness of the world about her. Even though she probably won't seem to recognize you, she still may come to wherever you are. Then she may stop and simply stare, but "through you," not "at you." Especially if she is beyond the toddler years she may seem to be looking for something and may mumble phrases that are difficult to understand. She may walk down the stairs and may even try to leave the house. If she is

FIGURE 11:

Spectrum of Behavior in Children
at the End of a Period of Stage IV Sleep
LISTED IN ORDER OF INCREASING INTENSITY

Normal termination of Stage IV (brief body movements; perhaps eye opening, mumbling, chewing)

Sleeptalking

(Enuresis)*

Calm sitting up in bed, looking about, blank expression

Calm sleepwalking (semi-purposeful; child may appear to be looking for something and/or may walk towards parents or light; actions may seem to be to fulfill a need such as hunger or urge to urinate; inappropriate urination common, e.g. into closet or shoe)

Agitated sleepwalking (trying to get out of room, possibly "away from something")

Extended periods of confused wild thrashing (thrashing, moaning, yelling, kicking, screaming; may be prolonged, child may act bizarrely or seem "possessed")

Sleep terror (terrifying "blood-curdling" scream, look of fear and panic, eyes wide open, heart racing, sweating profusely)

Full-blown sleep terror (scream with look of fear and panic, leaping out of bed, running wildly "away from something," significant chance of accidental injury)

*It is unclear where enuresis should be listed on this spectrum or even if it should be considered truly a part of this spectrum at all (see Chapter 12).

very calm she may respond to your simple questions ("Are you okay?") with single-word answers ("Yes"). If you tell her to go back to bed she may, or she may let you guide her back to bed, perhaps with a stop in the bathroom to urinate. Sometimes, because of confusion, a boy (or less frequently a girl) may urinate in the wrong place. If so, it may not simply be in the middle of the floor, but more likely he will urinate into a boot, a wastebasket, or even into the closet. Once back in bed, younger children will usually return to sleep without ever completely waking. Older children and adolescents may wake briefly and feel embarrassed at finding themselves in unexpected places with people staring at them, but they too usually return to sleep promptly.

If your child's partial arousal is more pronounced, she may continue to walk in her sleep but no longer calmly and quietly. She may jump out of bed and hurry about the room or house in an agitated manner. She may appear upset, confused, and disoriented. Perhaps she will feel along the wall for the doorway leading out of her bedroom. She may yell out angry phrases such as "Get outta here!" She may even seem almost frantic. Still, although she appears somewhat apprehensive, she does not seem to be really terrified. In this agitated state she is unlikely to respond to your questions. She will not recognize you, and if you try to hold her she will only become more upset and push you away. You can't wake her, but after one to forty minutes (usually between five and twenty) she calms down, wakes briefly, and goes back to bed. She will remember little or nothing of the preceding period and will not describe any dream.

Infants and very young children are unlikely to show the same type of agitated sleepwalking, but some of their more intense arousals can seem even more bizarre and may be quite frightening for parents. The toddler or young child may arouse with prolonged moaning, then begin to cry, sob, or even scream. She may then thrash around the bed wildly with eyes open and with a peculiar look on her face. She will sweat profusely and you may notice that her heart is pounding. She may continue to moan, cry, and thrash for up to forty minutes, and on rare occasions for as long as an hour. The thrashing and rolling about may be very strange, unlike anything you have ever seen when she is awake, and unlike the behavior you may have come to expect for her nighttime wakings. You may assume she is having (or has had) a bad dream. However, she does not calm when you walk into her room and she may seem unaware that you are even there. She is not comforted when you try to hold her, and instead of clutching you tightly, she may even push you away. If you try to wake her by shaking her or by putting cold water on her face, the thrashing may get worse.

Some parents become so frightened that they rush their child to the hospital, only to have the episode end before they get there.

These episodes are commonly known as "night terrors" or "sleep terrors," but these terms are misleading, since your child doesn't appear to be "terrified." She does not even appear to be in pain. She looks agitated, confused, and upset. Many parents say that during these episodes their child looks "possessed," because of the very strange facial expression, the wild thrashing, and the lack of response when they try to help. After about ten to forty minutes your child will stretch, yawn, and lie back down. If she is sitting, she will now let you help her to a lying position and tuck her back in bed. If she wakes fully, she will be calm and want only to return to sleep. Only if you insist on trying to keep her awake, perhaps to be sure she is all right, will she remain awake for more than one or two minutes. She will not have any memory of the episode or of any dream either then or in the morning. She is fine, although you may still be upset.

A similar partial waking with extended crying and inability to be calmed may also occur in infants, appearing perhaps as early as six months of age. These episodes don't seem so strange at this age, because the thrashing is less wild and because we tend to expect infants to have some periods of uncontrollable crying. Many parents of babies with these episodes simply assume their child has had a bad dream. This is an easy mistake to make, especially since their child is too young to deny it.

These "wakings," in infants and toddlers, are important to recognize, however, because they are different from all the ones I discussed in Chapters 5 through 9. They have nothing to do with habits, associations, or limits, and the treatment for them is much different. Sleep schedule considerations, however, may be important.

In some children we see very intense arousals, which do perhaps deserve to be called "sleep terrors." They happen most often in adolescents, although pre-adolescents may show mixtures of patterns—extended wild thrashing along with screaming and a look of terror. Typically a sleep terror will start very suddenly. Your child lets out a loud "bloodcurdling" scream and sits bolt upright in bed. She looks terrified—her eyes are bulging, she is sweating, and her heart is racing. She may yell out phrases that suggest fear of attack or entrapment: "It's gonna get me" or "The ceiling is falling." These episodes are usually shorter than the extended thrashing of younger children and often end within one to five minutes. Your child then wakes briefly but quickly returns to sleep. Most often on waking fully she will have no recollection of anything frightening, although sometimes she may have a vague "memory" of something that seems to fit the phrases she mumbled during the episode itself. Thus, your child may say that "something was going to get me." Nevertheless, she cannot describe this in any of the detail that you would expect if she had actually been dreaming. In the most intense episodes your child may jump out of bed and begin to run wildly. She will act as if she is trying to get away from someone or something, and she will seem to be in a real panic. She may knock over furniture or even people, break lamps or windows, and fall and injure herself. The major part of the event may be over in less than a minute, though your child may remain confused for some minutes more.

The Significance of These Arousals at Different Ages

All of these events occur during a partial waking from non-REM sleep. The more intense or long-lasting ones almost certainly arise from Stage IV. Until age five or six most of these episodes are "developmental." This means that they are not usually caused by physical or emotional problems but instead are only reflections of the normal maturation of your child's sleep stages. Because Stage IV non-REM sleep is very deep in young children, deeper than in older children and much deeper than in adults, it is likely that stimuli triggering arousal at the end of the first or second sleep cycle are sometimes insufficient to fully break the grip of the ongoing deep sleep state. As a result the child is left in a mixed state, half asleep and half awake. The triggers themselves are probably only the normal inherent mechanisms that control the end of one period in Stage IV sleep and the start of the next sleep cycle. These are part of your child's biological rhythms which are controlled by her "internal clock." Occasionally the triggers are external, for example an episode may begin when you make a noise walking upstairs or when you cover your child with a blanket. This is most likely to happen if you disturb your child near a time that a period of Stage IV sleep is about to end anyway. Ringing a loud buzzer an hour after sleep onset may trigger a sleep terror in susceptible children. Similarly, many children, even those who were not previously sleepwalkers, can be made to do so simply by lifting them up at this time and placing them on their feet.

Under age five or six, therefore, most of these episodes are of little significance, physically or emotionally. When they begin in or persist into the middle childhood years or adolescence, however, they may show different characteristics, be of different significance, and have different causes. Sleepwalking may look the same at any age, but the older child may show more agitation. Extended periods of wild thrashing become uncommon with increasing age, but in an older child the more clearly defined sleep terrors may appear. Also in an older child, these events can no longer simply be thought of as "developmental." Underlying emotional factors now are likely to be relevant, especially if the arousals are frequent. But before we discuss these matters more fully, it will be helpful for you to have a basic understanding of what this state of partial waking is all about.

More About "Partial Wakings" from Deep Sleep

Stage IV is a state with some paradoxes. It seems to be the state furthest away from waking. People waked from Stage IV sleep report no dreams and little or no memory of any ongoing thoughts. Generally it is a state from which it is difficult to be waked, even with meaningful words ("Fire!") or noises (crying, crashes). Trying to wake a child from Stage IV may seem almost impossible, even with vigorous stimulation. As mentioned in Chapter 2, if such a child falls deeply asleep in the car or at a neighbor's, she can often be carried back home, undressed, and put to bed with only a partial waking and no memory of being moved.

As difficult as it may be to wake someone fully from Stage IV, we have already learned that such a period usually ends suddenly, although this does not lead immediately to full waking. Under any circumstances, a full transition from Stage IV to waking takes time, especially in children. What does happen rapidly and more easily is a change from Stage IV to the start of the transition to waking, that is to a state of partial waking. This state is intermediate between sleep and waking and has some of the features of full waking and some of deep sleep.

Most often this transition is brief. Your child wakes slightly, turns over, pulls up the blanket, and goes back to sleep with little or no awareness of waking. But sometimes all does not go so smoothly. Your child may wake partially, then walk, thrash, scream, or run. If she does, you might like to know what she feels like at the time.

What a Sudden Partial Waking Feels Like

It may help you to understand if you imagine that, one hour after you fall asleep, there is a loud alarm, a gunshot, or a terrifying scream. You "wake" instantly. But your head will still be filled with "cobwebs" and you will have some difficulty figuring out what is happening. If you wake with the fire alarm ringing, you may find your heart racing, feel yourself scared, and know that you have to do something. Yet you still find that it takes several seconds (or longer) to become clear-headed enough to act appropriately. That period of a few seconds during which you feel yourself afraid but are foggy and not fully alert, is an *approximation* to what children experience during a sleep terror.

If you have to get out of bed two hours after going to sleep to give your child medicine, the alarm clock may "wake you," and you get up calmly and walk into the bathroom. But instead of getting the medicine, you use the toilet and then start to return to your bedroom. You may then feel that there is something else you are supposed to do, but you are confused. You may stop and look about with a blank or dazed expression on your face. Still you are not sure what it is you are looking for, where you should be looking, or why you are even out of bed in the first place. Finally you wake more fully and remember all about the medicine. But what you had been doing before this, from the moment your alarm went off until you were finally able to think clearly, is perhaps an approximation to what your child experiences as she walks in her sleep.

Even though you may not be clear-headed during these partial wakings, you are closer to full waking than your child when she is sleepwalking or having a sleep terror. You are forming memories, and your behavior, although possibly comical, is unlikely to be bizarre. This is because your Stage IV sleep is lighter than your child's. However, if you went to sleep drugged with sleeping pills or alcohol, then waking would be more difficult for you and what you did on "waking" might be more similar to your child's sleepwalking or sleep terror episodes. And you might well return to sleep without much of a memory of the waking.

Now we can come back and talk in more detail about the different characteristics, significance, and causes of these events at different ages. If your child shows nighttime behavior similar to any of the children I will describe, it should now be easier to understand and you will learn how you can best deal with it.

Partial Wakings in Young Children

Let's take a closer look at two of the children I described at the beginning of the chapter. Despite an easy bedtime, Lisa, a one-and-a-half-year-old girl, would wake several hours after going to sleep, usually about the time that her parents were retiring. Although she generally seemed happy during the day and would wake in the morning in good spirits, at the nighttime waking she would cry and thrash about in her crib. Her mother or father would go in and lift her up, but she would not seem to be comforted. Instead, the thrashing increased in intensity, she would arch her back, kick, and could not be calmed. At times her parents noticed Lisa's heart seemed to be beating rapidly, she would be sweating, and her eyes would be wide open, but she looked more uncomfortable or frustrated than truly frightened or panicky. They would generally try walking her, talking to her, or shaking her in an attempt to wake her, and on a few occasions even tried cold compresses or screaming at her. Regardless of what they did, it would usually take ten to fifteen minutes for her to calm down. At times the episodes lasted twenty to thirty minutes. Eventually Lisa would begin to quiet, stretch, and yawn; and now her parents found they could wake her into a more normal state and reassure themselves she was in fact all right. After doing this, however, they found they might have difficulty putting her back down, and she was reluctant to go back to sleep for some time. Once back asleep, she would usually sleep through until morning. These episodes occurred four or five times a week.

Lisa's parents were concerned. They wanted to help her, but what they were doing was only making matters worse. They, like most parents, were filled with a desire to "do something." However, the best response would have been to do nothing. They were interested to learn that Lisa was not crying in the midst of a bad dream. Crying occurs *after* a bad dream, not during it (see Chapter 11). And, she was not crying after waking from a bad dream either. In fact she was not awake at all and she was not frightened or in pain. Her parents came to realize that if she were awake and scared or in discomfort, she would want to be held and would let herself be comforted. Lisa was having partial wakings from deep sleep and there was little her parents could do to help at the time. And in fact there was no need to. Nothing worrisome was happening to Lisa.

Once Lisa's parents understood this, they were able to watch the crying spells without interfering, and without feeling guilty. I told them to go in, respond to her only if she wanted to be held, but otherwise just watch. They were to "keep their distance." Once Lisa stopped crying they were to help her lie down and cover her, but that's all. They were not to try and wake her fully. There was no need to see if she was all right. She was.

Lisa's parents noticed two improvements almost immediately. Although the "wakings" continued, they were shorter-lasting, because her parents simply let them run their course without intervening, which actually had seemed to make the thrashing last longer. Secondly, after each episode ended, Lisa went right back to sleep. This is what one would expect. In the past, however, her parents had insisted on waking her after the events subsided. She would reach such full waking, and be the center of so much attention, that she was unable or unwilling to return to sleep immediately. Soon the wakings ceased to be a problem. Because the parents usually did not go to bed until after the episodes occurred, their own sleep was not disrupted. Eventually most of the "wakings" were fairly mild, with only a little whining and thrashing, and Lisa's parents didn't even find it necessary to go to her at all.

Eldridge, almost three, had been waking frequently at night for the past year. Although his bedtime was about 7:30, there was always a prolonged period of stalling and he would not usually get to sleep before about 9:00 P.M. Within two to three hours he could be heard moaning and moving about. Soon he would be screaming, crying, sobbing, and sweating profusely. He would toss, turn, and thrash wildly about his bed, get caught in the sheets, bump the wall, and sometimes do somersaults. Occasionally he would stiffen, although never rigidly. The events were similar from night to night but never identical. Eldridge did not seem to be frightened or in any discomfort but rather appeared quite confused or, as the parents put it "out of it." He might mutter a few phrases such as "I don't want to" or "Go away," but much of his speech could not be understood. Much to his parents' concern and frustration they were unable to comfort him at these times. In fact, he did not seem to recognize them and he would push them away when they tried to hold him. Although worried, they sometimes became angry when Eldridge pushed them away as they were trying to help. Even though they could not comfort him, they would continue trying to wake him by calling loudly to him and shaking him until the event finally ended. Eldridge's episodes usually lasted only a few minutes, although some nights the thrashing continued for fifteen to twenty minutes. Then he would relax completely, stretch, and yawn. When the parents persisted they could wake him at this point, but he was quite sleepy and only interested in returning to sleep. He always was unaware that anything unusual had occurred and he would return to sleep promptly. Sometimes Eldridge would have another episode an hour or two later, but it was almost always shorter-lasting and less intense than the first. The rest of the night was usually quiet. He occasionally had a similar arousal during the day after he had been napping for about an hour. Shortly before they brought Eldridge to me his parents tried eliminating his nap in hope of improving his sleep, but the nighttime wakings only became worse. During the day Eldridge was happy and well behaved and I found the family situation to be stable and supportive.

Eldridge, of course, had the same problem as did Lisa, except that his arousals were more intense. He was bigger and could thrash about more, and at his age his failure to respond to his parents or to talk meaningfully seemed more unusual. His parents also had not known how to handle the problem. They always tried to "snap him out of it," and because the episodes did end in a few minutes, they thought they were "finally waking him" from the midst of an ongoing bad dream.

I gave Eldridge's parents the same advice I gave Lisa's—to keep their distance during the arousals, and then let him go back to sleep without questioning him. I suggested they go into his room when he was having an episode just to be sure he didn't hurt himself. They did not have to worry about "spoiling" him, as some people had warned them, because they were not going in to meet the demands of a wakeful youngster. And they should not question him about the events, then or in the morning, since he would have no memory of them, and their questions could only make him anxious. He would realize that he was doing something at night about which he was unaware, over which he had no control, and about which his parents were concerned. Anxiety over these partial wakings conceivably can lead to an increase in their frequency. It certainly will not help. Now Eldridge's parents felt less upset about getting up at night and they no longer felt angry. They were not involved in struggles with their son and getting rebuffed. Still, the partial wakings continued, so we decided to make two other changes. Eldridge was encouraged to begin napping again and his parents began to enforce the 7:30 bedtime after a pleasant bedtime ritual. Now that he was getting enough sleep, he was no longer overtired at night. The frequency and the intensity of the nighttime partial wakings decreased considerably and over the next few months the arousals disappeared almost completely.

In youngsters up to about age six, and less frequently in older children, assuring adequate amounts of sleep at night may be the most important treatment. You might expect an overtired child to sleep better than usual, but paradoxically such a child is more likely to sleepwalk or have sleep terrors. This happens because a sleep-deprived child has a greater need for deep sleep. This need or drive may prevent the deep sleep system from giving way at the end of the first or second sleep cycle, and a mixed state of partial waking may occur.

It is also important to insure that your child is on a regular schedule.

If your child is having episodes of partial waking at night, do everything you can to keep her nap- and bedtimes regular. Her biological rhythms will become more stable and can work in harmony. The timing of her arousals at the end of the first and second sleep cycles will be more appropriate. Now she will stir when deep sleep is "ready" to give way to a lighter state, not before.

Assuring adequate sleep, providing a normal schedule, and keeping your distance are the best ways to treat arousal problems in young children (see Figure 12, page 148). Please understand, however, that although these remedies *may* help, they won't always do so. You may just have to learn to live with your child's nighttime wakings. I find that once parents understand what is happening, they can accept the inconvenience much more easily. Some medication will alleviate the problem, but the side effects generally outweigh any possible benefits. I usually recommend the use of medication for children only if they seem at risk of injuring themselves, and this is unlikely before late childhood or adolescence.

When it is said that "sleep terrors" are most common at age three to four, what people are speaking of are the kind of events seen in Lisa and Eldridge. They probably occur with similar frequency in younger children but when they occur in infants they are more likely to be dismissed as "bad dreams." In most cases children outgrow them by age five or six.

Psychological factors are rarely relevant at this age, but they can be. If there is significant ongoing stress in your home, or if the episodes began after some specific stress such as a divorce, death in the family, or after a family member's hospitalization, then you should probably consider consultation with a professional counselor.

Partial Wakings in Older Children

The situation in older children and teenagers with frequent sleepwalking or sleep terrors is different. Here psychological factors are usually relevant. There is no specific age below which all such arousals are "developmental" and above which all are "psychological." But if your child is beyond six and her nighttime wakings persist, recur, or appear for the first time, there likely is a psychological component to her problem. This does not necessarily imply that she has *major* emotional problems. In fact, this is usually not the case. Emotional problems are most often minor and have to do with how your child has come to deal with her feelings. Typically she will be a well-behaved youngster

FIGURE 12 Sudden Partial Wakings

Behavior	Typical Age	What To Do	General Suggestions
Extended periods of crying, sobbing, moaning with wild bizarre thrashing	6 months–6 years, occasionally in older children	• Go in to be sure your child does not injure herself. • Let the episode run its course. Keep your distance. Don't forcibly "help." Only hold her if she recognizes you and wants to be held. Do not shake her or otherwise vigorously try to wake her. • Watch for the relaxation and calm that signals the end of the episode. You may then help her lie down and you may cover her. Let her go back to sleep. Do not wake her or try to ask her what was wrong or what she had been dreaming about. Similarly, don't question her in the morning. Don't make her feel strange, different, or bizarre.	• Make sure your child gets sufficient sleep. Consider an earlier bedtime. Restart a nap if it was abandoned without good reason. • Make sure that her sleep and daily schedules are fairly regular and consistent. • Counseling may be considered if events are frequent and if they began around known stresses, or if significant ongoing stresses are present, or if your child is older than age six (since by middle childhood psychological factors are frequently relevant). Professional consultation may help in this decision.
Calm Sleepwalking	Any age from the time the child learns to crawl or walk	• Talk quietly and calmly to your child. She may follow your instructions and return to bed herself. • If she does not seem upset when you touch her, you should be able to lead her back to bed calmly. She may want to stop at the bathroom to urinate. Although you might be able to wake her, nothing is gained and there is no point trying. • If she spontaneously wakes after the episode (which older children and adolescents commonly do), she will likely be embarrassed. Do not make any negative or	• For young children, insure adequate sleep and a normal schedule. Occasionally this will help older children as well. • Make the environment as safe as possible to avoid accidental injury. Floors should not be cluttered, objects should not be left on the stairs, hallways should be lit. If your child's walking sometimes goes unnoticed, put a bell on her door so you will be aware whenever she leaves her room. Young children may need a gate by their door or at the top of the stairs. If your child tries to leave the house, an extra chain lock above her reach should be in-

Behavior	Typical Age	What To Do	General Suggestions
		teasing comments. Don't mention it in the morning either, unless she asks. Don't make her feel peculiar or strange. Treat the sleepwalking matter-of-factly and let her go back to bed.	stalled. If she sleeps in a bunk bed, the bottom bunk is safer. • Consideration for counseling as with extended thrashing.
Agitated sleep-walking	Middle childhood through adolescence	• If the agitation is marked, restraint will only make the event more intense and longer-lasting. Keep your distance. Only hold her if she is starting to do something dangerous. • When she calms, treat her as you would a calm sleepwalker.	• Same as for calm sleepwalking.
Sleep terrors (scream, look of panic and fear, possibly wild running)	Late childhood, adolescence	• Let the screaming subside and then simply let your child return to sleep. Do not try to wake her. Do not question her in detail and do not embarrass her if she reaches full waking (as some adolescents may do). • If there is wild running and risk of injury, you may have to intercede, but be careful. Both she and you could get injured. Talk calmly and block her access to dangerous areas, but actually holding her may be very difficult and can lead to even wilder behavior.	• She may be safer sleeping on the first level of the house or in a finished basement room. • If there is threat of, or actual, window breakage, consider replacing the glass with Plexiglas. ® • Use the same general precautions as for sleepwalkers. • Consult your physician for possible use of medication, especially if there is wild running. If medication is used, it should be viewed as a temporary solution used mainly for protection. • Counseling should be considered. This is true even if psychological factors seem minimal but arousals are frequent, intense, and dangerous.

who finds it very difficult to express outwardly any feelings she might consider bad—anger, jealousy, guilt, hate.

You should, however, consider how often your child has nighttime arousals and in what context they occur. One episode of sleepwalking or other partial arousal per year is trivial and probably of little consequence. It should not raise concerns of possible psychological problems. And some children have thrashing or terrors only when they have a fever. Here their sleep disruption is caused by illness, not stress.

The more frequent and the more intense the episodes are, the more likely it is that a child is under some emotional stress, but the frequency and intensity of the episodes do not always correlate with the degree of emotional upset she is feeling.

The Arousal or the Terrors: Which Comes First?

There is a difference of opinion among researchers studying sleep terrors. Some believe the "terror" comes first and causes the sudden arousal. Others think that the arousal comes first and this leads to physiological changes usually associated with fear. This distinction is especially significant after the age of five or six, when emotional factors are more likely to be relevant.

Thus, some feel that the arousal is triggered by a frightening thought, idea, urge, or image that suddenly enters into "consciousness" during the deep sleep state when a child's emotional defenses are down. This fearful thought would cause the child to scream and have a partial waking. However, this theory does not explain why a sleep terror can be triggered by a noise. And it does not explain why sleep terrors tend to occur at the *end* of the first or second sleep cycle rather than interrupting an ongoing sleep stage prematurely.

Others maintain that the arousal comes first, caused in some way by an underlying sleep disorder or even by a sound. Increased heart rate, sweating, and other bodily changes usually associated with fear occur simply as part of this sudden arousal from Stage IV. Thus a child wakes partially and finds herself sweating and her heart pounding, and *responds to* this agitated state by crying out, running through the house, or muttering incomprehensibly. She wakes with the *physical* symptoms of fear and quickly tries to find an explanation for it.

Think again how you feel when a fire alarm wakes you at night. You may find yourself with heart beating rapidly and a sensation of fear before you even know what has happened or if there is actually anything to be afraid of.

I believe that the latter explanation, which says that the arousal comes first, best explains why children don't report having any definable thoughts and why, as the event ends and heart rate and other bodily functions return to normal, the child no longer seems afraid and in fact has no lingering fears. Yet this does not mean that emotional factors are not relevant; they are. But instead of directly triggering the events, as suggested in the first theory, I believe emotional stress acts indirectly. Emotional factors probably do not trigger the arousals but they may well affect how a child responds to arousals that occur normally during the night. The actual trigger to the arousals themselves remains the underlying biological system that controls the timing of sleep stages. This explains why the events occur when we would normally expect the first or second sleep cycle to end.

Thus in a sleep terror or sleepwalking episode it is likely that the child's emotional state affects how she responds to finding herself in a state of partial arousal rather than triggering the arousal itself. This differs from a true nightmare, in which stressful daytime events may appear in a dream in symbolic form and generate enough anxiety to wake the child. After such a nightmare a child will still feel fearful and can usually remember the dream.

How Emotions Affect Nighttime Arousals

I want to help you understand more clearly how a child's psychological state can affect her nighttime arousals. Imagine exploring an old cemetery on a dark drizzly night. You cannot see around you well; you do not know who or what is there. You feel defenseless and nervous. Then you hear a sudden unexpected sound. You may jump, cry out, and feel quite frightened. You might even run without ever learning if there was really anything to be afraid of. If you believe in ghosts, you may decide that you heard one, but you could not describe anything in detail. You "made up" the ghost to fit your feelings of fear at the time. Yet the same sound, if it occurred in the daytime in the security of your own home, might not have startled you at all. The sounds were the same in both settings but your psychological state was not. It was your state of mind that determined your different manner of response.

What happened in the cemetery occurred despite the fact that you were awake and clear-headed to start with. If something similar could happen in sleep, you might only reach partial waking, and a sleep terror or sleepwalking might result.

Now imagine yourself sleeping comfortably in your own bed. You have not been feeling particularly worried about anything. An hour after you fall asleep there is the noise of a twig breaking outside. Although this may trigger a brief arousal, neither you nor anyone else (unless you were being monitored in a laboratory) would likely be aware of it and you would return immediately to deep sleep. But what if, instead of being at home, you are in battle surrounded by an enemy over whom you have *little control* and against whom you are *on constant guard?* In a moment of apparent calm you fall deeply asleep. One hour later the same twig breaks. Now it is unlikely that you will ignore the noise and return to sleep after a momentary lightening of your sleep stage. Instead, you might bolt upright and find yourself intensely panicked. Initially you would be confused and you might even cry out.

The difference between these two situations was your psychological state when you fell asleep. Fearful thoughts did not trigger either arousal; the noise of the twig snapping did. However, in the second situation you knew that by going to sleep you were letting down your guard, and you responded to the arousal much differently.

Calm sleepwalking would occur for similar reasons, except that in this case the threat of letting down one's guard at night is not so great. Imagine this time that you are still on guard, but for something important rather than dangerous. Perhaps you are a biologist waiting at night in the woods for the arrival of a certain rare species of bird. You fall asleep and one hour later you hear unusual sounds, perhaps of a bird, perhaps not. Ordinarily these would not wake you, but in this setting you sit up promptly and begin to look about, even though you are initially very confused and are not even sure what it is you are looking for. You may not even remember hearing the sounds that woke you. In the first few seconds you may react very inappropriately, possibly making noise instead of remaining absolutely silent. During this time you feel the need to get up and to look for something but are not yet awake enough to think clearly or understand what is happening. This is probably quite similar to what a sleepwalker experiences. Here too the only reason the sound had any real effect on your sleep was that you went to sleep prepared to arouse, because you were still on guard.

In younger children, extended thrashing episodes or sleepwalking usually mean the child is having difficulty making a smooth transition from one period of Stage IV sleep to the next sleep cycle. This difficulty almost always results from the depth of Stage IV sleep characteristic of a young child's level of development. But in older children who should be able to make this transition smoothly, their exaggerated response to the arousal is more likely based on psychological factors.

These older children often are in situations in which things they do not want to happen are occurring *outside of their control.* There may be moves to new neighborhoods, changes to new schools, and especially losses—a divorce, separation, or death in the family. Even if the family is intact, there may be loss of warmth, love, and nurturance. Parents may be rigid, demanding, and uncompromising, with high expectations for their child's behavior, school performance, and athletic success. The child is often quite angry about the circumstances but doesn't express the anger outwardly. Instead, she remains *on guard,* probably feeling that expression of her feelings may only be followed by more unpleasantness in her life. She may already blame herself for her parents' separation or other family problems. And she may carefully avoid causing her parents any displeasure. Such a child often will appear to be extremely pleasant and well behaved—if anything, too well behaved. Occasionally her anger will show in passive ways that feel safer to her. She may stay in her room after school and not talk at mealtimes. Or she may do poorly in school when she could do well. Such children expend enormous quantities of energy during the day guarding their emotions, which they view as the enemy, and keeping them in check. At night, in sleep, these defenses must be relaxed.

It is perhaps somewhat easier now to see how such a child might react to a partial arousal after the first or second sleep cycle. Like the soldier in battle who wakes suddenly at night, she finds herself confused and out of control with her defenses down. Before she knows what is happening she feels very fearful. This fear response is generated at a low level in the nervous system and does not require complex thought processes for it to occur. If this is true, then ultimately the solution is for the child to learn to be able to go to sleep without being on guard so that normal nighttime arousals may be handled in stride. She must learn that her feelings are not dangerous and that there is no need to guard against expressing them. Accomplishing this goal is no easy task and often requires a period of psychotherapy or counseling.

Treating Emotional Causes

The decision as to whether or not a child needs counseling is thus based on several factors. If a child seems to be feeling a great deal of stress, then she should have help regardless of the degree of nighttime disturbance. If your child has several major episodes each week, then psychotherapy may be helpful even if she doesn't appear to be under much stress otherwise. If your child's nighttime episodes are dangerous, then treatment is urgently needed and psychotherapy, at least an initial evaluation, should be part of it. This is true even if no stresses seem apparent and your child seems to express her feelings openly. If therapy helps reduce the arousals, then it will certainly be worth it, even if you feel that your child is very happy and without any significant "psychological problems."

Christopher, you will recall, was an eight-year-old boy who had been having abnormal nighttime wakings for almost two years. Christopher had been a good sleeper until, two months after his father's death, he moved to a new neighborhood. At that time he began to get up two or three times a week and walk about several hours after his 9:00 P.M. bedtime. He wandered about calmly and quietly without any crying, talking, or signs of agitation. He would have a "strange look" on his face and was not very responsive to his mother's questions. Usually his sleepwalking appeared to have no purpose, but on some occasions he seemed to be "looking for something." Although he did not seem to recognize his mother, he would let her lead him back to bed, usually after a stop in the bathroom, where he would urinate. On two occasions he urinated in his room, once into the wastebasket and once into a shoe in his closet. Twice he actually walked out of the house and was led back home by neighbors. Over the next year his nighttime wakings stayed the same, although he faced considerable new stresses. His mother was away for two weeks because of emergency surgery, and shortly after that she remarried and his family moved again. Finally his mother became pregnant, and shortly before the birth of his sister, Christopher's nighttime episodes became more intense. Instead of happening a few times a week, they were now occurring several times a night and the initial event was of a different character.

About one hour after falling asleep, Christopher would sit up suddenly, cry out briefly, and appear frightened. He would not respond to his mother, did not want to be touched, and muttered incoherently. He would calm in a few minutes, then allow himself to be coaxed back down into bed and would fall asleep rapidly. A similar event would occur one hour later and a third an hour after that. Once Christopher calmed after the final episode, he would get up and begin to walk about the house as he had when he was younger. Several more episodes of quiet sleepwalking might occur over the next few hours. After 4:00 A.M. his sleep seemed to be deep and arousals were rare.

When I saw Christopher he was a nice quiet youngster, but despite his calm exterior he seemed very tense and anxious. I learned that his father and stepfather were alcoholics and there was some violence within his home. He had many angry feelings toward people around him but was afraid to express them. He was quite frightened at his lack of control of the world about him and was surely distraught that his parents could not seem to control themselves. He devoted much of his own energy toward rigid self-control. He worried that if he did not control his feelings, there would be dire consequences.

Christopher and his mother both needed counseling. In the meantime I suggested that the family put a lock high up on the front door so that he could not walk out of the house. I explained in detail what happens during nighttime arousals so that other family members would be less angry at Christopher.

In the beginning Christopher's mother was not able to be supportive. She was still angry at Christopher for waking her. For this reason I decided to try to reduce the episodes until their therapy had gone further. Usually I would not recommend medication, but I felt it would help in this case. I prescribed imipramine (Tofranil) for Christopher, a drug that is sometimes, but not always, helpful. His nighttime arousals disappeared almost completely. Three months later he and his mother had made real progress in therapy and the tensions at home had eased, so we stopped the medication. The nighttime arousals returned, but they were much less frequent and Christopher never had more than one per night. His mother now felt that she could deal with them without anger. Over the next nine months his arousals decreased even further and now, at nine, he has episodes only occasionally.

Christopher's daytime behavior was typical of many children with emotionally induced sleepwalking or sleep terrors. He was a nice youngster who did not yell and scream but kept his feelings inside. His nighttime arousals varied within the spectrum described in Figure 11 (page 138) from calm sleepwalking to episodes close to full sleep terrors. And the progressive increase of symptoms after age six did suggest that psychological factors were involved, although the stresses Christopher faced were unusually severe. As he learned to handle his daytime stress in an appropriate manner, he showed a progression toward the milder end of the spectrum, with calm walking instead of screaming, sitting instead of walking, and so on.

Shannon's nighttime arousals were even more striking than Christopher's. At age twelve she had been having them for just over three years. Although there had been periods of up to several weeks without any episodes, they usually happened nightly. She had not had any major problems when sleeping at a friend's home, although that possibility continued to worry her. She would go to sleep at 10:00 P.M. but about an hour and a half later would sit up and cry out with a single long guttural scream. She would then get out of bed and run about frantically and hysterically, touching the walls and furniture like a blind woman trying to get out of a burning room. At times she would even fall on the floor and thrash, kick, and roll about. Sometimes she would run wildly out of her room and even downstairs. Her mother had noticed that she could trigger one of these wakings if she disturbed Shannon in any way sixty to ninety minutes after she fell asleep. For this reason she was careful to stay out of her room at that time and not even attempt to cover her with a blanket.

Her family felt that although Shannon did seem somewhat frightened during some of these events, she did not seem truly terrified. Instead she seemed more to be angry, frantic, and very confused. She would only push people away if they tried to hold or restrain her. She even seemed to get angry when spoken to, replying "Don't bug me" or "Leave me alone." She had tried to leave the house once or twice, but never successfully. Infrequently the events were less disturbing, with simple talking and sitting in bed and hardly any signs of agitation.

When Shannon was nine, these events lasted up to half an hour, but by age twelve most were over within five to ten minutes. Toward the end of the episodes she would calm, urinate in the bathroom, alert in a sleepy fashion, and return to sleep. She had no memory of the events at that point or in the morning.

Shannon's family tried to be supportive, but her parents were preoccupied with their own problems, which they were beginning to solve with the help of a marriage counselor. Shannon had recently started seeing a psychologist as well. She did not seem to have significant emotional problems and, at least outside of the home, she was extremely well behaved. However, she was not a spontaneous youngster. She seemed angry at her parents for the tensions at home and she felt a lack of warmth and nurturance. She had difficulty expressing these feelings and was afraid that if she did, matters would only get worse.

Shannon's arousals fell somewhere between angry agitated sleepwalking and full sleep terrors. She also had episodes of extended thrashing. Although psychological problems were not major, they could clearly be identified and the family had already sought help for them. I helped the family most by reassuring them that Shannon was physically normal and by telling them that these types of arousals were common. Except for prescribing medication, there was little I could do promptly to reduce the frequency of wakings. But I preferred to avoid the nightly use of drugs and the family agreed. Instead, we decided to find a dose of medicine that would prevent these episodes and allow Shannon to take it only when she slept over at a girlfriend's home, when a friend slept at her house, or when she went to camp. Otherwise the events would be allowed to continue. We were hopeful that as she continued to work with her psychologist, and as her parents continued to resolve their own problems, the wakings would gradually decrease. In fact, they did diminish, but very slowly. I was prepared to start regular medication if her arousals intensified to the point that she became in danger of hurting herself. Fortunately this never occurred.

I did not expect Shannon to hurt herself, because that would be unusual for a twelve-year-old, unless she tripped over something left on the floor. I would have been more concerned if the same symptoms were present in a child several years older, because injury occurs most often in teenagers.

David was seventeen and during the eight years before I met him his parents had divorced, then each had remarried. At the time that his parents separated David was known to talk in his sleep frequently. He did not begin to have intense arousal episodes until he was twelve, when his father remarried. Then about once a month he would leap out of bed suddenly about midnight and begin yelling. His mother would find him standing in his room, apparently upset, as if "something was going to happen to him." He did not seem to be terrified, although he occasionally mumbled phrases such as "I've got to kill him." David's mother could not wake him, and within three to four minutes he would return to bed and fall rapidly back to sleep. When David was fifteen his mother remarried and his arousals became more intense. Now they would start with a "bloodcurdling scream." David would jump out of bed, knock over furniture, and run about as if trying to "escape from something." He no longer simply looked upset. Now he appeared truly terrified. He injured himself a few times, although usually the scrapes and bruises were very minor. However, on a number of occasions his mother saw him head toward the window. Once he leaned out the window and another time broke a windowpane, cut his hand, and required several stitches. At the end of each episode David would wake fully and was always quite embarrassed to find himself in a disarrayed room with his family members staring at him.

David's parents described him as being "very controlled," "holding things in," and "handling things too well." He did not seem to be working up to his potential in school. I found David to be pleasant and cooperative but somewhat depressed. He was easy to talk to and, in fact, he was able to express some of his feelings, though he clearly was not fully in touch with all of them, particularly those of sadness and anger.

Although David's episodes occurred infrequently, their character was quite worrisome. I felt that he might injure himself seriously. I have treated other adolescents like him who had actually jumped through windows. In David's case I recommended medication without much ambivalence. I chose diazepam (Valium) which was the drug I felt most likely to suppress his arousals. When David was on the medication, the arousals stopped completely, but I viewed this as only a temporary measure to assure David's safety. In the long run we wanted to have David sleep at night, calmly and safely, without drugs. To this end psychotherapy was recommended and begun even though David was not seriously disturbed. But his psychological characteristics, taken in the context of his nighttime symptoms, were enough to justify this approach. Our plan is for David to remain on the medication until he has had more time to benefit from the counseling. Then we will gradually decrease the medication, hoping that the arousals will not recur, or if they do that they will be milder and not require medication at all or only a small dose.

Variability of Arousals

As you have seen in the cases I have described, a child's nighttime arousals may be different on different nights or at different times in her life. Often a child shows a progression along the continuum described in Figure 11, from quiet arousals to major sleep terrors, usually because of changes in current life stresses and the manner in which she deals with them. But day-to-day changes in a child's life may be subtle and difficult to recognize and night-to-night changes in the occurrence or intensity of arousals may occur without any identifiable change in daytime stress. In fact, nighttime symptoms usually tend to wax and wane over weeks and months without any recognizable daytime changes. Therefore, it is not easy to predict when a child will have nighttime episodes, based only on the knowledge of what current stresses she seems to be facing—an upcoming examination, an operation, or perhaps a separation from the family. In fact, nighttime episodes may actually *decrease* at a time when your child starts to misbehave, have outbursts of temper, and become uncharacteristically uncooperative during the day. When she allows herself to express her feelings in the daytime, even inappropriately, she will have less need to guard against these feelings at night and will have more continuous sleep.

What About Other Causes?

It is certainly possible that hormones or other biological factors affect the character of the nighttime arousals. Also many children with these sleep disorders have close relatives with a history of similar nighttime arousals. In very young children this may explain the occurrence of the arousals entirely. In older children, a family history of the disorder may explain why only some children who struggle to avoid expressing their feelings develop these sleep problems. It is likely that after about age six, a child needs both a biological and an emotional predisposition for frequent sleep terrors or sleepwalking to occur. Just as stress is more likely to lead to an ulcer in a person with a familial predisposition to ulcers, sleep terrors or sleepwalking are more likely to occur in a child who not only has difficulty dealing with and expressing her emotions but who also has close relatives known to walk, thrash, or scream in their sleep. Similarly, it is likely that the specific type of arousal shown by a child—that is, where on the spectrum of increasing intensity it occurs (from sleeptalking to terrors)—also involves both psychological and inherited factors.

Some Final Words

The state of extended confusion or sleepwalking is unusual and has many features otherwise seen only during epileptic seizures (which these events clearly are not). Specifically, a child's unusual and confused behavior goes on over an extended period of time during which she has little ability to respond to people or events in the environment. She does not seem capable of rational thinking, and she forms little or no memory of the events. What seems even stranger is that no amount of stimulation can shorten an episode, at least a major one, and bring the child to full waking. It will simply run its course and usually will only be intensified if one tries to hold or otherwise restrain the child. The child seems to perceive any intervention as threat or attack instead of help. Perhaps this is so because she feels her parents closing in on her but she does not recognize them.

You should now understand these unusual phenomena more fully. However, I cannot entirely explain why some of the arousals should be so extended in time or why forceful waking is usually impossible. But whatever the reason, try to be content to wait. All episodes, regardless of their length, will eventually end fairly suddenly and on their own. You can learn to recognize when your child reaches this point. There is a general relaxation, stretching and yawning, and readiness to return to sleep rapidly. At this time older children may wake fully, either spontaneously or in response to your efforts. Not only will they have no memory of the preceding event, but they will seem calm and usually unperturbed. If your child seems upset at this time it is usually because she sees that you are or she is embarrassed that she has done something strange again, something that her family regards as "bizarre," and something over which she seems to have no control.

It is for this reason that such a child may become quite angry when questioned repeatedly about the nature of her "dream." She is concerned about loss of control during the day and finds out that she has acted without any control during the night. This knowledge can cause her even more anxiety, increase her worries at bedtime, and possibly even lead to more arousal events. This is one of the reasons I recommend you do not try to wake a child after one of the events and certainly do not question her at that point or in the morning. In fact, it only makes sense to tell your child about them on a regular basis if she is asking or if she is old enough to make her own decision as to psychotherapy and medication.

The children you have read about in this chapter represent only a small number of those I have seen with similar problems. This sleep problem is not as unusual as you may think. However, because the disorder is not often discussed among parents, or between children and their friends, some parents view their children as "strange" or "abnormal," and some children worry that they themselves are weird. You and they should be relieved to know these episodes are very common and are usually outgrown.

Most toddlers have occasional confused partial wakings of varying intensity. The actual number of children who have extended thrashing spells, sleepwalking, and full night terrors is not known, but at least 15 percent of children have had at least one sleepwalking episode. Extended partial wakings and thrashing in children are probably much more common. Of course, fewer children have very frequent and intense episodes, but wild sleep terrors with running about are by no means rare.

It is relatively easy to feel empathy for a child who wakes at night in distress and accepts your efforts of comfort. But when you attempt to help your child and she only pushes you aside, you may react with anger if you do not understand what is happening. If you watch your child thrash about for an extended period of time as if "possessed," you may become extremely frightened. It is important that you understand what is happening during these partial arousals so that you will not react hastily to your child out of anger or fear. Now you should be able to simply watch the episodes proceed, realizing that nothing serious is happening. Do your best to avoid overreacting, and control your urge to try and wake your child forcibly. And don't question her, since she will not have any memories to describe.

If your child seems susceptible to these episodes, pay attention to their frequency and character and try to identify any stresses she might be under. The infant or toddler who has occasional thrashing episodes doesn't need treatment. Just keep your distance, let the event run its course, and then allow your child to return to sleep. Make sure your child gets enough sleep and has a regular schedule. Drug treatment is almost never advisable.

Sleepwalking is similar. You can often lead a calm sleepwalker back to bed; but if she is agitated, you may have to first wait until she calms. For her safety, remove any obstacles on the floor and stairs. If your child is young, a gate may be necessary by the stairs and possibly across her bedroom door. If your child is older and she tries to leave the house, put an extra chain lock high up on the door, and you may want to attach a bell to her bedroom door and to the outside doors to let you know if they are opened. Although injury is unusual during calm sleepwalking, it certainly can occur. It is more likely if there is agitation. Leaving the house, of course, is especially worrisome.

Even full sleep terrors should be allowed to run their course if possible. However, if your child is about to hurt herself or others or to damage the furniture or walls, then you may have to intervene. But do so as gently and with as little physical restraint as possible. Trying to restrain an agitated seventeen-year-old could lead to everyone's getting hurt.

If you are worried that your child's episodes are unusually frequent, intense, or dangerous, by all means consult your doctor. Very rarely medical problems may be responsible for some of the arousals—pain from heartburn (acid moving up out of the stomach into the esophagus) or middle ear disease. But when medical factors are involved, the child will usually have wakings at other times as well, not just from Stage IV. She will have a more general sleep disruption, with only some of the arousals being sleepwalking or sleep terrors.

Very rarely nighttime epileptic seizures can mimic this disorder. You should be suspicious if your child's arousals are very different from those described in this chapter. If they occur near morning instead of closer to bedtime, if they begin with full waking and your child's realization that something is about to occur, or if she has good memory of the entire event or of its beginning instead of its end, she should be seen by a physician. If the episodes are always exactly the same, if there is marked body stiffening with one arm extended and the head turned to the same side, or if there is prominent repetitive body jerking, you should also be concerned. Discuss these with your doctor.

Although I have prescribed medication for children having very frequent episodes—two or three every night—because of the disruptive effect in the household, I always do so reluctantly, because, in a sense, I am treating the family more than the child. However, the child who is having many intense episodes and who is at significant risk for self-injury, does deserve the most urgent intervention. With such a child it is important first to protect her by suppressing the nighttime episodes through medication. If your child is like this, you should see your doctor promptly. You should also consider counseling, although you need to understand that the therapy is needed to identify and treat certain psychological problems and not simply to cure the arousal events. Although stopping the arousals may be a prime goal, you cannot judge the success of psychotherapy simply by keeping track of the frequency or intensity of the nighttime episodes. Sometimes improvement in sleep follows progress in therapy very slowly. It may take some time for your child to learn new ways of dealing with important feelings so that she is able to go to bed without worrying about what may happen if she relaxes her emotional defenses in sleep. Similarly, a child who develops sleep terrors after surgery is like a soldier who develops sleep terrors during a period of battle. She may continue to have them for some time even after returning to the safety of home, where she no longer has to be on guard at night for nurses with needles or doctors with scalpels. Such a pattern, once learned, may be slow to change.

Nightmares

What Are Nightmares and Why Do They Occur?

Nightmares are dreams—very scary dreams that wake your child and leave him or her feeling frightened, anxious, and with a profound sense of dread.

Although nightmares occur during sleep, for the most part they are caused by, and reflect, emotional conflicts that take place during the day. These are the usual struggles faced by all children at each stage of normal development. All children have nightmares at one time or another.

The specific content or "story" of your child's nightmares depends on several factors: his stage of physical and emotional development at the time; the particular emotional conflicts facing him at that developmental stage; and the occurrence of specific daytime events which seem particularly scary or threatening.

The anxieties that lead to nightmares during sleep are the same ones that may lead to fears at bedtime and during periods of wakefulness at night. These are discussed in Chapter 4. Concerns about separation are common in young toddlers. Your child worries about being away from you. He may have nightmares when he first goes to daycare, at a time when you must be out of town or hospitalized, after he is temporarily "lost" at a store, or when he feels that he "loses" you to a new brother or sister.

As your child grows a little older he is more concerned about loss of your love than about temporary separation from you. In his third year, for example, during toilet training, your child may struggle with his own impulse to soil while at the same time wanting to please you. He may worry that if he gives in to his impulse and soils, you will disapprove. His dreams at that time may well reflect the associated anxiety.

From age three to six your child typically has to resolve many aggressive and sexual impulses. He may feel jealous of your attention to a new baby and wish to hit him or her. And he will discover that he enjoys the pleasant sensations he feels when touching his genitals. But he may also find that he is frightened by his desire to do these things, especially if he thinks he will be punished severely for this behavior or not helped to control himself. If, however, you teach your child that such *urges* are normal and show him that you will help him learn what is acceptable behavior and that you will supportively help him control any temptations to truly wrongful behavior, then he will be more able to relax. Otherwise the scary feelings associated with these impulses may take on the form of "monsters" that frighten him both at bedtime and during dreams. Such a three- to six-year-old may also be quite disturbed by seeing violent behavior or overhearing loud arguments at home. He may sense that you cannot control your own behavior appropriately and worry that you will be unable to help him stay in control without being either too strict and punitive or too lenient and permissive.

Sexual stimulation at this age can also lead to significant anxieties and nightmares. Your child could have overt contact from a caretaker, sibling, or peer or simply witness or overhear parents during intercourse, which he doesn't understand and may perceive as violent and aggressive. Or he may feel conflicts deriving from his desire to replace his father, or a girl her mother, as the other parent's partner. Such anxieties may be further stimulated when the child is allowed to sleep in the parents' bed routinely. Martin, a five-year-old boy I saw, would come into his parents' bed each night, crawl between them, and begin kicking until he literally kicked his father out of bed. His father would then go into the son's bedroom to sleep. For the father it was the easiest thing to do and he got more sleep, but Martin was not sleeping well at all and was having many nightmares about threatening monsters. When I discussed the situation with the parents, they agreed it would be better to insist that Martin always return to his own bed, and Martin (despite initial protests and struggles) was ultimately much more comfortable with this kind of control. Before long his nightmares disappeared altogether.

Your child at this age may also be struggling to understand the concept of death, and he may have serious concerns about falling asleep and never waking again. Harold, age six, never had any difficulty sleeping until he went to his uncle's wake. He was told not to worry, because his uncle "would look just like he was sleeping," and in fact the boy learned that the uncle had "died in his sleep." Harold's nightmares after this experience were clearly related to his concern about death and his confusion between sleep, death, and the risk of dying during sleep. Once Harold was encouraged to talk more openly about his feelings regarding his uncle's death and funeral, and after his parents corrected some of his misconceptions through discussion and reading him a book on death written for children, Harold's bad dreams disappeared.

Frequent nightmares are not common at ages seven to eleven. The conflicts of the preceding years should be largely mastered or "repressed," and new stresses are likely to be handled more in stride. If your child continues having nightmares, it may be that he is still struggling with conflicts that were not resolved at an earlier age.

During puberty and throughout adolescence significant new conflicts and anxieties emerge. As your child changes to an adult, physically, sexually, emotionally, and cognitively, he has to face a great many stresses every day. There seems to be some increase of nightmares at this time, although it is difficult to say for certain, because adolescents are less likely to talk to other family members about their dreams or wake them during the night.

Nightmares are part of the normal process of growing up. Since nightmares are dreams, they must occur in REM sleep. Although REM sleep is plentiful in newborn babies and is associated with eye movements and little smiles, we do not know if any of the images, sounds, feelings, or thoughts of dreaming are also present at birth or if actual dreaming does not appear until later in the first year. But dreams, and even nightmares, unquestionably do occur during the second year of life, a fact which becomes progressively clear as the child develops speech and hence the ability to describe them.

The nightmare of a one-year-old is likely to be of simple content. Typically a child will recreate and re-experience a recent frightening event. Even though a one-year-old cannot describe his dream well, he may be verbal enough to suggest that he just had a dream about a recent blood test, car accident, or bee sting. Your child at this age does not understand the difference between a dream and reality and so, on waking, will not understand that "the dream" is over. He may continue to be afraid, acting as if the threat from the dream is still present. For example, he may be convinced that the bee is still in the room, saying, "Buzz buzz here."

By age two, dreams are clearly more symbolic, and monsters or wild animals will typically represent your child's impulses and fears. By this age he begins to understand the concept of a dream, but not well enough to fully appreciate the difference between dreaming and reality. He may admit to "dreaming" of a monster yet still insist that "the monster hasn't gone yet."

As your child grows, his dreams become more complex. At the same time he becomes progressively better able to distinguish dreams from the real world. By about age five he may wake from a dream with immediate and full understanding that "I just had a dream." It will still be harder for him to reach this point after waking from a nightmare. Your child's ability to accept a dream as "just a dream" continues to develop, and by age seven he may even be able to handle an occasional nightmare without waking anyone for support. Still, on waking from a nightmare, the feeling of fright is very real. As one child said: "Mom, I know what happened in the dream wasn't real, but the dream was real!" He knows he only had a dream, but he still feels the fear that was associated with it. Rationally he knows nothing happened but emotionally he is not so sure. Thus Betsy, an eleven-year-old girl, had to get up during the night to check that her younger brother was all right after dreaming that he had died. This, even though she "knew" full well that it was "only a dream."

How to Help Your Child If He Is Having Nightmares

As we have seen, nightmares are mainly a symptom of daytime emotional struggles. There are a few occasions in which this is not true. For example, your child may have nightmares when he is ill and has a high fever or as a side effect of a particular medication. Although most nightmares do reflect ongoing emotional conflicts, in most cases neither the nightmares nor the conflicts are "abnormal." Rather, the normal emotional struggles associated with growing up are at times significant enough to lead to occasional nightmares.

If your child has nightmares now and then, a straightforward approach is usually sufficient. A very young child mainly needs physical comforting, an older child needs reassuring words as well. If your child is less than two years old, remember that he does not yet understand the concept of a dream. So you won't have much success by trying to show him "it was just a dream." He simply needs to be held and comforted in the same way as he would after any frightening event in the daytime. By age two his concept of a dream is still only rudimentary. Holding him is still most important, but soothing, reassuring words will also help. At this age he may also be comforted if you listen sympathetically while he describes his dream or fears to

you. At age three or four it may be useful to remind your child that
he was dreaming, though his fear still needs to be treated with empathy and reassurance. Even if it was not important to him to sleep with
a night light on and his door open when he was younger, it may be
now. In this way, when he wakes from a dream, he can see about his
room and not feel isolated from the rest of the house. This will make
it easier for him to become oriented and accept the fact that the dream
is over and he is safe. After waking from a very scary dream, he may
even want a brighter light turned on.

Still, the main point to remember is that when your child wakes
from a nightmare, he is truly frightened and needs full reassurance
and support. If he is afraid to go back to sleep, you may have to stay
with him for considerable time. Occasionally lying down with him or
even taking him into your bed won't hurt and may be the most reasonable approach at times, but don't make a habit of this, since it can
lead to more anxiety and further sleep disruption. When your child
has had a nightmare, be supportive in a firm and convincing way that
will show your child that you are in control and will make sure that
nothing bad happens. It is not the time, however, to be extremely
firm. It would not be wise to shut your child's door when he clearly is
too afraid to stay alone. But neither should you be overly lenient. You
should not feel compelled to fulfill all of your child's requests in a
chaotic effort to allay fear. Don't spend thirty minutes after he has
had a bad dream shining lights into all corners of the closet, under the
bed, outside the window, and in the drawers. Ultimately this will not
reassure him. Instead, let your child know calmly and clearly that you
will take care of him and protect him. This is more important than
trying to convince him that the monsters are not real. Now is the time
to hold your child and in this way let him know that you can and will
keep him safe. Often even a thirteen-year-old who feels too big to be
hugged in the daytime may appreciate such reassurance when he
wakes frightened after a nightmare. An older adolescent may still want
some physical contact or at least someone sitting close by.

If your child is having frequent nightmares, you will have to work
with him during the day to solve the problem, not after he wakes
frightened from a dream. Try to determine what is worrying him and
see if you can help relieve his anxiety. For example, if your one-year-
old has difficulty leaving your side, activities such as "peek-a-boo," in
which your disappearance and reappearance is made a game, may
help your child feel comfortable when he is apart from you. If your
two-year-old is having nightmares during a period of toilet training,
even when the training has been going well, try relaxing the toilet

training efforts for a while and allow and encourage messy play such as fingerpainting. For three- to six-year-olds, you may find that children's books about sleep and dreams (see Appendix A) will help them better understand these concepts. You can begin to talk directly to your child at this age about his fears and concerns. You should also screen the books, movies, and television shows that your child sees. Certainly avoid very scary ones. But because of the amount of "sex and violence" that now regularly appears in prime time television (or in the advertisements during the shows), you will also have to monitor "non-scary" shows. Even if your four- or five-year-old "enjoys" these shows and does not seem frightened by them when he is awake, they may still stimulate enough anxiety to cause nightmares when he is asleep.

By all means allow your child, at any age, to express his feelings, but teach him appropriate limits. Avoid moral condemnations. Don't make him feel guilty about having angry or sexual feelings, but help him learn acceptable ways to express them, for example by talking angrily but not hitting. He may also be reassured to learn that you used to have fights with your sister or brother or that everyone finds that it feels good to touch his or her genitals or have an erection.

With the older child, work toward better communication, frankness, and willingness to discuss his concerns, even if they have to do with difficult issues such as sex, drugs, or divorce.

Occasionally nightmares are a symptom of more significant emotional difficulties. Since nightmares do tend to decrease after age five or six, their persistence after that should raise special concern. Regardless of his age, if your child's nightmares continue to be frequent and persist for more than one or two months, and if you can't identify and help him resolve the stress he is feeling, then you should seek professional help. This is especially true if your child also has unreasonable fears during the daytime, such as unwillingness to separate from you; refusal to be in his bedroom alone; reluctance to go to school; or phobias of needles, heights, or fires. As a parent you should expect to take some part in the counseling, but the form of the sessions and your degree of involvement will depend on the age of your child, his particular daytime difficulties, and the kinds of general family stresses that may be present. Sometimes it is only necessary for you to have help learning how to recognize and deal with the cause of your child's anxiety. Other times the issues are more deep-seated. These are less responsive to simple changes, and longer-term therapeutic efforts will be needed. The counseling sessions may be mainly for your child alone or for the whole family. Sometimes when a young child seems to be reacting mainly to stress between his parents, counseling for them alone may be the most helpful.

Nightmares or Sleep Terrors?

If you are to do anything about your child's "nightmares," you must first be sure that nightmares are in fact the problem. If he cries out in the middle of the night and seems frightened, then you may assume he just had a bad dream. But you should also be aware that he might have had a sleep terror. It is important to decide which of the two is occurring, because what you should do for each is quite different.

Nightmares and sleep terrors are easy to confuse and in the past the terms "nightmares" and "night terrors" were sometimes used interchangeably. We now know, however, that nightmares are scary dreams that occur within well-established REM sleep and which are followed by full waking. Sleep terrors, on the other hand, occur during a partial arousal from the deepest phase of non-dreaming sleep. Although in principle it should be easy to differentiate between the two, in fact the distinction is not always so obvious, especially when your child is young.

The differences between nightmares and sleep terrors are discussed below and summarized in Figure 13, pages 172–73. You will recall that nightmares usually occur toward the end of the night when REM sleep is most intense, and sleep terrors happen during the first few hours after your child has fallen asleep when non-REM sleep is deepest. After a nightmare your child, if he is old enough, can describe a dream, but after a sleep terror there is no dream to report. When your child wakes from a nightmare he will cry if he is young or he may call for you if he is older. He will recognize you immediately and will want you to hold, comfort, and reassure him. He will remember the dream both right after it occurred and in the morning. A child having a sleep terror is not fully awake. He may cry out regardless of his age, but the cry may sound more like a scream, or he may talk, moan, and cry all at the same time in a confused and seemingly nonsensical way. During the episode he will not recognize you or allow you to comfort him. If you try to hold him he may push you away and become more agitated. And he will have no recollection of the episode when he does wake, either at the end of the sleep terror or in the morning. He will have no memory of a dream or that he was yelling and thrashing about. In the morning he may only have a vague memory of being awake briefly after the terror, perhaps talking to you.

A child who has been frightened by a nightmare will remain

frightened and often be reluctant to go back to sleep alone in his bed afterwards. He may even be afraid to go to bed for several nights following an especially scary dream. After a sleep terror, however, a child does not have this fear. On waking he will actually relax, all signs of fear or agitation will disappear, and he will return to sleep rapidly. And since he is unaware of the episodes, he will not be reluctant to go to bed on subsequent nights.

Why It Is Sometimes Difficult to Tell the Difference

Despite the differences between nightmares and sleep terrors, it may be difficult to determine which of these your child is having. First of all he may be too young to describe a dream—especially if he is under two. If so, you may simply be assuming he has had a "bad dream" whenever he wakes crying and upset. You may also think your older child has had a nightmare whenever he wakes thrashing or screaming, even though he does not describe a dream after he quiets down. And if your child wakes partially from non-dreaming sleep, calling out, "Mommy, Daddy, help me," you may believe, incorrectly, that he must be fully awake and talking about a nightmare that just occurred. You are more likely to make these mistakes if you know little about sleep terrors.

It is also true that if you struggle to wake your child from a sleep terror, you may be unaware of his initial confusion and lack of receptiveness. If he pushes you away you may conclude that he is "still dreaming" and "fighting off the monsters." If you are successful in waking him as the event ends, you may actually scare him by your own apprehension and nervous questioning. At that point, he may become frightened by your behavior. If so he may be reluctant to let you leave, just as he would after an actual nightmare. If you tell him that he has been acting bizarrely he may be even more frightened, since he is unaware of having done anything. Even if he hasn't been frightened, he now has been fully waked and may be enjoying the attention. And if you keep asking him what he was "dreaming" about, he may actually make up a story to satisfy you. He may now be fully awake, and quite anxious—but not from a nightmare or from the actual sleep terror. He is anxious because you are so upset. Now, instead of returning to sleep rapidly as expected, he may have difficulty doing so or be unwilling to try.

When the sleep terror begins suddenly, is very intense, then ends quickly (features not usually seen until adolescence), your child may wake spontaneously and find himself with heart racing and other feelings he is used to associating with fear. In an effort to explain these feelings to himself, he may create a vague, poorly defined "image" of a threatening situation, which he may describe to you as "The walls are closing in" or "It was going to get me." Reasonably enough, you may assume he had a nightmare, but if he has had a sleep terror he will not be able to give you a full dream report with a story line, characters, and places. Even though he feels some "fear," the feeling will usually fade rapidly and he will be able to return to sleep quickly if you yourself are calm.

Lastly, on occasion a child waking from a nightmare will initially behave in a manner similar to a child who is having a sleep terror. He may appear confused and very frightened and may not at first seem responsive to your efforts to comfort him. In fact, it could take several minutes for you to calm him. He may point to places in the room and refer to animals or monsters but be too upset at that point to describe a coherent dream. This happens most often with a very young child who does not fully understand what a dream is, that the "monsters" are not real, and that the dream is over and he is safe at home, not in continued danger.

But most often a very young child who has had a nightmare will cry out and reach up to be lifted out of the crib as soon as you come into his room, and he will cling tightly to you. If he is old enough he may get out of bed and run into your room seeking reassurance. Although he will appear very upset, he will not be thrashing and unresponsive like a child having a sleep terror. In fact, even though his fear may be marked, we have noted in the laboratory that the change in heart rate and other physiological measures in nightmares is actually less than during sleep terrors. The time it takes to calm your child may vary, and he may be unwilling for some time to stay alone in the crib or bed and go back to sleep.

An older child or adolescent will probably not cry or scream on waking from a nightmare and may be able to calm himself unless the nightmare was extremely distressing.

It is much more common for parents to misinterpret sleep terrors as nightmares than the other way around. I recently saw two children, Meredith, two, and Bernard, sixteen, whose parents were having trouble deciding what to do about their children's wakings. Meredith's parents told me they often had to go in and reassure their daughter, who would wake crying after a nightmare. But Meredith's wakings always happened within three hours of her falling asleep. Furthermore, on closer questioning, I learned that she was not reassured by her parents' presence and would often push them away as they tried to hold her. They were quite upset at these wakings and would try very hard to wake her, then to reassure her. Meredith would often not go back to sleep for an hour, during which time one of the parents would stay with her playing or reading stories. I was certain Meredith was only waking partially from non-dreaming sleep and not having nightmares, so I suggested that the parents go into her room at these wakings but avoid interacting with her unless she clearly recognized them and asked for help. Meredith's episodes became less prolonged and they ended with a quick return to sleep rather than with the extended waking that had actually been stimulated by the parents.

Similarly, Bernard's parents were concerned about his "terrible nightmares." They said Bernard would wake suddenly two hours after falling asleep, scream, and then mumble phrases such as "It's after me." On speaking to the boy myself, however, I learned that he never had any true dream recollections, only an occasional vague sense of attack. Psychologically he showed the characteristics usually seen in adolescents with frequent sleep terrors (see Chapter 10). Once his family understood that Bernard was having sleep terrors instead of nightmares, they were much better able to deal appropriately with the episodes at night. Bernard had some counseling, and over the next year the sleep terrors gradually disappeared.

After reading the chapters on nightmares and sleep terrors, you should now be clear on the differences between them, their causes, and the best ways of handling both. At the time of a sleep terror, the key is to be as uninvolved as possible, but when your child has had a nightmare, warm, supportive involvement is the best treatment.

FIGURE 13 Nightmares vs Sleep Terrors

	Nightmares	Sleep Terrors
What is it?	A scary dream. It takes place within REM sleep and is followed by full waking.	A partial arousal from very deep (Stage IV, non-REM) non-dreaming sleep.
When do you become aware your child had or is having one?	After the dream is over and he wakes and cries or calls. Not during the nightmare itself.	During the terror itself, as he screams and thrashes. Afterwards he is calm.
Time of occurrence	In the second half of the night, when dreams are most intense.	Usually 1 to 4 hours after falling asleep, when non-dreaming sleep is deepest.

FIGURE 13 **Nightmares vs Sleep Terrors** (*continued*)

	Nightmares	Sleep Terrors
The child's appearance and behavior	Crying in younger children, fright in all. These persist even though the child is awake.	Initially the child may sit up, thrash, or run in a bizarre manner, with eyes bulging, heart racing, and profuse sweating. He may cry, scream, talk, or moan. There is apparent fright, anger, and/or obvious confusion, which *disappears* when he is fully awake.
Responsiveness	Child is aware of and reassured by your presence; he may be comforted by you and hold you tightly.	Child is not very aware of your presence, is not comforted by you, and may push you away and scream and thrash more if you try to hold or restrain him.
Return to sleep	May be considerably delayed because of persistent fear.	Usually rapid.
Description of a dream at the time or on waking in the morning.	Yes (if old enough).	No memory of a dream or of yelling or thrashing.

Chapter 12

Bedwetting

B edwetting, or nocturnal enuresis, is a very common and frustrating childhood sleep problem. In most of the disorders we have discussed it is the parents who become quite worried and upset, but with bedwetting the child is very often even more frustrated and unhappy than the parents.

We know that bedwetting is a problem in all societies and has been recorded down through history. Although figures differ somewhat between cultures and among various groups within a culture, approximately 15 percent of all five-year-olds and 5 percent of all ten-year-olds still wet their beds. Even by adolescence 1 to 2 percent of children are not consistently dry. About 60 percent of all enuretic children are boys. Although the causes of enuresis are only partially understood, several methods of treating the disorder have proven quite successful.

The Impact of Enuresis

If your child wakes partially every night, sits up in bed, looks around, and then goes back to sleep, we do not consider that he or she has a disorder. Even if you are aware this is happening, you are probably not concerned. But if your child wakes partially every night, moves around, and then urinates in her bed it is another matter.

In disorders such as sleepwalking and sleep terrors, you are aware of your child's walking, screaming, or thrashing *as it occurs*. But in enuresis, *at the time* your child is wetting, neither you nor she is aware that this is taking place. So it is not the actual act of urination that concerns parents and children—it is its *consequences*, namely that the sheets and pajamas get wet, your child wakes, you must get up, and the bed linens must be changed. This is frustrating and annoying to both you and your child. If the nightly urination continued, but magically nothing got wet, then enuresis would not be the problem that it is. It would hardly be considered a problem at all. We are not troubled by a child who quietly gets up for a drink of water most nights, but we would be if she often spilled it in her bed. Thus, enuresis only becomes a "problem" when your child is old enough to be out of diapers.

There are several other factors that set enuresis apart from sleep disorders such as sleepwalking and sleep terrors. A child only knows she has had a sleep terror or has walked in her sleep if you tell her. But she *always* knows if she has wet the bed. This is true even though she has no memory of wetting. In this case it is not you who tells her but the wet sheets. Also, since you are able to observe your child during an episode of sleepwalking or sleep terrors, it is easy to realize that she is unaware of her actions; you may be *worried* about her health and safety, but you probably won't be *angry*. On the other hand, it is left to your imagination to decide what your child's state of alertness is at the time she wets the bed. If you (incorrectly) assume that she is awake, aware, and thus consciously capable of urinary control, you may feel *anger and resentment* rather than *sympathy and concern*.

Your reactions as well as those of your child to her bedwetting episodes are very important. She needs you to be understanding and supportive or she will surely suffer. But even if you are fully supportive, even if you really don't mind changing the sheets, and even if you can be empathetic, perhaps because you used to wet the bed yourself, your child may still feel ashamed, embarrassed, and babyish. She may be reluctant to have friends sleep at her house and she may refuse to sleep at their homes or attend overnight camp. If her brother or sister tells friends that she wets the bed, she may be teased at school. The impact of enuresis can be very far-reaching then because it may affect your relationship with your child, her own self-image, and her interactions with other children.

For many families enuresis does not really seem to be a significant problem, especially if the bedwetting does not occur every night and if the child is only five, six, or perhaps seven years old. If this is so in your family, there is no need for you to intervene. Your child will probably outgrow the problem. Just be sure the wetting is not more bothersome to your child than you think. However, the older the child and the more frequent the wetting, the more likely it is that both child and parents will want to find a solution.

The impact of a child's bedwetting on the family varies considerably from one family to another. I try to take this into account whenever I see a child with this problem. We cannot always eliminate the bed-wetting, but I am able to counsel family members. If we can improve family relations and the child's view of herself, then the child and her parents are much happier. Very often we are successful in decreasing or eliminating bedwetting episodes as well.

Some parents misunderstand the nature of bedwetting and react to their child in a hostile, punitive, or otherwise inappropriate manner. Such was the case with George, a six-year-old boy who still wet his bed almost every night despite the fact that he had been toilet trained since he was three. He did have occasional dry nights, but he had never remained dry for more than one week. His parents had become quite frustrated with his inability to control his bladder during the night and got angry at him for his continued wetting. They punished him on occasion and frequently denied him special privileges, hoping that this would bring about some control. They insisted George wear a diaper to bed so that the sheets would not have to be changed. He had to sleep on a small cot, since his parents said they would not buy him a regular-sized bed until he stopped wetting.

George's parents were caring people and they loved George very much. But they did not understand bedwetting and were reacting in a way that seemed sensible to them, even though the problem was not improving. Finally they realized they needed help.

Fortunately, George was still young, but I knew that if the punish-ment continued everyone would suffer. I started by discussing the nature of enuresis with the entire family. George was surprised and delighted to hear me explain that it was not his fault, that punishment would not help, and that he should not wear diapers or be required to sleep in a cot. I told him that many children his age still wet the bed. He had thought he must be the only one. His father admitted, with much embarrassment, that he used to wet the bed as a youngster himself—something not even his wife had known.

The parents were anxious to correct their previous mistakes, and I supported their efforts carefully during frequent initial visits. We em-barked on a program of behavior modification which I will discuss at length later in this chapter. The results were fairly good. George's bedwetting did not cease entirely, but it did decrease significantly. But even before the wetting decreased, the family was functioning much better. The parents no longer felt guilty about "having" to punish George and to exclude him from family functions, and George no longer felt guilty about wetting.

In some cases the parents are not overly concerned about the bedwetting but the child is very unhappy. Recently I saw Veronica, an eight-year-old girl who wet the bed several times a week. Hers was a stable and happy home, and her parents were quite understanding; in fact, they accepted her bedwetting without complaint, and although they would have preferred her to be dry they were not very disturbed by the problem. Veronica's father had also been enuretic until age ten and he had discussed this with his daughter without embarrassment. They sought my help not because of their own concerns but because of Veronica, who was very bothered by the wetting. Veronica was a lovely girl who expressed her concerns forthrightly. She was very anxious to begin a program that might help her be dry at night.

Here the family needed little counseling. It was still worthwhile to reassure Veronica that her problem was far from unique, but because she wanted to stop wetting, we started her on a behavior modification program as well, with good results. Veronica, with her family's help, followed through on every part of the treatment, and they reported back to me frequently—weekly at first—until the problem was solved. In her case the most important factors were her strong motivation and her parents' full cooperation. Motivation and cooperation help, but they aren't always the answer. Other equally motivated youngsters have failed to respond. At times enuresis is very resistant to all types of intervention.

Enuresis is particularly upsetting for older children and adolescents. Larry, a twelve-year-old boy, was very upset by his bedwetting, to the point that it was affecting his whole life. He was very down on himself, and some of the children in the neighborhood teased him cruelly. It was important that Larry get help. Simply knowing that other children his age were bedwetters would not be reassurance enough.

Larry used to wet every night, although when I first saw him it was happening less—about three or four times a week. Both parents had been quite understanding and had tried to help him with various techniques, including behavior modification, responsibility training, bladder training, and even diet changes, but his problem had persisted. Larry changed and laundered his sheets and pajamas by himself, so the parents did not have to get up at night or have extra work in the daytime. Larry was becoming withdrawn. He never slept at a friend's house and never invited a friend to spend the night at his. He wanted very much to go away to camp but would not consider it until he stopped wetting.

Some supportive counseling was useful to Larry, but I knew he really needed to get the wetting under control. I suggested the family try the technique of conditioning with a "bell and pad" (see below), but this also failed. Finally we decided that a trial period of medication was justified. We found the minimum dosage necessary to suppress Larry's wetting, and then allowed him to use it for three months. He was delighted and he began to come out of his shell. When the medicine was stopped, the wetting resumed. But now Larry knew he could have a dry night whenever he wanted. He agreed not to take the medicine on a regular basis but saved it for sleeping at a friend's house and he took it with him to camp. Even though he still wets many nights at home, the knowledge that he can control it when necessary, albeit by medication, makes all the difference.

What Causes Enuresis?

It is difficult to say what causes enuresis because there seem to be several contributing factors. In each child it may be impossible to say which of these factors are most important.

1. Maturation

For your child to be able to control her urination (which we call urinary continence), that part of her nervous system controlling her bladder has to mature to a certain degree. During infancy your child will have little awareness of her bladder filling and that there is a "need" to urinate. Her bladder will empty when it is full simply by a reflex contraction. But some time between ages one and a half and two and a half, your child should begin to recognize when her bladder is full. She may stop playing when she has this feeling, and may have a facial expression that you have come to recognize and associate with impending urination. At this point, however, she still can't postpone the flow of urine. She can feel it coming, but she can't stop it. She will develop the ability to postpone urination over the next year. If you are toilet training her during that time, she will be able to get to the bathroom and remove her clothing in time to use the toilet. Finally, by age three or perhaps four, your child will be able to urinate at will, even when her bladder is only partially full. Also, she will now be capable of interrupting her urinary stream after it has started. She can go to the bathroom before leaving the house, even though she does not feel the urge to urinate, and she can "catch herself" when she realizes she is starting to urinate at the wrong time. When this occurs you can expect your child to have urinary control at night too, or at least that her nervous system has developed sufficiently for her to be *able* to be dry day and night. If she continues to wet despite this degree of maturation, other causes are probably responsible.

In fact, most children are dry at night before age four, but the actual age at which nighttime dryness is attained varies from child to child. Your child's bladder size increases considerably between ages two and four and a half, making it easier for her to hold her urine for the whole night. Some babies are already dry at night before one year of age, but this happens fairly rarely. By two and a half about half of all children are dry, and by age three about 75 percent no longer wet their beds. Although "delayed maturation" is often blamed for ongoing enuresis, it is unlikely that children of five or older continue to wet for this reason. If your child is dry at night even occasionally, it suggests that she has the ability to recognize that she is about to urinate and that she can postpone or prevent it until she is in the bathroom or until her bladder stops contracting and the urge ceases.

2. Small Bladder Capacity

Many bedwetters urinate more frequently during the day than do non-bedwetters, and in smaller amounts. This would suggest that their bladders are smaller than normal and less able to hold all their urine at night. But when examined under anesthesia, these children are found to have bladders of normal size. So we know that for some reason these children must feel the *sensation* of a full bladder and the need to urinate before their bladders are actually full. Not only are bladder contractions beginning too soon, but they may be very strong. At night this may lead to wetting. "Bladder training" techniques described later in this chapter are based on these observations—that the bladders of many enuretic children *function* as if they are smaller than they actually are.

3. Sleep Stages and Enuresis

We now know that bedwetting does not take place during a dream. If your child wakes describing a dream about water, and her sheets are wet, it does not mean that she wet because of the dream. The wetting episode came first, and the feeling of wetness from the sheets and pajamas then stimulated the particular dream. Although some bedwetters seem difficult to wake, most studies suggest that enuretic children do not sleep more deeply than non-enuretics. But it may still be that a child who wets during sleep has not learned to recognize the sensations from a full bladder, or from a partially full bladder that is already contracting, as a signal important enough to trigger a full waking. You will recall, from the discussion of sleep stages in Chapter 2, that a stimulus that is important to you (like your baby crying) is much more likely to wake you than an unimportant stimulus (like a bird chirping or a cat screeching). Somehow you have learned to make this distinction, even when you are asleep. Your child must also learn to make these distinctions automatically in her sleep. If she does not interpret the sensation of impending urination as "important," then she will not wake and may wet the bed instead. We believe conditioning and behavior modification techniques work by helping your child learn to pay closer attention to these signals.

Because most bedwetting occurs in the first third of the night, usually during or immediately following an arousal from non-REM sleep, it would seem that enuresis is similar to the arousal disorders described in Chapter 10. It may be that in the confusion of the partial arousal from deep sleep, urination occurs without the child's awareness. Children who have confused thrashing, sleep terrors, or sleepwalking episodes often also wet their beds. The bedwetting may occur at the same time as these other events, for example, in the midst of a sleep terror, or it may occur on separate nights altogether. As mentioned in Chapter 10, a child may even urinate inappropriately—into a wastebasket, clothes hamper, or boot—while sleepwalking.

Although not enough is yet understood on the possible link between bedwetting and the other arousal disorders, we do know that in some bedwetters spontaneous contractions of the bladder increase during non-REM sleep. It may be that these contractions both trigger the partial arousal and lead to subsequent bedwetting.

4. Medical Factors

The enuresis discussed in this chapter is "functional"—that is, bladder *function* is altered, but the bedwetting is not caused by any medical disorder. Most bedwetting is functional. But you should not simply assume your child's wetting does not have a medical cause until this has been excluded. All enuretic children five years of age or older should have a thorough physical examination before non-medical treatment begins. Even though medical factors are only rarely responsible for bedwetting, your child should also have a urine specimen examined to determine whether she has an infection that needs attention. Urinary infections are more common in enuretic children, especially girls, and should be treated, even though in most cases the bedwetting is not caused by the infection and may persist after the infection has cleared up.

Urinary tract abnormalities and some neurologic conditions may occasionally cause bedwetting, but these problems are usually accompanied by other symptoms, which your physician should notice. If your child has problems during the day such as dribbling, incontinence, frequent strong urges to urinate, or frequent or painful urination, then she may have an infection or abnormality that will require a doctor's attention.

Similarly, if your child begins bedwetting after many months of dryness, a condition called *secondary enuresis* or *onset enuresis*, as opposed to *primary enuresis* in which there never has been a long period of dryness, then there is more likelihood that medical factors may be involved. But if these are ruled out, then a child with secondary enuresis can be expected to respond very well to the same techniques we use to help primary enuretics achieve urinary continence.

5. Food Sensitivity

There has been a great deal of interest in the role of food sensitivity in a number of childhood health problems, bedwetting among them. On a few occasions nighttime wetting has decreased when certain foods were eliminated from a child's diet. It seems likely that some foods cause bladder irritation with increased bladder contractions and decreased bladder capacity in certain children. Unfortunately, *very* few children respond at all to diet manipulation.

6. Emotional Factors

You may be concerned that your enuretic child wets her bed because she is emotionally disturbed. Fortunately this is unlikely to be the case. Although it is true that bedwetting is somewhat more frequent among children with emotional problems, the vast majority of enuretic children are quite well adjusted. Many of them are of course feeling very bad about their wetting, and they may have emotional problems, but these are more likely the *result* of the bedwetting than the *cause*.

7. Environmental Influences and Early Childhood Experience

A child's early experience may affect her ability to be dry at night at the expected age. For example, studies of very large groups of children have shown an increase in enuresis in lower-income families, in middle children, and in children faced with early stresses such as divorce or chronic illness. Stresses during the third year, when a child is usually being toilet trained, are particularly disruptive. And if the toilet training itself is handled in a punitive manner, a child is also more likely to become a bedwetter. But although bedwetting is less common in children who were toilet trained lovingly and with care by supportive parents in stable family settings than it is in less fortunate youngsters, the difference is slight. Don't assume your child wets her bed because you have not been a good enough parent or that you somehow could have prevented it. At best the early family environment can provide only a very partial explanation for this disorder.

8. Heredity

I believe heredity is the single most important contributing factor in children with enuresis. There is a significant incidence of wetting in children whose parents were also bedwetters. For example, while only 15 percent of all children are bedwetters, this figure increases to about 45 percent if one parent used to wet the bed and 75 percent if both parents did. It is not known what is inherited, but it may be some of the factors described above, such as a small functional bladder capacity or a tendency to partial non-REM arousals.

Approaches to Treating Enuresis

Throughout recorded history there have been references to enuresis and various methods of treatment for the disorder. Our methods of treating the problem are now very humane and caring, although in the past enuretic children have been subjected to some pretty unusual "cures."

As early as A.D. 77, Pliny the Elder recommended "giving boiled mice" in the food of young children incontinent of urine. And in 1544 "cocke trachea or hedgehog testicles" were a suggested remedy for "Pissying in the Bedde." Byzantine potions included a fragrant wine made of hare's testicles, and in the nineteenth and twentieth centuries we have tried plenty of our own elixirs and potions, most of which have been no more effective than the "flowers of the white oxe" administered hundreds of years earlier.

Besides potions, some primitive cultures tried special rituals to cure enuresis. In one, the enuretic child had a frog tied around her waist and then had to lick the hooves of a newborn lamb. An enuretic in the Navajo tribe was forced to stand naked with her legs apart over the burning nest of a phoebe, swallow, or nighthawk, since it is known that birds do not wet their nests.

Although our treatments are now very different, some parents like George's still make the mistake of using punishment, ridicule, and shame in an attempt to stop the bedwetting. It is important that you understand that it is *not* helpful to treat an enuretic child this way. It will not help the bedwetting and may even prolong it. And if your child continues to be treated unjustly, she may suffer emotionally.

If your child is wetting her bed at night, she does so while she is asleep and has no knowledge that she is doing it. She does not do it to misbehave or upset you. Enuretic children are most unhappy about their problem and would be delighted to change it. George Orwell was one of the most famous self-admitted enuretics. He described his dilemma quite eloquently:

> I knew that bedwetting was (a) wicked, and (b) outside my control. The second fact I was personally aware of, and the first I did not question. It was possible, therefore, to commit a sin without knowing you committed it, without wanting to commit it, and without being able to avoid it.

You will be encouraged to know that most enuretic children will be able to reduce the frequency of bedwetting, and many are able to control the problem entirely. But before you begin your treatment program, you must understand that solving the problem will require patience, persistence, and everyone's cooperation. Results may be very slow in coming, and there are sometimes relapses after a dry period. All of the behavioral methods of treatment require a good deal of consistency and cooperation, and they will only work if both you and your child want them to and are willing to accept the temporary inconveniences. Your child can't stop the wetting without your full help and you can't make it stop if she isn't interested in participating. Again I must emphasize that an initial visit to a doctor is important. Don't begin a program of therapy until you are sure your child does not have a medical problem that needs attention.

Today we treat enuresis four main ways: with reinforcement and responsibility training, bladder training, conditioning, and medication. The first three are behavioral approaches and can be undertaken simultaneously or in succession. Many families start with reinforcement and bladder training methods, then try conditioning if the first two are not successful. Medication therapy can only be done under a doctor's supervision and is, or should be, recommended very rarely.

Before trying any of the behavioral approaches, get the family together and discuss your plans. Everyone will need to feel comfortable about working together to solve this problem. If there is resentment or teasing your plan will have less chance for success. If you have been punishing or criticizing your child for bedwetting up to now, explain to her that you were wrong and that you now understand she was not responsible for the wetting. Let her know that you want to work *with* her to help her control the nighttime wetting and feel better about herself. This is easier said than done; even the most well-meaning of parents may show subtle disapproval when the bedwetting continues. So you will need to monitor your own behavior carefully too.

1. Reinforcement and Responsibility Training

There are two related goals here. First you want to help your child learn to be more in charge of herself. She should feel good about this and so it should be presented as a privilege and an opportunity, *not* as a punishment. Once she becomes accustomed to responding promptly and automatically to her own general needs, responsibilities, and obligations during the day when she is awake, she will have an easier time doing the same at night when she is asleep. Hopefully your child will then begin to interpret the sensation of the need to urinate as an "important" signal requiring *her* to wake *herself* enough to be able to prevent wetting and, if necessary, to walk to the bathroom.

Second, you want to further reinforce your child's motivation to react to these nighttime signals and help her learn to recognize nighttime bladder sensations as important. You should do so by reward, not punishment. Most of us will put more energy and concentration into earning a reward than avoiding a punishment. And if the family works together in a spirit of cooperation, the treatment works even better.

Begin by discussing with your child ways in which she can assume more general responsibility around the house—clearing dishes from the table, taking out the garbage, or walking the dog. Most important is that she take on more responsibility around the enuretic event itself. She should change her own pajamas and, when she is old enough—about seven—help change the sheets and do the laundry. However, I don't think it's a good idea for such a young child to have the entire responsibility for these chores. It will seem more like a punishment, and you are trying to foster an atmosphere of cooperation and mutual concern.

At the same time, you must treat your child in a manner that is appropriate for her age. Do not treat her like a baby. Under no circumstances should she be left in diapers, like George, and she should sleep in a regular bed. Use waterproof pads under the sheet to protect the mattress. Do not restrict her in any way because she still wets; instead, give her extra privileges for taking on the new responsibilities.

Also, most children should avoid drinking *large* amounts of fluid after 6:00 P.M., although this alone will not solve the problem. Severely restricting fluids is harsh and of no value.

Next, set up a system for recording and rewarding dry nights. A star chart, specially drawn or kept on a calendar, is often successful, at least up until about age ten. Give her stars for dry nights and special prizes once she has earned enough stars. You can structure the system to suit your child's age and interests, but you may want to base it on this one, which has worked well for us. Choose one color star for dry nights, another color to be used at the end of the week if there have been four dry nights, and a special sticker for seven consecutive dry nights. Instead of stars, your child may prefer some of the many stickers now available—animals, special characters, 3-D, or scented stickers. Let her help choose them. Agree on a special (though inexpensive) treat or prize for every two seven-day stickers. Have your child stick the stars to the chart or calendar, and congratulate her when she has earned one, but once again, do not scold her or in any way make her feel bad after she has wet the bed.

These changes alone may lead to improvement. But whether they do or not, you will be doing your child a service. Her view of herself, and of you, will improve and she will see that she does not have to feel guilty about bedwetting, or be punished for it.

2. Bladder Training

You may begin bladder training at the same time you start responsibility training, or postpone it for a while if you wish. This is how you proceed.

- Do not restrict your child's fluid intake during the day (such restrictions have never proven helpful), although once again it is reasonable to avoid large amounts of liquid near bedtime.
- On the first two days, collect the urine each time your child urinates at home and measure the volume. Note the amount of time between urinations.
- Record the largest volume of urine over the two-day period and use that as the "record to beat."
- If your child urinates more often than every three to four hours, have her try to increase the intervals a half-hour each day until she achieves a three-to four-hour minimum.
- Once a day, at the same time each day, have her hold her urine as long as possible, at least to the point of some discomfort. Then when she urinates measure the volume. This will help to gradually increase bladder capacity during the day as she tries to beat her previous "record." There is no specific volume that will guarantee nighttime continence, but ten to twelve ounces are reasonable goals. Or try for a 50 percent improvement over the initial "record."
- At least once each day have your child practice starting and stopping the stream of urine several times.
- When your child has been dry at night for two consecutive weeks, reinforce the success with a program of "overlearning."

Encourage her to drink more and more fluid during the day and up to two to four glasses at bedtime so that she will get better and better at controlling her bladder.

3. Conditioning

Conditioning techniques have been very successful in treating enuresis, although this method has been used more in Europe than in the United States. The system consists of a "bell and pad," several of which are available commercially here. Two pads which fit on the bed are separated by a thin sheet. The pads are connected to an alarm, and when the sheet becomes wet, an electrical connection is made between the two pads and the alarm rings. Current models are safe, with little danger of burns.

The object in conditioning is for your child to wake up as soon as she begins to wet the bed. The system works on the theory that your child will then learn to associate the feelings she has just before urinating with the need to wake. To use this method successfully you will need your child's full cooperation and understanding. Therefore it is unlikely to be much help before she is at least seven, although a few younger children have been able to profit from it.

To use the conditioning bell and pad system, both the parents and the child should understand how the mechanism works, but the enuretic child should take responsibility for testing it and turning it on when she gets into bed at night. It will help if she wears very thin pajama bottoms or none at all, since thicker fabric will absorb urine and delay the start of the alarm.

If the alarm rings at night and the child does not wake immediately, it is up to the parents to wake her. Leave the alarm ringing, however, until the child gets up and turns it off herself. She can then go to the bathroom to complete her urination, help remake the bed if necessary, and reset the alarm. It is crucial that you use the system *every* night and keep accurate records of the results. It seems the biggest cause of failure with this device is lack of commitment to follow through for whatever time is needed. Often the conditioning will take a number of months, so be prepared to continue for four to five months, although most children will respond earlier. In general, 25 percent of children improve within two to six weeks, 50 percent are dry by three months, and 90 percent are dry by four to six months.

You can also use "overlearning" in this program after your child has been dry for two weeks. Increase her fluid intake in the evening up to sixteen to thirty-two ounces before bedtime and continue to use the bell and pad until she has stayed dry for twenty-one consecutive nights.

It is important that you know there is often a relapse when the pad is discontinued. If this happens to your child, you simply use the pad again exactly as you did before. Several courses of conditioning therapy are sometimes necessary when the problem is a stubborn one.

4. Medication

For children who are severely enuretic and have not responded to behavioral approaches, we occasionally prescribe medication to help bring the problem under control. Imipramine (Tofranil) has been the most useful drug in controlling enuresis, although no one knows for certain exactly how and why it works. The drug may work by its effect on sleep (perhaps affecting the likelihood and characteristics of non-REM arousals) or by its known direct effect on the bladder (which is to decrease contractions and increase bladder capacity). Taken in appropriate doses this medicine is relatively safe, although side effects of irritability, nightmares, and mood changes are occasionally reported. Overdoses of the medication, however, are quite dangerous and can be fatal. So if your doctor prescribes imipramine for your child it must be handled *very* carefully. Do not leave it out where children can get into it and be sure that your child does not try to increase her own dosage in an effort to be dry at night.

I believe this treatment should only be used rarely on a nightly basis, but I will consider it for the older child who hasn't had any success with other methods and who is having social and psychological problems because of bedwetting. Once an effective dose is found, it may be best to use the medication only on certain occasions (as Larry did) to allow a child to attend camp or sleep at a friend's home without fear of embarrassment. I always begin treatment with a very small dose and increase it gradually until we get an effective response or until I have reached the maximum dosage I feel is safe. The results are usually prompt. The child will often be dry on the first night; in any case there is usually reduction of wetting by the end of the first week of therapy.

Other Methods

5. Lifting

You may already be "lifting" your child, that is taking her to the bathroom at some point after she has fallen asleep, probably when you are about to go to bed. This is sometimes successful in eliminating wetting at night, especially if your child only wets once each night and if the time of wetting is regular, predictable, and not too late in the night, but it is unlikely to have any long-term benefits.

The fact that you are arousing your child rather than letting her learn to wake from bladder signals may actually postpone her achieving nighttime continence. On the other hand, if it does work it means at least that your child is dry, there is less frustration and fewer sheet and pajama changes. Often this technique will not be successful because your child will already be wet when you go in or she will wet again later in the night. If you do find lifting useful, I suggest that every three months you go for two weeks without lifting to check your child's progress and to give her a chance to learn nighttime control.

6. Dietary Changes

I rarely suggest major dietary changes to try to decrease wetting, because improvement is rare and a lot of work is involved. If you do want to try this method, however, you may follow the same diets that are described in books on dietary therapy for hyperactive children. Ask your librarian for help. But remember, if there is improvement it may be coincidental or it may be a response to increased family cooperative efforts rather than any specifics of the diet. In any case, do not leave your child on a severely restricted diet. Gradually add back the foods you have eliminated. Be sure that a particular food is responsible for increased wetting before you make your child do without it.

Conclusion

Enuresis may be a difficult problem to eliminate entirely, and it is certainly a frustrating one when it persists. Although the treatments described in this chapter do not guarantee success, when they are carried out *diligently* most children show significant improvement and many stop wetting altogether. Although enuresis is only a minor sleep disorder in terms of the event itself, it may have major consequences because of its impact on the child and family. For this reason it is important that you understand the problem and respond to your child's needs in an appropriate way. Even if you must wait until the bedwetting is finally outgrown, it is important that your child feel that you are doing so in a warm and caring manner. You should work *with* her in a positive fashion as part of a team. By so doing, you will help your child avoid months or years of unnecessary suffering, your own interactions with her will remain good, her self-image will improve, and she will get along better with her friends. And the more you are able to show your child that you and she are working together, the more likely it is that your attempts to reduce wetting will be successful.

Part Five

OTHER PROBLEMS

Headbanging, Body Rocking, and Head Rolling

M any children engage in some sort of repetitious, rhythmic behavior at bedtime, after waking during the night, or in the morning. They rock on all fours, roll their heads from side to side, bang their heads against the headboards of their beds, or repeatedly drop their heads onto their pillows or mattresses. At night this may continue until they fall asleep, and in the morning it may persist until they are fully awake. If your child is like this, you may be comforted to know that headbanging, body rocking, and head rolling are very common in early childhood and, at least at this age, are usually normal. If your child exhibits any of these behaviors there is little need for concern about emotional difficulties or neurological illness. However, if these symptoms persist or begin in older children, there may be other implications.

When the Rhythmic Behaviors Begin

Most young children rock back and forth occasionally and about 20 percent of children do so more consistently, rocking back and forth on all fours at least once a day. Still, their rocking occurs mainly during waking hours, often while they are listening to music. About one-half of these children also rock in bed before going to sleep and some mainly confine their rocking to this time. About 5 percent of children exhibit other rhythmic behaviors, particularly headbanging and head rolling, most often at bedtime, after waking at night or in the morning, or during sleep. Body rocking and head rolling are equally common in both boys and girls but headbanging appears three times more often in boys.

These rhythmical behaviors most often begin very early—usually within the first year. On the *average*, body rocking starts at six months of age, headbanging and head rolling at nine months. Still, there is a considerable range. Head rolling and sometimes rocking may even appear within the first three months of life. Headbanging may start as early as four months or as late as the beginning of the second year. Often body rocking or head rolling starts first and headbanging begins several weeks or months later.

These rhythmical behaviors may last only a few weeks or months, or they may be more persistent; even so, they usually disappear within a year and a half of their onset. It is uncommon to see them after three years of age.

What the Behaviors Look Like

If your child bangs his head he probably gets up on all fours and rocks back and forth, hitting his forehead or the top of his head into the headboard of the crib or bed. Or he may sit in bed and bang backwards into the headboard. Some children will lie face down and lift their heads, or head and chest, then bang or drop back into the pillow or mattress again and again. Occasionally a child may stand in his crib, hold on to the side rail, and hit his head there. Now and then a child will assume a very awkward posture to allow himself to rock, bang his head, suck his thumb, and hold on to a stuffed animal all at the same time.

Some children only rock; they move back and forth but without hitting their heads. Most often they do this on all fours, but some rock in a sitting position. The child who head rolls usually lies on his back and moves his head rhythmically from side to side. He may also bang his head on the side of the crib at the same time.

Parents usually find headbanging most frustrating. Timothy, for example, was a two-year-old boy who had been healthy and developing normally. However, his parents had become concerned about his behavior in bed at night. Starting at seven months of age, he began to rock back and forth vigorously on all fours for about twenty minutes before falling asleep. Before long he had begun to bang his head and was still doing so at age two.

Every night after getting into bed Timothy would rock vigorously, banging his forehead into the headboard at the end of his bed. Although he usually stopped within fifteen minutes and fell asleep, some episodes lasted as long as an hour. During the rocking and banging, the crib would often move across the room. It was constantly being damaged and had to be replaced twice.

Timothy's parents were worried that he would injure himself, and so they put padding at the end of the crib, but he would either manage to push it aside or find another hard spot on the crib into which he could bang. When his parents placed his mattress on the floor, he simply crawled over to the wall and began to bang his head there.

Children like Timothy, who do most of their rocking or banging in bed at night, mainly do so at bedtime, but they may behave in the same way in the morning after waking, before naps, or as they try to return to sleep after nighttime wakings. Some children go to bed without any rocking or banging but still show these behaviors after spontaneous wakings during the night. Similar rhythmical rocking or headbanging may occur during the day in certain children—usually at times of stress or pain, but more often when they listen to music. When a child rocks or bangs his head at night, he is usually drowsy, and the behavior will stop once he is sound asleep.

Only very occasionally do these rhythmical patterns actually seem to persist into the deeper stages of sleep. If you go into the room when your child is rocking and find that he remains oblivious to you even when you speak to him, then he is likely asleep. If at these times he responds only after you speak loudly or shake him and then seems temporarily confused, he certainly was asleep. He was not simply rolling his head as he tried to go back to sleep after a brief arousal, or to get your attention, or because of anxiety. In these cases the rocking or banging seems to be somewhat different. Instead of being semiconscious movements that your child finds soothing and helpful while falling asleep, these behaviors are unconscious and apparently represent a true sleep disturbance. Still, they are usually without major significance. But this type of rocking or headbanging that occurs during deep sleep may be slow to disappear and may persist well beyond the age of three. However, as your child grows, it will progressively diminish in intensity and duration, it will shift to periods of lighter sleep or drowsiness, and eventually it will almost certainly disappear entirely.

What Causes the Behavior?

We all know that rhythmical stimulation is very soothing for a baby as it is for all of us. A child rocking in bed or rolling his head from side to side—or an adult swaying to soft music—may simply be providing himself with a feeling of pleasure or comfort. We believe that in young children the feeling is soothing, like rhythmical thumb sucking or being rocked in a rocking chair. It is less clear, of course, why forceful headbanging would be so "soothing," but it seems to be. Possibly the child finds the loud rhythmical sounds, or even the regularly recurring impacts, comforting in a way most adults would not.

Teething often begins at about the same time as headbanging or rocking. When the rocking or banging is short-lived, it may in fact be in response to the discomfort. But there is a tendency to ascribe too many sleep disorders in infants to teething and it is unlikely to be the cause of rhythmic behaviors if they persist for more than a few weeks. We find that temporary headbanging or rocking may also appear or recur when your child is facing an important developmental hurdle such as learning to stand or take his first step. When this happens, the behaviors at night seem to help release tension he may feel during the day.

When rhythmic behaviors begin before eighteen months and disappear for the most part by age three or four, they are not usually a sign of emotional problems. Most often children with these habits are quite happy and healthy, with no discernible problems or significant tensions in their families. It is true, however, that these types of behaviors do occur more frequently in children with certain neurological or psychiatric disorders. Retarded, blind, and autistic children are more inclined to rock their bodies or bang their heads. But when headbanging or rocking is associated with a major disorder, it is almost always obvious that the child is not normal. So if your child is developing normally, there is no reason to worry about a major disturbance because he begins one of these rhythmical motor patterns at an early age.

When these behaviors begin after about eighteen months of age or when they persist or recur in an older child, they may have a different significance. Still, if the symptoms are mild—perhaps brief non-vigorous head rolling or a few minutes of mild banging into the pillow before sleep—they are probably simply learned habits associated with drowsiness and falling asleep, or perhaps automatic behavior patterns that occur only in the drowsy state, and are not of any importance. Many older children and even adults, for example, will roll one or both legs from side to side for a few minutes while falling asleep.

However, if your child's rhythmical patterns are strong, last longer than ten to fifteen minutes, and recur repeatedly during the night, then you should investigate further. If your child is autistic or retarded, you will already be aware of his condition. But less serious emotional difficulties could be responsible. Your child may be using the rocking or banging to get attention. If you go into his room or call out to him to stop when he rocks or bangs his head, you may have inadvertently reinforced that behavior. Your child has learned that by making rocking or banging noises in bed he can assure himself some interaction with you. Or his rhythmic nighttime behavior may be his way of dealing with anxiety. He may feel alone and frightened about being apart from you, especially if you live in a house and he sleeps upstairs (or downstairs) on his own, or he may be upset by important changes in his life or ongoing tensions at home.

Jessica, for example, was an eight-year-old girl I saw who had gone through a brief period of rocking in bed before her first birthday but stopped soon after. Six months before her mother brought her to see me, she had adopted a pattern of "thumping" every night for thirty to sixty minutes before falling asleep. She would lie in bed face down, lift her head, and let it fall into her pillow repeatedly.

Jessica was healthy and seemed happy enough, although a little withdrawn. I learned that the previous year had been a time of great difficulty for Jessica's family. Her parents had separated and were in the process of working out the details of a divorce, Jessica and her mother had moved into a smaller apartment, and her mother had returned to work. On speaking with Jessica alone I learned that she felt that she had caused her parents' separation and she believed they might be angry with her for that. She was afraid she might cause her mother more unhappiness, and, if this happened, she would suffer even more loss of love. It was clear that the recurrence of Jessica's headbanging was in response to her current emotional struggles.

Treating the Problem

In the infant and young toddler, rhythmic patterns are of little significance and you will not need to intervene. The behavior will likely disappear before long. If the rocking or headbanging is especially severe, as with Timothy, then for the sake of more quiet at night, less damage to the furniture, and fewer complaints from the neighbors, you may want to consider several approaches, though these are only occasionally successful. Try putting a loud ticking clock in your child's room or a metronome set to beat at the same tempo as the rocking or banging. If your child will pay attention to the rhythmical ticking, he may lie still. Encourage him to enjoy rhythmical activities during the day, such as using swings or hobby horses, listening to music, or rocking in a chair. But it is most important to keep in mind that this is one time that the advice "Don't worry, nothing troublesome is happening, and it will be outgrown" is sound. Timothy's parents accepted this, made no changes (other than to stop worrying), and in fact after six months the banging had almost stopped.

A normal child will not injure himself seriously while headbanging, although he occasionally may bruise his forehead and, very rarely, there may be a small amount of bleeding. Concussions, fractured skulls, or brain injuries just do not occur. The main damage is to furniture and walls. On the other hand, retarded youngsters who bang their heads vigorously sometimes do injure themselves. If your child is retarded or autistic, you may have to consider having him wear a helmet or other restraints. Padding around the bed will reduce the noise and you will probably worry less, but a child like Timothy, intent on banging, will often remove it or find another spot.

For the child who simply rocks, but rocks vigorously for prolonged periods, it may be best to let him sleep on a mattress on the floor. This will avoid the crib's being shaken back and forth and "walked" across the room each night. You won't have to put up with the noise, nor will you have to keep replacing broken cribs. Unfortunately, putting a mattress on the floor often does little for the child who bangs his head. It certainly will not help if he bangs his head into the mattress. But if he bangs against the end of the crib or bed, then placing the mattress in the middle of the room may help. Still he likely will only crawl over to the wall and bang his head there. Occasionally this change will result in less banging, especially in the middle of the night, when a child may settle instead for vigorous rocking.

Vigorous headbanging or rocking in older children is usually related to emotional factors and you should take a more active role in helping to solve the problem. Your child may, for whatever reason, feel the need for extra attention. His rocking or headbanging gets you to come to his room, even if it is only to tell him to stop. You may notice that if he sleeps at a friend's house or if you sleep in his room, he does not rock or bang. If this is the case with your child, it is important that you respond to his need for attention but not to the nighttime behaviors, or you will only reinforce them. Thus, it is best to ignore the rhythmic behavior at night (as you would a temper tantrum) but do be sure to set extra time during the day to spend with your child. Show him that you enjoy his company but don't wait for him to demand attention. The time before bed is especially important. If you and he have some special time together, then he will probably need you less after he says goodnight. It may help if you stay in a room near his when he goes to sleep and if you promise to check him before you go to bed. During the day the two of you can even work together to help him stop banging or rocking, perhaps by keeping a star chart with rewards for a sufficient number of quiet nights. If you feel that you cannot meet your child's needs for attention because of pressures in your own life, or if your child's need for attention persists despite what you feel is plenty of good time together during the day, you may want to seek professional advice.

It may also be that your child's rocking or headbanging is his way of dealing with anxiety. If he is concerned about major issues such as an impending divorce, or about family fighting or illness, you will quite likely be aware of the cause of his feelings. On the other hand, if his life seems superficially happy and stable, you may be unable to identify the cause of his upset. In any case, if your child is tense, then the nighttime becomes extra difficult. When he goes to bed and the lights are turned out, he is left with his own thoughts and fantasies. If they are frightening or upsetting he may do anything to avoid them, including rocking vigorously or banging his head. By concentrating on these behaviors, it is much easier for him to avoid worrisome or scary thoughts. If your child is having a difficult time, he will also need extra attention, and so the behaviors may have a dual purpose—helping him deal with being alone with his thoughts at night and getting you to come in to give him some extra attention and possibly reassurance.

If the rhythmical behaviors begin at the time of a major change in his life—after a separation or serious illness perhaps—try to discuss the situation openly with him and encourage him to express his feelings of anger or guilt. If his anxiety is relieved, his need to rock or bang will be lessened. If he is too young for this, be extra attentive and loving so that he will know his world is safe and caring and that he was not responsible for any of the problems. It is sometimes hard to provide all this support on your own. If your attempts to help your child meet with little success, or if you feel that you do not know the source of the problem or how to deal with it, then do consider counseling. Depending on the issues involved and the age of the child, the counseling may include you, your spouse, your child, or all of you together.

In Jessica's case, it was apparent that she was very anxious because of her confused feelings regarding her parents' separation. In the beginning her mother had been reluctant to discuss the matter with Jessica because of her own anxiety and because she felt that not discussing it would be "easier on Jessica." However, Jessica's mother sought counseling for herself, which was very helpful, and the tension at home began to ease quickly. She spent more time talking with

Jessica and together they found it easier to discuss feelings related to the divorce. Jessica's mother was surprised at how much Jessica had to say about her father's leaving, and Jessica admitted that she felt responsible. Jessica said that she had been unwilling to discuss things before because her mother had always avoided the topic. Now Jessica could express her feelings, and her mother was able to correct her misconceptions and reassure her. Jessica said that she wanted to stop "thumping" and so she and her mother began to work on a star chart in which Jessica earned rewards for nights without banging. Keeping the chart provided Jessica and her mother with a chance to spend special time together during the day as Jessica added the stars and they talked about her success. Jessica did not receive the extra attention at night at the time of the "thumping" and she was not rewarded for banging. She received the attention during the day and she was rewarded for *not* "thumping."

Now that Jessica and her mother were working together, their daytime interactions improved, and they felt better about themselves. Jessica's anxiety was reduced and she was able to work on the star chart with a true motivation. The rocking disappeared within four weeks, except for an occasional episode lasting only a few minutes after waking on some nights. Happily, in this case, once the parent and child understood the source of the problem the anxiety diminished, they were able to work together, and a change in the nighttime behavior followed quite quickly.

Often, however, a child is faced with ongoing stress, usually in the home. In such cases treatment will likely take longer and counseling for the child or the entire family will be indicated. I believe it is always more important to treat the emotional problem than it is to try and quickly stop the rhythmic behavior. In fact, once emotional tensions ease, the nighttime behavior usually decreases or disappears by itself.

Chapter 14

Noisy Breathing, Snoring, and Sleep Apnea

If your child snores loudly in his or her sleep, you may have dismissed it lightly, joking that no one would ever be able to share a room with him or her. Or you may be very worried. Watching and listening to her each night, you may have come to believe that she is struggling to breathe—perhaps at times unable to breathe at all—and that she is not "just snoring." You may even sit by her bed or take her into yours when she has a cold to make sure that she doesn't stop breathing. Yet your friends or even your doctor may have told you that snoring is nothing to worry about. But each night you watch and listen—and no matter what anyone has told you, you still worry.

Although snoring used to be dismissed as simply an annoyance, we now know that it is often associated with major breathing problems in sleep. So if your child snores you may have reason to be concerned. She may have a disorder called "sleep apnea," and if so, she should have medical attention.

What Happens in Sleep Apnea

Although physicians have been aware of sleep apnea for many years, it is only since the growth of sleep laboratories in the 1970s that we have begun to recognize just how frequently this disorder occurs. The problem is especially frequent in men over forty years of age and in women after menopause. However, a great many children suffer from this disorder as well. Nevertheless, the problem of sleep apnea in children has been largely overlooked, perhaps because children's *daytime* symptoms are less obvious than are adults' or because most sleep centers see primarily adult patients.

"Apnea" means the absence of breathing. In a child with sleep apnea, an unusual phenomenon occurs repeatedly throughout the night. Once asleep, her upper airway narrows or closes off so that she cannot breathe properly; little or no air will pass through the obstruction no matter how hard she tries to breathe. If there is some airflow, the child will snore. The sounds may be soft and squeaky if only a tiny amount of air gets through, or loud and raspy if the airflow is a bit better. If the airflow becomes blocked completely, there will be a very quiet period—because she isn't breathing at all. While the airflow is decreased or absent, oxygen levels in the bloodstream drop until, usually after eight to thirty seconds, she arouses, semiconsciously adjusts the muscles of her tongue and throat to open her airway, and takes in several less obstructed breaths. If her breathing was completely blocked before this, these breaths will be accompanied by loud snoring or snorting. Thus you would hear loud snores with intervening silences. If the obstruction had been partial, with ongoing snoring, these less obstructed breaths may be quieter, with just a little snoring or deep heavy breathing, and you would notice periods of snoring interspersed with heavy breathing. After taking these few breaths and returning her oxygen to better levels, she falls back to sleep (without any awareness of the partial waking) only to have her breathing become obstructed once again. The child with sleep apnea tries vigorously to breathe, and her sleep may be quite restless. In extreme cases she may sit up or sleep bent forward on her knees in an effort to improve respiration.

In the past, doctors often did not recognize sleep apnea in children until the strain from the intense respiratory efforts coupled with the lowered oxygen levels led to diminished heart function. Fortunately, this is uncommon. Most children with sleep apnea do not develop heart complications; this occurs mainly in children with such severe obstruction that their breathing is also impaired when they are awake.

In sleep apnea the actual obstruction usually takes place in the back of the throat behind the base of the tongue. Here the airway can be blocked by collapse of the walls of the throat, which are floppy in this region, and by the tongue falling backwards. While awake, we hold our tongue forward and the throat taut so that we can breathe. But in sleep, when we lose some of the ability to do this, a collapse of the airway can occur. Under certain conditions, for example when there is an abnormal narrowing higher up in the airway that forces a child to breathe very hard, this collapse is more apt to happen.

To give you an idea how such an obstruction occurs, imagine for a moment what it is like to breathe through a straw, so that the straw represents your respiratory system (see Figure 14). The end of the straw away from you would be the air inlet (like your nose) and the end in your mouth the source of suction (like your diaphragm). As long as the straw is formed normally you can breathe without difficulty. However, if you bend the straw in the middle several times so that it becomes floppy you will find that if you breathe in too rapidly, the weakened part of the straw will collapse. Still, if you breathe slowly and regularly it will not.

Now imagine pinching the far end of the straw. In order to breathe through that narrowed opening at the end you would have to suck harder than usual and the floppy part would surely collapse and cause an obstruction. This is analogous to what happens in a child whose upper airway is narrowed perhaps because of enlarged tonsils or adenoids. In order to get enough air she has to breathe harder, but in the process the floppy area in the back of her throat may be sucked closed. This will not happen when she is awake and able to control the muscles of the tongue and throat to keep the passage open. But it may occur when she is asleep. If this does happen repeatedly during the night, then she has sleep apnea.

Although we cannot always pinpoint the cause of sleep apnea, any narrowing of the upper airway or increased floppiness in the throat tissues can precipitate this condition. Many adults with sleep apnea are overweight and have thick, short necks. Obesity can also be a major factor in sleep apnea in children, at least in part because of deposits of too much soft fatty tissue in the walls of the throat.

Sleep apnea may also be caused by oral or facial abnormalities—the most common being an abnormally small receding lower jaw (called micrognathia or retrognathia). Sleep apnea may occur in a child with Down's syndrome, since she may have a tongue too large for the size of her mouth and because the neurological control of the muscles of the tongue and throat may not be completely normal. In some children the "abnormality" may have been created artificially by surgery. Sometimes the roof of the mouth (palate) is connected surgically to the back of the throat (making a "pharyngeal flap") to help correct certain speech problems, especially in children born with a cleft palate. Abnormalities of the nose such as a deviated septum or tumor are unusual causes of sleep apnea. Nasal obstruction from allergies may lead to some snoring, but is very unlikely to cause significant apnea. For most children with sleep apnea, however, enlarged tonsils and/or adenoids are the source of the problem.

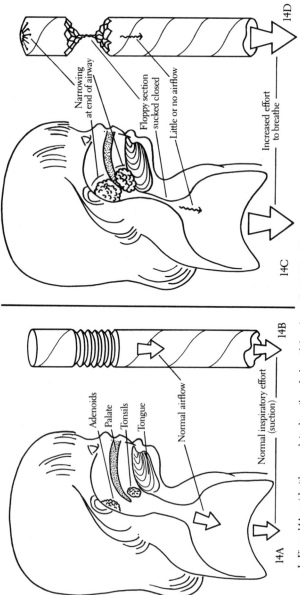

Adenoids
Palate
Tonsils
Tongue

Normal airflow

Normal inspiratory effort
(suction)

14B

14A

Narrowing
at end of airway

Floppy section
sucked closed

Little or no airflow

Increased effort
to breathe

14D

14C

In Figure 14A, a girl with normal sized tonsils and adenoids breathes well with little effort. One could do the same, breathing through a straw of sufficient caliber (Figure 14B).

In Figure 14C, the air passages are narrowed by markedly enlarged tonsils and adenoids. Now the girl must breathe in strenuously in an effort to get air past the narrowing. But, the floppy part of the airway just below the tonsils and adenoids only gets sucked closed and there is little or no airflow (apnea). This is similar to breathing through a straw that is pinched off at the far end (Figure 14D).

FIGURE 14 Obstructive Sleep Apnea

Enlarged Tonsils and Adenoids

Your child's tonsils are pink roundish glands that are easily seen at the back of her mouth just above her tongue and against either side of her throat. They may become quite swollen when infected. Afterwards they usually shrink down again, but sometimes they remain large.

You can't see your child's adenoids, which are located against the back of her throat above the roof of her mouth. They are similar in appearance to her tonsils. When the adenoids are enlarged they may block normal airflow through your child's nose and she may be forced to breathe through her mouth. Her speech may take on a nasal quality and her nose may run constantly. Also, the tube that normally drains her middle ear cavity may become obstructed, fluid may collect, and your child may have a temporary hearing loss and repeated ear infections.

Not all children with enlarged tonsils or adenoids develop sleep apnea. This is probably because of the anatomical and physiological differences among children. The size and shape of a child's throat may determine whether or not enlarged tonsils will significantly block her breathing at night. And a child's ability to switch to mouth breathing automatically during sleep may determine whether or not her large adenoids will lead to any nighttime breathing difficulties.

In children with difficulty breathing because of enlarged tonsils and/ or adenoids, snoring is often present for many years. It can increase in severity over time or remain fairly stable. Occasionally symptoms begin suddenly in association with a bout of tonsillitis. Often breathing difficulties are worse in the winter months when colds are more frequent.

I have seen many children like Melody, a three-year-old girl. She was happy and alert during the day except for some occasional tiredness in the afternoon. She was well behaved and played cooperatively with her friends, but her parents were quite worried because of what happened to Melody during the night. At three months of age Melody began to snore, and over the years her snoring became progressively worse. She snored most of the night and could be heard all over the house. Melody seemed to be struggling to breathe during sleep, her mouth would be open, and at times her upper chest would actually be pulled inwards rather than expanding with each breath. Her parents noticed that sometimes Melody's chest seemed to go in and out without any apparent airflow, and at these times they would shake her awake to help her start breathing normally again. After such periods without apparent breathing Melody would shudder and make strange snorting sounds as the air finally entered her lungs. When she had a cold her breathing troubles were even worse.

Her parents had discussed this problem with their pediatrician on several occasions, and he did comment that Melody's tonsils were large and that her adenoids were also probably enlarged because she tended to breathe through her mouth all the time. Nevertheless, he felt that removing her tonsils and adenoids was not necessary, because "snoring itself is nothing to be concerned about and will be outgrown," and because Melody had not had repeated throat or ear infections.

At our center we work closely with ear, nose, and throat specialists as well as with doctors from other disciplines such as oral surgery, nutrition, and plastic surgery. With this cooperative approach we are able to diagnose and treat children like Melody so that such problems are not passed over as unimportant.

To find out for certain what was happening to Melody when she slept, we had her come into the laboratory one night with her mother so that we could record her sleep. We monitored her stages of sleep throughout the night as well as the airflow in and out of her nose and mouth. We recorded her chest and abdominal movements as she attempted to breathe. And with a special device called an oximeter that clipped painlessly to her ear, we were able to measure the amount of oxygen in her bloodstream. Our findings in Melody were generally typical of those we have seen in many other children with similar stories, although Melody's problem was fairly serious.

During the night Melody had 350 *episodes* in which her breathing was either completely or partially obstructed for periods lasting eight to fifty seconds. She spent *one-fourth* of her sleep time struggling with these obstructions. Melody did sleep fairly well in the early part of the night during the deeper stages of non-REM sleep when her breathing was fairly good and her snoring only moderate. But during the rest of the night the obstructions and recurrent arousals disrupted her sleep severely. During most of these obstructions her blood oxygen level dropped significantly. As expected, the most severe obstructions occurred during REM sleep, when the muscles of her throat were most relaxed and when the control of her breathing was least automatic.

Watching Melody struggle to breathe throughout the night was heartbreaking. Given Melody's sleep disruption, it was surprising that she was not more tired and irritable than she had been during the day! Melody's mother was relieved to learn that her concern was justified and that we would not let Melody continue to suffer.

Obesity

Sleep apnea also occurs frequently in children who are markedly obese. Most physicians are familiar with the "Pickwickian syndrome," which, loosely defined, refers to a child who is both very fat and very sleepy. The term derives from the character of Joe in Dickens's *The Pickwick Papers*, "a fat and red-faced boy" who always seemed to be "in a state of somnolency." When Mr. Pickwick was told that Joe "goes on errands fast asleep, and snores as he waits at table," he responded, "How very odd!"

Odd, perhaps, but uncommon, no. In fact it is common enough that we now routinely perform sleep studies on most *very* obese youngsters who come to our hospital.

Vaughn was such a youngster. He was a twelve-year-old boy with two obvious problems: at almost 180 pounds he was quite obese, and he was always falling asleep during the day despite the fact that he seemed to get enough sleep at night. He often fell asleep in school while working in class, and he often fell asleep at home when trying to do his homework. As a result he had to repeat one grade. His teachers and parents viewed his sleepiness as laziness and reacted with anger instead of sympathy.

When they came to see me, the family did not at first mention any snoring. They were more concerned about his sleepiness. But in response to my questioning, they said that for years Vaughn had snored very loudly for the better part of each night.

When we studied Vaughn's sleep we found his sleep apnea was even more severe than Melody's. He had over 600 apneas, each lasting about twenty to seventy seconds. The degree of oxygen deprivation was quite profound, and often it did not even return to normal levels during the arousals that followed each obstruction. He had no deep sleep at all, and there weren't even brief periods of regular breathing. No wonder he was so sleepy in the daytime.

Like Vaughn, most obese youngsters with sleep apnea are otherwise normal. Often these children's parents are similarly obese. Emotional factors are likely to be important, either as a cause of the obesity or as a reaction to it. Sometimes the obesity may be a secondary effect of a particular medical disorder, endocrinological (hormonal) condition, or medication.

Treating Sleep Apnea

The methods we use to treat a child with sleep apnea depend of course on the cause of the disorder. If, as in most children, enlarged tonsils and adenoids are at fault, we usually recommend they be removed.

For example, Melody's tonsils and adenoids were much too big and even though she had not had problems with ear or throat infections, we felt the severity of her sleep apnea more than justified removal of that tissue. After the operation Melody's improvement was remarkable. Her breathing became completely quiet at night and her sleep returned to normal. In fact, her mother told me that her child's breathing was so quiet at night that for the first few weeks after surgery she would go in to check her to make sure she was all right. It seemed strange not to be able to hear her breathing in the other room. Although Melody's parents had never considered her to be unusually sleepy and irritable during the day, they did see a pleasant change after the surgery. Melody's spirits improved, she complained less, and she was full of new energy that she used in appropriate ways.

If Melody had been born in the 1940s, it is unlikely that she would have suffered so long. In fact, it is very likely that sleep apnea occurs in children now more often than it did then because doctors now are less inclined to do tonsillectomies—and with good reason. In the past tonsils were often removed simply because they were large. We now know, however, that many children have huge tonsils or adenoids without any problems at all. They should not have surgery. It is only when complications develop that the tonsils or adenoids should be removed. The complications that occur most frequently are chronic middle ear disease, recurrent strep throat, and sleep apnea. The first two are usually diagnosed, but sleep apnea often goes undetected.

If, like Vaughn, your child is obese, the treatment must include a program of weight loss, and this alone may be curative. If other factors are also involved, they may need to be treated as well. For example, we discovered that Vaughn's tonsils were considerably enlarged. After they were removed he did show significant improvement, but we still felt his breathing at night was unsatisfactory. Fortunately, after several months of closely supervised dieting, Vaughn had lost forty pounds. He was now having only a few obstructions at night, his sleep was fairly continuous without recurrent arousals, and he was getting enough of the deeper sleep stages. But the change that was most *apparent* to everyone around him was that Vaughn was now able to stay awake all day without signs of sleepiness or "laziness" and was doing much better in school, to the delight of his parents, his teachers, and especially himself.

Although dieting is a "straightforward" approach, it is not an easy one. Satisfactory weight loss is best accomplished under the supervision of a carefully run *medical* program. Such programs not only supply proper diets and close follow-up by a nutritionist, but they also provide necessary counseling services and support groups. If your child has any medical condition causing or caused by her obesity, this will be treated at the same time. Long-term hospitalization with closely supervised dieting or special stomach and intestinal surgery are recommended only rarely, in extreme cases.

If the cause of the sleep apnea is an oral or facial abnormality, corrective surgery may be helpful. For example, if your child has a markedly recessed chin, it can be brought forward, and the teeth readjusted, by oral surgical and orthodontic procedures. This is a major undertaking, however, and although a cosmetic improvement is fairly well assured, there is yet no absolute guarantee that the apnea will be satisfactorily reduced. Still, newer *pre*-operative techniques are continually improving our ability to predict results. If your child has apnea because a pharyngeal flap had been created surgically, then this flap may have to be "taken down" again—that is the connection between the palate and the back of the throat removed—or at least narrowed so that there is more room for air to pass around it.

If your child is not obese and does not have enlarged tonsils or adenoids or another surgically remediable abnormality, then treatment for sleep apnea can be more difficult. Unfortunately, medications are not usually very helpful. In severe cases it may be necessary to do a tracheostomy, in which a tube is inserted into a hole made through the neck below the vocal cords (larynx) and into the windpipe (trachea) to provide for satisfactory breathing at night. This tube is then plugged during the day to allow for normal speech. (When the tube is plugged, exhaled air passes around the tube in the trachea in the normal way and up through the vocal cords and out the nose and mouth.) A newer procedure called a "pharyngoplasty" involves tightening the walls of the throat to make them less floppy. This holds some promise for certain people, although we do not yet have much experience with this procedure in children. Another approach, which also has not been used much in children, involves wearing a tight-fitting mask over the nose at night through which air is delivered under pressure. This pressure prevents the airway from collapsing by counteracting the suction created when the child inhales. Air is blown in through the nose and this tends to balloon open the part of the throat that would otherwise collapse. This technique may prove to be a useful temporary aid to obese children until they lose enough weight.

Fortunately most children can be treated by removal of tonsils and adenoids and/or by weight loss. A smaller number can be cured by other corrective oral or plastic surgery procedures. Very few require a tracheostomy. Since a tracheostomy is a major procedure and one that requires significant ongoing care afterwards, it is generally performed only on patients with fairly severe disorders. On the other hand, a tonsillectomy and adenoidectomy is a relatively simple procedure and will probably be recommended even when the sleep apnea is mild. However, it is difficult to treat a child with *mild* sleep apnea if she does not have enlarged tonsils and adenoids that can be removed or excess weight that can be lost. If such a child's daytime symptoms are minimal, it probably is best for the physician to do nothing but follow that child closely to be sure more worrisome problems do not develop and that the sleep apnea does not become progressively more severe.

Some Words of Caution

The symptoms of sleep apnea in children are generally obvious at night (if you watch carefully) when the breathing disturbance is most marked, but daytime symptoms may be less noticeable. Adults with this disorder often have overwhelming sleepiness during the day, but this happens much less often in children, at least in those who are not very obese. Young children do tend to get a reasonable amount of deep sleep despite their breathing difficulties. In fact, you may not recognize the subtle daytime symptoms until they disappear after the obstruction is corrected. Then, as with Melody, sleep improves and daytime behavior becomes even better. Remember that "sleepiness" in the child may appear as any number of behavioral problems— hyperactivity, irritability, difficulty concentrating, forgetfulness, school problems, or general "laziness"—instead of as constant yawning and frequent napping. Children with sleep apnea may also have problems with bedwetting, and they may have other sleep disruptions such as nightmares, sleep terrors, and sleepwalking. Occasionally an electrocardiogram will show that the heart is working too hard and rarely a child's blood pressure may be elevated. Adults with sleep apnea may also complain of headaches on waking in the morning. Or they may have periods of "automatic behavior" during the day in which they act in a manner similar to sleepwalking, going about some routine activity without apparent awareness. Hypertension among adult patients is common. However, apart from the snoring, sleep disruption, some sleepiness, and bedwetting, most of these other symptoms which are common in adults occur only rarely in children (see Figure 15). Children who are very obese are more likely to have all of the symptoms usually seen in the adult.

You should be aware that this disorder can be serious and should always be treated by a qualified physician. When allowed to go untreated in adults, sleep apnea may be fatal, primarily because of heart complications. Abnormal beating develops in a heart compromised by age when oxygen levels decrease during apneas. An even more common cause of death in adult sleep apnea patients may actually be automobile accidents—because of falling asleep at the wheel. Fortunately your child's heart is very resilient and, although your concern is understandable, the chances of her simply not waking in the morning are *exceedingly small*. Still, the danger exists, especially if she takes any strong medication, such as phenobarbital, which decreases the automatic drive to breathe and which makes it harder for her to wake.

The sleep apnea discussed in this chapter should not be confused with "sleep apnea" in infants. Newborns, especially those born prematurely, may have episodes of apnea (or not breathing) that are truly life threatening. In most cases, however, this does not involve airway obstruction. Rather, the baby simply stops trying to breathe. These episodes of apnea occur intermittently, not hundreds of times each night. Despite much research trying to show that a similar phenomenon is a cause of the Sudden Infant Death Syndrome (crib death) in older infants, no definite conclusions can yet be made.

If you believe your child does suffer from sleep apnea, you may have a problem getting the proper treatment for her. Unfortunately it is not always easy for doctors to recognize that a child has sleep apnea. Many physicians are still unaware of the frequency with which this syndrome appears in children, and few hospital complexes have the facilities to study children's sleep. In addition, most doctors have never had the opportunity to watch a child with sleep apnea during the night. Your doctor will see your child during the day when she is awake and probably breathing quite well. You may have to work hard to persuade your pediatrician that your child has a problem that needs attention.

Ask your pediatrician for a referral to an ear, nose, and throat specialist for his or her opinion. Make a tape recording of your child's snoring so the doctor can listen to the breathing difficulty. You may want to try to find a sleep center in your area so that you can discuss your child's symptoms with doctors there (see Appendix B). Even if they mostly treat adults, they may still be able to evaluate your child satisfactorily.

Be persistent, and you will get the attention you need for your child. And if necessary, ask your child's doctor to review the information in this chapter so that you can work together to solve your child's sleep disorder.

FIGURE 15 **How to Tell Whether Your Child Has Sleep Apnea**

A. Main Symptoms
 1. Snoring
 • Loud, raspy, squeaky, snorty
 • Can be heard throughout the house (if you have to stand by bedside to hear it, sleep apnea is unlikely)
 • Present every night (not just occasionally with a cold)
 2. Difficulty Breathing
 • Works hard or struggles to breathe
 • Mouth kept open (often, but not necessarily, true)
 • Upper chest may be pulled inwards rather than expanding during inspiration
 • Restless sleep
 • Repeated episodes of respiratory difficulty followed by moving about (even "shuddering"), partial waking, and briefly improved breathing (with loud snorting, snoring, gasping, or heavy breathing)—then return to sleep with resumption of breathing difficulties
 • May be times when attempts to breathe are strong (chest and abdomen move in and out) but actual breathing (airflow) seems completely, or almost completely, blocked

B. Associated Symptoms Common in Children
 1. Tonsils or adenoids known to be enlarged (or frequent sore throats or ear infections), obesity, or abnormalities of the jaw, mouth, or throat
 2. Mild daytime sleepiness, irritability, difficulty concentrating, school problems
 3. Bedwetting

C. Other Symptoms, Seen Mainly in Adults
 1. Overwhelming daytime sleepiness
 2. Morning headaches
 3. Automatic behavior (carrying out routine daytime activities without apparent awareness)
 4. Cardiovascular problems (high blood pressure and electrocardiogram abnormalities)

D. Diagnostic Findings in Sleep Laboratory Study (which should be carried out if above symptoms are suggestive)
 1. Recurrent respiratory obstructions
 2. Lowered oxygen values
 3. Major sleep disruption
 4. Possible cardiac rhythm disturbances

Chapter 15

Narcolepsy and Other
Causes of Sleepiness

For the two years preceding his first visit to me, Timothy napped for forty to sixty minutes every afternoon. He usually went to bed after dinner, about 7:00 P.M., and slept through until 6:30 A.M. Perhaps this may not seem unusual—but Tim was ten years old. Sometimes he also fell asleep in school for ten or fifteen minutes, but he could usually fight off the sleepiness until he got home. He was in the fourth grade when I saw him and was beginning to have both social and academic problems at school. His teacher was concerned and thought he should see a counselor.

Jacqueline, eighteen, was also unusually sleepy for her age. She slept ten hours at night and had at least two twenty-minute naps most days. Sometimes her sleepiness appeared very suddenly and was almost impossible to fight off unless she was active at the time—walking or moving about—and even then it was very difficult. After her naps she usually woke feeling fairly refreshed. Her sleepiness had begun when she was fifteen, and by the time I saw her she had noticed two new symptoms. Occasionally, just as she was about to fall asleep at night, Jacqueline found that she could not move at all, except to breathe and move her eyes. This continued for several minutes or until someone touched her or talked to her. Also, when she laughed very hard, and sometimes when she felt angry, she became weak. She would have trouble holding her head up, or her knees would start to buckle. She sometimes even fell to the ground. Jacqueline was very frightened by these new symptoms, but was embarrassed to talk about them. At seventeen she had fallen asleep while driving and was involved in a car accident—fortunately a minor one. Since that time she had driven the family car as little as possible. She quit college after her freshman year because she could not stay awake in class or complete her assignments.

Both of these children have narcolepsy. Although excessive sleepiness is a major symptom of this disorder, narcoleptic children usually have other symptoms as well. They may have sudden attacks of weakness during the day (cataplexy) and temporary paralysis and occasional hallucinations while falling asleep or waking (sleep paralysis and hypnagogic hallucinations). In fact, cataplectic attacks of weakness such as the ones Jacqueline had, in her case triggered by laughter, are a principal feature of this disorder. Timothy had not yet developed cataplexy, but he almost certainly would later on.

Narcolepsy doesn't usually appear until at least the mid-teens, although younger children like Timothy do develop the disorder. In fact, both Tim and Jacqueline had had symptoms for several years before I saw them, diagnosed their conditions, and began treatment, treatment which precluded years of unnecessary suffering for Tim and allowed Jacqueline to go back to college. In fact, most narcoleptic patients go eight to ten years or longer before being diagnosed. This happens not because earlier diagnosis is not possible but because symptoms are often misunderstood or unrecognized.

Not all sleepy children have narcolepsy. Sleepiness is also a symptom of other sleep disorders, various medical problems, and depression. Frequently, abnormally sleepy children are thought to be simply "lazy" or "sluggish," and the physician may be as much in error as the family. But sleepiness is a serious complaint and should not be dismissed easily or humorously. If your child seems sleepier than he or she should be, be sure to investigate further. And, if he seems very sleepy day after day without obvious cause, you should be very concerned and see that he gets medical attention.

Is Your Child Abnormally Sleepy?

First of all, you have to decide if your child really is excessively sleepy. Extremes are obvious, but the milder the sleepiness, the harder it is for you to be sure it is "abnormal." Approximate norms for hours of sleep for children of various ages are listed on page 19. If your child sleeps up to two hours longer than the average for his age, but seems fine during the day, then he probably just has a long sleep requirement. If he averages even more than that, however, there may be some cause for concern. Thus, an eight-year-old who sleeps fifteen hours every night but is wide awake and cheerful during the day may still be just a long sleeper, but such a pattern is somewhat worrisome and the child probably should be seen by a physician. Continued naps in children of elementary school age are another clue to the presence of excessive sleepiness. Napping decreases significantly after age three and is uncommon by age five. Any child six or older who still takes regular naps or who starts napping again (however short the naps) may well be abnormally sleepy.

It is harder to decide if your child is too sleepy if he only *looks* tired but does not actually fall asleep except, perhaps, when riding in the car. He may be irritable, yawn, and drag about, but stay awake. Or he may have difficulty sitting still and keeping his attention focused at school and at home. He may just be having unexpected difficulties in school. It is often at this point that parents, teachers, and even doctors misdiagnose excessive sleepiness in a young child as something else. They may believe the child is overactive, learning-disabled, or simply lazy. And although we now have ways of quantifying sleepiness in the laboratory, it *is* often difficult to recognize just by observation. Deciding whether your child is sluggish, lazy, unusually active, or excessively sleepy is not always easy. So if your child has any of the various symptoms of sleepiness, it would be wise for you to be suspicious.

Non-narcoleptic Causes of Sleepiness

Some of these causes of sleepiness are easy to identify, others are not. If you decide your child is sleepier than he should be, then the next question to consider is: is he sleepy because the amount of sleep he gets is inadequate or its quality poor, or is he sleepy *despite* adequate amounts of normal sleep? Without laboratory study it may be impossible for you to answer this question for sure, but you can make some important observations.

First consider the amount of sleep your child gets. Keep track of his sleep patterns for several weeks. If your ten-year-old is hard to wake after nine hours of sleep and is sleepy during the day, but wakes spontaneously after eleven hours on the weekend and then is alert all day, it means that nine hours is simply not enough sleep for him. If your teenager goes to sleep at 2:00 A.M., wakes at 6:00 A.M. for school, and naps every afternoon, it should be clear why he needs those naps. He may simply stay up late because he likes to, or he may be unable to fall asleep earlier because of a phase shift (see Chapter 9). Teenagers also have the ability to binge on sleep on the weekends, especially if they do not get enough sleep during the week. On weekends they can sleep fifteen hours at night and possibly nap during the day. But they don't do so seven days a week, and if your teenager does, you should be suspicious. Pay close attention to weekends and holidays to help you judge how much sleep your child gets when he does not have to get up for school or day-care.

Next, try to determine whether your child is sleeping well once he goes to bed. This is much more difficult to determine outside the laboratory, but if your child is very restless or seems to wake often during the night, whether he remains awake for extended periods or not, his sleepiness could still be a result of inadequate sleep, inadequate deep sleep, or poor quality of sleep.

If your child is sleepy despite getting enough of what seems to be good sleep, you should look for other causes.

Many medications also cause daytime sleepiness. Antihistamines used to treat allergies, or many of the medications used to treat seizures, are just some of the drugs that have sleepiness as a side effect.

Illness of any sort, of course, may also leave a child feeling fatigued and to some extent truly sleepy. Viral infections, especially mononucleosis and hepatitis, and any illness with high fever, are especially noted for doing this. But the sleepiness should not persist for much longer than the time of the fever, or for more than several weeks in the case of the slower-resolving viral infections. Children with anemia, hypothyroidism, or other chronic conditions are inclined to be tired, but even with these problems truly excessive sleeping is not common. Similarly, high or low blood sugar levels are rarely the cause of significant sleepiness. More serious illnesses, including cancer, may certainly make a child appear "run down" and to some extent cause him to sleep more.

If your child is *never* wide awake you should be greatly concerned. If he sleeps long hours at night and repeatedly during the day and is still never fully alert between naps, he needs medical attention. Assuming this is not the temporary consequences of an acute illness or a recently started medication, such a sleepy child must be evaluated for serious medical and psychological conditions as well as for the basic sleep disorders such as narcolepsy and sleep apnea.

Treating Some of These Causes of Sleepiness

If your child's sleepiness is mild and seems related to inadequate sleep at night, you need to help him increase his sleep time. For example, if he refuses or is unable to go to sleep until very late, or if he is waking frequently at night because of his particular sleep associations, a delayed sleep phase, or poor limit setting, you should handle matters according to the methods outlined in the earlier chapters of this book.

In these cases the main problem is *sleeplessness*, and the daytime *sleepiness* is only a consequence.

If it seems that your child simply has a long sleep requirement, your family may have to make a few adjustments to allow for it. This may not always be easy or even fully possible. An adolescent who needs ten hours of sleep and who must get up at 6:30 for school would have to go to sleep at 8:30. If he needs twelve hours, his bedtime would have to be 6:30. Such early bedtimes are obviously not feasible. You will have to arrive at a compromise in such situations. Perhaps your child can have a somewhat earlier bedtime, say 9:30, on weekdays, and be allowed to sleep late on the weekend or take naps. Such a remedy is less than ideal, but it may still be quite workable. If your child's bedtime used to be 11:30 P.M., the extra two hours of sleep each night can make a big difference.

If your child's sleepiness results from illness, medication, or a medical condition, then you should work with your doctor to find ways of alleviating his symptoms. A change in medication or an alteration of dosage regimens, for example, may be helpful.

Evaluation at a Sleep Disorders Center

If neither inadequate sleep nor known medical factors seem to provide an explanation for your child's sleepiness, then a full evaluation becomes crucial. This may still reveal an undiagnosed medical disorder, an emotional problem (depressed children often withdraw into sleep), or a primary sleep disorder (one in which basic sleep mechanisms are directly involved).

If at all possible, your child's sleep should be evaluated directly in a sleep laboratory. I realize that many medical centers still do not have the facilities to carry out sleep studies, especially in children. However, sleep disorders centers are becoming more widespread (see Appendix B); and even if the one nearest you mainly sees adults, they can probably still test your child, particularly if he is ten years or older.

There are two sleep studies useful in evaluating a sleepy child. In the first study the child is monitored during the night. These are some of the things we look for:

1. How long does it take the child to fall asleep? (A truly sleepy child is unlikely to lie awake for a long time, even in the laboratory.)
2. How much sleep does the child get: a normal amount, too much, or too little?
3. Does he go through all the normal sleep stages and do they last the

expected lengths of time? In particular, are the deepest phases of non-REM sleep, Stages III and IV, present and sufficiently long? (Most recuperation takes place in these stages, and they are very important for feeling well rested.)

4. Are sleep stages well maintained or is sleep broken by frequent arousals? (Even if normal amounts of sleep are obtained, if sleep is fragmented, sleepiness can result.)
5. Is the pattern of cycling from one stage to the next normal?
6. Does REM sleep occur at the expected time or does it start too early? (In narcolepsy, and to a lesser extent in depression, REM tends to appear very soon after the start of sleep. In fact, we find that children with narcolepsy often enter REM sleep within ten minutes of falling asleep at night and especially during naps. We refer to this as a "REM Onset," "Sleep Onset REM Period," or SOREMP.)
7. Does the child have sleep apnea, and if so what is its severity?
8. Are there any brain wave (EEG) abnormalities, including patterns seen in patients with epileptic seizures or tumors?

A second study, the Multiple Sleep Latency Test (MSLT), is carried out, if possible, on the day after the initial sleep study. This measures a child's actual degree of sleepiness and his tendency to enter the REM state rapidly. Once again the child is monitored as he was at night, but not continuously this time. Instead, he is allowed to lie down in a dark, quiet room every two hours and is given twenty minutes each time to fall asleep. The first nap occurs at 10:00 A.M. and the last at 6:00 P.M. If the child does fall asleep, he is allowed to sleep for ten minutes.

Most children will fall asleep only occasionally during this test, and the amount of time it takes them to fall asleep, averaged over the five trials, will be greater than twelve minutes. Abnormally sleepy children will fall asleep during the majority of the trials and will do so in about five to ten minutes. Narcoleptic children usually fall asleep within two to three minutes during all or almost all of the naps, and at least two of the naps will have REM onsets.

If you have your child tested in a sleep clinic and the sleep study and MSLT are completely normal, then it is unlikely that he is truly abnormally *sleepy*. That does not mean he isn't *tired* in the daytime. ("Tired" and "sleepy" do not mean the same thing. You may be tired after a game of tennis or running around the block yet not feel the least bit sleepy.) His fatigue may still have a medical or an emotional basis. Once your doctor rules out medical factors, then you should consider carefully the possibility that your child's sleepiness is a symptom of an underlying emotional condition.

If the laboratory testing confirms that your child is very sleepy (that is, if he falls asleep rapidly on each of the naps in the MSLT), but the sleep itself is normal at night and during the day, then again, once medical factors are eliminated, psychological causes must be considered likely.

While adults suffering from depression usually do not sleep well, youngsters, and especially adolescents, may react to depression quite differently. They tend to withdraw into their inner world of sleep as a way of escaping from problems that just seem too difficult to face. How they do this is not known, but the sleep is real and long-lasting. They may sleep deeply at night and have repeated naps during the day. They may even spend most of the day in bed. If this is happening to your child, *don't* wait for the problem to blow over. Instead you should seek medical and psychological help promptly.

Narcolepsy

Narcolepsy and sleep apnea are the two main non-psychiatric sleep disorders that cause children to be *very* sleepy in the daytime. You will recall that in sleep apnea the problem is an inability to maintain normal breathing in sleep and the sleep disruption is secondary. Although the daytime sleepiness may be marked, in children this is often subtle. But in narcolepsy, sleepiness is more clear-cut, and in this disorder it is the sleep systems that are directly affected.

Narcolepsy is *not* epilepsy. It is a completely different disorder, even though some of its symptoms occasionally resemble certain forms of epileptic seizures. Narcolepsy is characterized not just by sleepiness but by several other symptoms which I will discuss shortly.

The symptoms of narcolepsy usually start in adolescence or early adulthood, but they may begin in the primary grades in school. About 50 percent of narcoleptics are symptomatic by age sixteen. It is a lifelong condition, though the sleepiness may eventually become milder and some of the associated symptoms may even disappear. Narcolepsy and all its symptoms can be treated with naps and medication. Often treatment is very successful, but both the severity of the disease and the response to therapy can be quite variable.

In narcolepsy, sleep systems turn on inappropriately during the day, and they don't always work as they should at night. Although both REM and non-REM sleep are affected, most often it is the REM system that begins at the wrong time, and this accounts for most of the symptoms.

Sleep Disturbances in Narcolepsy

It is commonly believed that narcoleptic patients are "hypersomniac," that is that they sleep too much and very deeply. Although their sleep may be somewhat excessive, as it was with Timothy, the total amount of sleep most narcoleptics get in a twenty-four-hour period usually is close to normal. Often the nighttime sleep is broken by many brief and some not so brief wakings, in the same way the daytime waking is broken by several brief and some not so brief naps. Sleep is thus distributed across the twenty-four-hour day rather than being consolidated into a single block at night. This disturbance in nighttime sleep is an important characteristic of narcolepsy.

The other main characteristic of sleep in narcoleptics is that it is the REM system that most often begins inappropriately. As a result, the REM state frequently occurs immediately upon, or at least within ten minutes after, falling asleep. Because this does not happen every time, a study of one nap or one night's sleep is not sufficient to diagnose the disorder. But the five naps of the MSLT do allow such a tendency to be seen. If a child takes only a few minutes to fall asleep during the tests and if he goes right into REM sleep in at least two of the five naps, we can confirm the diagnosis of narcolepsy.

Ordinarily, after about three months of age, REM does not occur until after one complete cycle of non-REM, usually two cycles in children beyond infancy. One would only expect to see REM onsets under unusual conditions, such as during withdrawal from a medication that decreases REM sleep (this leads to a "REM rebound").

Partial Activation of the REM System

Sometimes narcoleptics have episodes in which REM sleep is not fully established. This can happen at bedtime, on waking, or during the day. This unusual phenomenon accounts for the other symptoms of narcolepsy—cataplexy, hypnagogic hallucinations, and sleep paralysis. In these states it seems that certain features of the REM state, namely dreaming and/or paralysis, are activated while the child is still fully awake or only partly asleep.

The Major Symptoms of Narcolepsy: Sleepiness and Cataplexy

These two symptoms are the hallmark of the narcolepsy syndrome. If your child has both of these, then a diagnosis of narcolepsy is fairly certain. Let's look at them one at a time.

1. The Sleepiness of Narcolepsy

Narcoleptic children are sleepy. They will fall asleep quickly whenever there is nothing happening to keep them awake. However, when they are up and about and not in monotonous, tedious, or boring settings, most narcoleptics can stay awake. They only *feel* very sleepy from time to time during the day. However, severe narcoleptics feel quite sleepy all of the time and have periods of "irresistible" sleepiness as well.

Narcoleptics do not really have "sleep attacks" as is often said. Marked sleepiness may come on fairly rapidly, but they can fight off sleep if there is enough motivation to do so and possibly if they have the help of another person. And if they do fall asleep, they can be waked. What happens is that they begin to feel extremely sleepy and they become progressively less able to stay awake. If a narcoleptic tries to stay awake, the sleepiness is only prolonged. If he gives in to the desire to sleep, he will feel relief both from the unpleasantness of having to fight off the sleepiness and, after the nap, temporarily from the sleepiness itself.

We have all felt irresistibly sleepy on occasion, but narcoleptics feel this way every day, and their desire to sleep is much more overwhelming. To give you an idea of how a narcoleptic person feels, imagine yourself after a big dinner, watching a boring program on television in a very warm room. Your eyelids feel heavy and you know that you cannot stay awake unless you get up and go for a walk. It may feel good to let yourself fall asleep. Trying to fight it off is very difficult, unpleasant, and leaves you with a headache. If you do fall asleep you will probably wake after fifteen to sixty minutes feeling very refreshed. The sense of overwhelming sleepiness will be gone.

And so it is with narcoleptics. Marked sleepiness comes on at various times during the day—not just after a big dinner but any time, although their sleepiness is more common and more pronounced in situations where anyone might find it hard to stay awake. Without physical activity narcoleptics find it almost impossible to fight off sleep. Even if they do manage to stay awake, they feel very groggy and their ability to concentrate or work is greatly diminished.

Typically a narcoleptic's naps are short—sometimes only a few minutes, occasionally up to an hour, but rarely much longer. And the naps often do seem to be considerably refreshing. In school, for example, a narcoleptic child may return to productive work after being allowed (or allowing himself) to nap for twenty minutes. However, if he has to fight off sleep he may be unable to concentrate for hours. Such a child may find it quite impossible to listen quietly and simultaneously to stay awake. He must move about, talk, and be disruptive or he will fall asleep. Either way he usually winds up in trouble with the teacher.

Thus although narcoleptics can fall asleep in almost any setting, they are most likely to do so in situations which require little physical activity and which provide little variety or interesting stimulation. A narcoleptic child sitting in class, riding in the car, or watching television may find that the desire to sleep comes on quickly and seems impossible to fight off. Such a child might also fall asleep during a baseball game, but it would likely occur while he was sitting on the bench or standing in the outfield waiting for someone to hit the ball. It would be unusual for him to fall asleep while running to catch the ball, although he could have a cataplectic attack at that time.

2. Cataplexy

This dramatic symptom is very disconcerting and even dangerous to the narcoleptic, yet it may seem strange and even humorous to the observer. Cataplexy is a sudden muscle weakness, or even temporary total paralysis, triggered by strong emotion, and it is often the key to an otherwise difficult diagnosis of narcolepsy. Typically the emotions that initiate a cataplectic event are laughter or anger, but any strong emotion or excitement can do it. In fact, cataplectic adults often learn to control their emotions rigidly, avoiding all expressions of laughter, anger, or excitement. Their nieces or nephews, however, may delight in trying to make them laugh or get upset just to watch him or her fall over at the dinner table.

Cataplectic attacks vary from one person to another in terms of frequency, severity of weakness, and the length of the attacks. If your child is cataplectic, the weakness may be so mild that he only experiences a momentary buckling of the knees, a sagging of the jaw, or a transient difficulty holding his head up. Or it may be so severe that he falls to the ground with a temporary but almost complete paralysis. He will be unable to move any muscles except those that control breathing and eye movement. In effect the paralysis is the same as that which occurs in REM sleep.

Most cataplectic attacks are short, lasting only a few seconds or a minute. Less often they last several minutes, and on rare occasions they can last up to half an hour. Episodes that continue for several minutes may lead into a period of sleep. Most narcoleptics have one to four cataplectic attacks each day. Some patients have them less often, but others have them many times each day with very little provocation.

When cataplexy is severe and frequent, it is a crippling condition if it is not treated. Even if attacks don't happen often they still may be very dangerous if the weakness is marked. Adults and children may have accidents around the home such as burning themselves by dropping a pot of boiling water, or hurting themselves by falling down the stairs. And dangers outside the home can be even greater. A child may fall down in the street if he is startled by an approaching vehicle. And an adolescent may have a cataplectic attack while driving a car.

Again, despite its resemblance to certain types of epilepsy, cataplexy is a very different problem. Although it is at times tempting to assume the weakness is imagined or "hysterical," especially when it is precipitated in unusual settings such as during fear or sexual intercourse, it is very real. Cataplexy is a *true* weakness, a *true* paralysis. It seems to be identical to the paralysis that occurs during normal REM sleep. We believe that the system that controls this REM paralysis turns on inappropriately and suddenly during the day instead of confining itself to REM sleep. Why cataplexy can be triggered by emotion is not yet known.

The age at which cataplexy first appears and its relationship to the onset of sleepiness varies greatly. Cataplexy and sleepiness may begin at the same time, or cataplexy can precede or follow the onset of sleepiness by several years. Most often, however, sleepiness appears first. Cataplexy usually follows within five years, but we know of much longer delays. Because of this, it is rare for cataplexy to appear in a child as young as five. By adolescence it is seen more often, but perhaps 85 percent of narcoleptics do not develop this symptom until after the age of fifteen.

Even if your child is cataplectic, this symptom may be difficult to recognize. Many children have trouble describing the weakness they feel during mild episodes. In fact, even if you see your child drop to the floor when laughing hard, you are unlikely to be alarmed. Most normal children will fall to the ground or flop down onto their desks or the table when they are laughing very hard and feeling silly. But you should be concerned if your child complains or seems alarmed about his weakness at these times, or if he experiences similar weakness when he is angry or startled. Cataplexy in older children is usually easier to recognize.

The Minor Symptoms: Sleep Paralysis
and Hypnagogic Hallucinations

3. Sleep Paralysis

This is a phenomenon very similar to cataplexy, but it does not occur during full waking. It happens most frequently just as a narcoleptic child is about to go to sleep, less often just as he wakes. Children like Jacqueline with sleep paralysis find themselves alert but unable to move.

Sleep paralysis thus also seems to represent only the *paralysis* part of REM sleep, but it occurs either just before or just after actual sleep and dreaming. Most episodes last only a few minutes. They either end spontaneously or are broken by some type of outside stimulation, typically touch (like Sleeping Beauty) or even sound. Generally sleep paralysis occurs only a few times a month. Only rarely does it happen every night.

Sleep paralysis may begin at any time in the course of narcolepsy. About half of all narcoleptic patients have repeated sleep paralysis episodes and one-quarter of them develop this symptom by age sixteen.

Not surprisingly, sleep paralysis can be a very frightening experience, especially the first episode. Children may feel they are dying. They are even more terrified when sleep paralysis occurs along with frightening hypnagogic hallucinations in which the dream system turns on along with the paralysis.

4. Hypnagogic Hallucinations

Occasionally, just as a narcoleptic child is beginning to drift off to sleep, he sees a very realistic but bizarre image, or what we refer to as a hypnagogic hallucination. Often he may hear sounds as well. (Other senses—smell, taste, touch—are less commonly involved in the hallucinatory experience.) The visual or auditory hallucinations may be pleasant or scary. A child might see only moving colored blobs or hear meaningless noises. More often the images are better formed. The child may visualize real scenes that appear true to daily life. He may believe he hears music or voices. Intruders may suddenly seem to appear either within his bedroom or in another location visualized as part of the hallucination. He may see burglars, strangely shaped or colored animals, or threatening monsters. This theme of intrusion and threat is common, and because the imagery is so realistic, it may be quite frightening. Depending on how close to sleep your child is, he may recognize these visions or sounds as unreal, or he may believe they actually exist. The child may also feel that he is doing something, such as running away or trying to fight back, even though he is not actually moving. If he has sleep paralysis at the same time as a hypnagogic hallucination, his terror may, quite understandably, be overwhelming.

Hypnagogic hallucinations occur just before falling asleep or just on waking (when we refer to them as *hypnapompic* hallucinations) but like sleep paralysis, they tend to happen mainly at the onset of sleep as a partial REM episode. Here, too, one component of REM is active —in this case the *dream* has begun while sleep and paralysis have not.

The occurrence of hypnagogic hallucinations usually makes a child feel anxious at the very least, and frequently quite frightened. If the hallucinations are frequent, going to bed may have such unpleasant associations that the child will resist bedtime intensely. A young child may have difficulty describing these experiences to you. Very often older children are afraid to talk about these hallucinations for fear of being thought "crazy," especially if they experience bizarre images of body distortion such as deformation or loss of a limb. Since many children will call out at bedtime that they are afraid of monsters in their room, it is possible to confuse your child's normal, vivid, waking imagination with an abnormal activation of the dream system itself.

Although we speak of hypnagogic hallucinations as involving the dream system only, this may be somewhat simplistic. More likely, perhaps, is that a transition from waking directly into REM sleep is not instantaneous any more than is the usual transition from waking to non-REM sleep. During the transition, sleep begins to become established before the child loses awareness of the environment. For example, if you are drowsy and daydream in a chair, on waking you may insist that you were not asleep at all. You will remember your daydream but believe you were having controlled rational thoughts of waking rather than drifting or irrational ones of sleep. In a narcoleptic, the transition to REM would be similar, but the character of the thoughts or images would be more bizarre and appear to be really happening. Awareness of these events would depend on how early in the transition to sleep the dream actually begins.

Many narcoleptic patients find that the best thing they can do is not to fight off the hallucination but just let full sleep overtake them. This probably doesn't end the dream, but "conscious" awareness gradually slips away. The fact that the dreams are so intense may well be part of the abnormality of the REM sleep system in narcolepsy, and this probably accounts for the fact that narcoleptics have more scary nightmares as well.

Although about half of narcoleptics eventually develop hypnagogic hallucinations, only 15 percent (25 percent if we include those with frequent terrifying nightmares) have them by age sixteen.

Sleep Paralysis, Hypnagogic Hallucinations, or Cataplexy Without Sleepiness

The symptoms of sleep paralysis, hypnagogic hallucinations, and cataplexy in a patient with narcolepsy tend to wax and wane in frequency and severity over time. But there is a general overall tendency for symptoms to decrease with increasing age and, in fact, any or all of them may eventually disappear completely.

Although these three symptoms are very characteristic of narcolepsy, each may occur independently as well. Sometimes they are just isolated symptoms and not part of the narcolepsy syndrome. In fact, many people have occasional "independent" sleep paralysis or hypnagogic hallucinations.

These symptoms of sleep paralysis or hypnagogic hallucinations, without excessive sleepiness or cataplexy, present no cause for alarm. In children, independent sleep paralysis most often occurs on waking. This is what would be expected, since waking from REM sleep is common among all children, whereas sleep-onset REM periods would only be expected in narcoleptics. Independent hypnagogic hallucinations, however, do occur on falling asleep and may be quite intense and even frightening, like those of narcoleptics. In these cases, it is not clear if they are occurring as part of the non-REM or REM system. Many people have "mini-dreams" as they fall asleep. These seem to occur in Stage I, in which we can have some thoughts or dreamlike imagery. But these are not usually very intense, frightening, or convincingly real. Perhaps occasional ones are. Or perhaps some people have a very occasional REM onset even though they do not have narcolepsy. In any case, when independent hypnagogic hallucinations do occur in children, they do so only occasionally.

Independent cataplexy is much more rare. Some researchers believe that this is still part of narcolepsy but with the sleepiness not yet apparent. This seems possible, since cataplexy does sometimes precede the onset of sleepiness by many years. In any case, if your child has symptoms of cataplexy, he should see a doctor. Cataplexy can be dangerous in and of itself, and symptoms resembling cataplexy can also be caused by other disorders.

The Importance of an Early Diagnosis

Although any of the symptoms of narcolepsy can be the first to appear, in 90 percent of children the initial problem is sleepiness. Cataplexy usually follows within a few years. Hypnagogic hallucinations and sleep paralysis are not always present and may begin at any point.

Sometimes the onset of symptoms seems related to a particular incident. Emotional trauma, for example, is occasionally associated with the onset of sleepiness. In these cases the initial diagnosis is usually psychiatric and the correct one may not be made for a very long time. Or one may just be aware that symptoms started during a certain year. Perhaps sleepiness first began interfering with daily life during the third year of high school. At the time, parents and child may have recognized the presence of sleepiness but still have been unaware that any *major* change had occurred.

If cataplexy begins and is significant, a patient will likely be brought to medical attention. Unless the symptom is misinterpreted as a form of epilepsy or hysteria, narcolepsy should be diagnosed or at least suspected. However, if your doctor knows little about the symptoms of narcolepsy, or if your child is not cataplectic or that symptom is very mild, the disorder can go undiagnosed for years. The personal cost of this delay in diagnosis can be enormous. A child's school performance and self-esteem may suffer tremendously. Such a child may go through most of his schooling with an undiagnosed handicap. In perhaps one-third of all narcoleptic patients, sleepiness begins early enough to interfere with performance in elementary or high school. A child or adult with undiagnosed narcolepsy may alter his plans for education and a career because of school difficulties. As he grows older he may develop significant social problems and feel he has to reconsider possible marriage plans. People may simply assume he is "lazy" or has "psychological problems." He may begin in psychotherapy in an attempt to treat the misdiagnosed symptoms, but this is sure to be unsuccessful, because the wrong thing is being treated. A psychiatrist cannot help lessen the sleepiness or eliminate attacks of cataplexy through psychotherapy, although he or she could help a patient better learn to cope with these conditions once narcolepsy has been properly diagnosed.

Thus it is very important to recognize narcoleptic patients as early as possible. At the present time we have no way of predicting which children will eventually develop narcolepsy, although there is some evidence that these youngsters' sleep habits may be different even before major symptoms emerge. Retrospective studies on adult narcoleptics suggest that many of them, as children, continued napping into grade school. Over 10 percent of them had also been misdiagnosed as being hyperactive as children (because they could not sit still and pay attention) and were treated with stimulants—the right drug, perhaps (truly "hyperactive" children may respond well to such medication), but for the wrong reason. So you should be especially suspicious if your child seems overactive yet still naps inappropriately.

Since the onset of sleepiness may be subtle, most parents don't seek help for their child immediately unless symptoms are very dramatic. Even when symptoms are not so subtle, the parents are correct in assuming that if sleepiness appears in their otherwise normal child, it may in fact pass. It often does, for whatever reason, after several weeks or months. When this happens, the sleepiness was not caused by narcolepsy but perhaps by a low-grade viral infection or a period of some emotional struggle. But sleepiness that persists beyond that should be evaluated.

The Cause of Narcolepsy

Although narcolepsy is not common, it certainly cannot be considered rare. About one in every 2,500 children will develop the disorder, and it occurs with equal frequency in boys and girls. This means that if you attend a baseball game with 40,000 other fans, about sixteen of them are already, or soon will be, suffering from narcolepsy.

We do know that narcolepsy is a genetic illness, but the pattern of inheritance is complex. If you, your spouse, or another of your children has narcolepsy, then each of your other children has a one in fifty, *not* a one in 2,500, chance of developing the symptoms.

Still, the specific biological abnormality that causes narcolepsy remains a mystery. It is not even known what is or is not inherited in persons destined to develop the disorder. Current research has been encouraging, and hopefully many answers will soon be forthcoming.

The Treatment of Narcolepsy

Sleep centers treating adults see many patients with narcolepsy. In our center where we treat children, we see very few. This happens for two reasons: symptoms often don't begin until the mid-teens; and people—families and doctors alike—do not recognize the symptoms as they emerge, do not ask the right questions, and are not worried enough by the daytime sleepiness to press for further evaluation. Sometimes they are concerned but just do not know how to proceed. Since sleep studies and MSLT's are not yet routine at most medical centers, especially in pediatric institutions, you may have to look for a center that does have this facility (see Appendix B). Again, even if the center nearest you treats primarily adults, they will have experience with narcolepsy and may be quite helpful to you.

The treatment of narcolepsy often requires the use of medication and so must be handled under a doctor's supervision. If you work closely with him or her, there are things that can be done with and for your child to alleviate the symptoms. Your child will always have the disorder, but it does not have to interfere so painfully with his schooling, work, and social life.

We handle the different symptoms of narcolepsy in different ways.

1. Sleepiness

We treat the sleepiness of narcolepsy with naps and medication. We encourage narcoleptic patients to take brief naps as needed during the day. The child who functions well if he is allowed to take two relatively brief naps during the day may not even need medication to combat the sleepiness. He should not have to try to fight off the sleepiness, since this will not help and it will leave him performing poorly. We usually have the family contact the school and discuss the disorder with teachers and counselors. They are almost always quite willing to provide a place and time for a child to nap, once they understand fully what the disorder is and how it should be treated. This allows the child to nap without feeling guilty or lazy. Teachers are also helpful in educating the child's classmates about the disorder and discouraging them from any teasing.

When medication is necessary, narcoleptics should still have naps as they need them so they can perform better during the day, feel less stress, and have less need for medication. We find that stimulants such as pemoline (Cylert), methylphenidate (Ritalin), and the amphetamines work best in alleviating sleepiness, although sometimes the drugs used to treat the other symptoms (see below) help reduce sleepiness as well. These drugs do have potential for abuse, but this is not a major worry in childhood when parents control the dosage. Some adults are inclined to abuse their medication, especially if their sleepiness is not well controlled, but most handle it appropriately. Nevertheless, it is important to remember that these are strong drugs with significant side effects. Although their use may be vital, one should be careful to keep to the minimum doses that still give satisfactory results.

If a child shows only very slight improvement in sleepiness on medication, this probably does not warrant continuing its use. A significant improvement in sleepiness, however, certainly does. Very often we do see dramatic improvement at school, at home, and socially when children begin taking stimulants. When a child is diagnosed as narcoleptic, a trial period of medication is sometimes a good idea just to see whether the child was sleepier than anyone suspected. After we see how a child responds to medication, we can best decide whether to use or postpone it.

Depending on the severity of the symptoms, the child may need medicine once or several times a day, and he may or may not be able to discontinue it on weekends or vacations. He should be followed closely by a doctor knowledgeable about narcolepsy, and medication decisions should be discussed frequently. Physicians should permit a teenager to drive only if sleepiness and cataplexy (see below) are satisfactorily controlled. Long drives, however, are to be avoided.

In the best of circumstances, a relatively low dose of the prescribed stimulant leads to satisfactory relief and the same dose remains effective over time. With Timothy, for example, we were able to significantly reduce his daytime sleepiness by allowing him to continue to nap after school (during school on occasion) and with a low dosage of methylphenidate. He has been taking the medication for over a year now and we have had to increase the dosage only slightly. As a result of this treatment Timothy is feeling much better about himself, and his school work has improved considerably. He no longer sleeps such long hours at night and he uses the hours after dinner to do homework, play, and just to spend more time with his family.

In less fortunate circumstances, a child needs progressively larger doses to get a satisfactory response. Eventually these doses become unacceptably large and the drug must be withdrawn and restarted at lower levels, or we try a different stimulant altogether. Other classes of drugs are sometimes useful in these circumstances.

Jacqueline, like many children, fell somewhere between these extremes. Her sleepiness also responded to medication, but she needed moderately large doses of pemoline. Still, there was no need to increase the dosage progressively. She did not want to stop the medication on the weekends, since this would have made it impossible for her to do her homework and it would have eliminated her social life. However, Jacqueline was back in school, doing well, and was quite happy.

2. Cataplexy, Hypnagogic Hallucinations, and Sleep Paralysis

The treatment of these symptoms is usually easier and can be accomplished with a safer class of drugs. Again, if your child's symptoms are mild, no treatment may be necessary. Hypnagogic hallucinations and sleep paralysis are annoying and frightening, but very often, once children understand why they occur, they can learn to accept them. However, if these symptoms are frequent and very frightening to your child, they do deserve medical attention. Cataplexy should be treated unless, perhaps, symptoms are extremely mild, because even though the milder forms may not lead to much embarrassment, they can still be quite dangerous.

Fortunately all of these symptoms usually respond well to a class of drugs called tricyclics, including imipramine (Tofranil), protriptyline (Vivactil), and several others. They possibly work because they tend to suppress REM sleep and hence all the manifestations of REM sleep, even during waking. Once we find a satisfactory dose, further increases, except to accommodate a child's growth, are usually not necessary.

Jacqueline's cataplexy and sleep paralysis, which were mild to begin with, were easily controlled with protriptyline. For her it was significant that she could allow herself to laugh freely in public without fear of embarrassment or of injuring herself. Timothy does not yet have any of these symptoms, but he and his family know what to look for so that treatment can begin promptly if and when these symptoms do develop.

The American Narcolepsy Association

If you know or suspect that your child has narcolepsy, you should contact the American Narcolepsy Association (ANA). They can provide you with important information and support. The ANA is a non-profit association whose directors, advisers, and members include narcoleptic patients, sleep disorders medicine specialists, and other interested individuals. The aims of the association are to provide support and information to narcoleptic patients, to increase public awareness and understanding of the disorder, to encourage government funding for research, and to keep the medical community informed. The directors are particularly concerned about trying to shorten the length of time from onset of symptoms to diagnosis and start of treatment. Also, they want to do everything possible to help a newly diagnosed patient adjust to his or her condition. Local chapters also exist in many states.

To learn how to contact the ANA for information and help, see Appendix B.

Appendices

Appendix A

Children's Books on Bedtime, Sleep, and Dreams

Bedtime

Aylesworth, Jim. *Tonight's the Night*. Chicago: Albert Whitman & Company, 1981. Daniel tries to find out exactly how it feels to fall asleep. (Toddler)

Barrett, Judi. *I Hate to Go to Bed*. New York: Four Winds Press, 1977. A little boy thinks about why he hates to go to bed, then why he likes to, as he tries to gain mastery over bedtime. (Preschool)

Brown, Margaret Wise. *A Child's Good Night Book*. Reading, Massachusetts: Addison-Wesley, 1943. Night is coming and all the animals, boats, cars, and children go to sleep. (Toddler)

Brown, Margaret Wise. *Goodnight Moon*. New York: Harper & Row, 1947. A wonderfully warm classic bedtime story of a little bunny going to sleep, saying goodnight to everything as darkness falls and sleep comes. (Toddler)

Coatsworth, Elizabeth. *Good Night*. New York: Macmillan, 1972. The sun sets, darkness comes and a star rises—a star that watches all the animals and a little boy go to sleep. (Toddler)

Cole, William. *Frances Face-Maker*. Cleveland: Collins World, 1963. Frances McGee used to stall when it was time for bed until her father made bedtime fun by having her play a game of making faces. (Preschool)

Goffstein, M. D. *Sleepy People*. New York: Farrar, Straus & Giroux, 1966. A sleepy family stretches, yawns, has a bedtime snack and goes to sleep. (Toddler)

Johnston, Johanna. *Edie Changes Her Mind*. New York: G. P. Putnam's Sons, 1964. Edie always hated to go to bed until her parents dismantled her bed and let her stay up late. (Preschool)

Katzwinkle, William. *The Nap Master*. New York: Harcourt Brace, 1979. Herman thinks "naps are for saps" until the Nap Master comes to his home and shows him that naps can be full of exciting dream adventures. (Preschool)

Kushkin, Karla. *Night Again*. Boston: Little, Brown, 1981. A child's quiet bedtime routine is described from prayers to hugs and kisses and the song of the stars. (Toddler)

Levine, Joan Goldman. *A Bedtime Story*. New York: E. P. Dutton, 1975. Arathusela lives in Brooklyn and always fussed about going to bed until her parents let her put them to bed. She learns what it is like when they stall. (Preschool)

Montresor, Beni. *Bedtime!* New York: Harper & Row, 1978. Daniel seems to have magic colorful adventures on his way to bed when his parents say "bedtime!" (Preschool)

Schuchman, Joan. *Two Places to Sleep.* Minneapolis: Carolrhoda Books, 1979. A boy whose parents are divorced lives with his father. On weeknights his father puts him to bed at home. On weekends his mother puts him to bed at her apartment in the city. (Preschool/elementary school)

Seuss, Dr. *Dr. Seuss's Sleep Book.* New York: Random House, 1962. Yawning then sleep with snoring, sleeptalking, and sleepwalking spread throughout Dr. Seuss's land of fantastic characters. "This book is to be read in bed." (Preschool)

Showers, Paul. *In the Night.* New York: Thomas Y. Crowell, 1961. A young boy who knows that many animals can see in the dark discovers that he too can gradually see about his room after his lights are turned out, thus gaining a sense of security and mastery. (Preschool)

Simon, Norma. *Where Does My Cat Sleep?* Chicago: Albert Whitman & Company, 1982. A little girl knows that she and everyone else have special places to sleep, but her cat sleeps "anywhere he wants." (Preschool)

Stevenson, James. *We Can't Sleep.* New York: Greenwillow Books, 1982. Louie and Mary Ann can't sleep because it's too hot, quiet, windy, noisy, light, dark, and lonely. But they fall asleep listening to their grandfather tell them of adventures he had as a boy when he had difficulty falling asleep. (Preschool)

Waber, Bernard. *Ira Sleeps Over.* Boston: Houghton Mifflin, 1972. Ira sleeps at Reggie's house for the first time and is embarrassed to bring along his teddy bear until he learns that Reggie sleeps with one also. (Preschool)

Warburg, Sandol Stoddard. *Curl Up Small.* Boston: Houghton Mifflin, 1964. A cozy and warm book describing how human and animal babies, in a big world full of many things to see and do, curl up safely with their mothers as the day ends and time comes for sleep and dreams. (Preschool)

Winthrop, Elizabeth. *Bunk Beds.* New York: Harper & Row, 1972. Instead of going to sleep quickly, Willie and Molly pretend they are having a series of adventures. (Preschool)

Zolotow, Charlotte. *The Summer Night.* New York: Harper & Row, 1974. A father and daughter spend time together outside on a beautiful and quiet summer night until she finally becomes sleepy and wants to go to bed. (Preschool)

Zolotow, Charlotte. *When the Wind Stops.* New York: Harper & Row, 1962. At bedtime, a little boy wonders where the sun goes when the day ends. He learns that the day doesn't end but moves elsewhere to return later like the wind and the waves and the seasons. (Preschool)

Zolotow, Charlotte. *Wake Up and Goodnight.* New York: Harper & Row, 1971. What happens in the morning when the sun comes out, and what happens at night when it gets dark and the time comes to sleep and dream, are described in warm and quiet tones. (Preschool)

Nighttime fears

Alexander, Martha. *I'll Protect You from the Jungle Beasts*. New York: Dial Press, 1973. A small child deals with nighttime worries by pretending to reassure his teddy bear as they walk through an imaginary forest; then, as fears creep in, the teddy bear grows in size to provide the child with the desired protection and reassurance. (Preschool)

Hoban, Russell. *Bedtime for Frances*. New York: Harper & Row, 1960. Frances is a little badger, put to bed warmly by her parents. But when she becomes frightened in her room, she needs firm reassurance from her parents so that she can relax and go to sleep. (Preschool)

Low, Joseph. *Benny Rabbit and the Owl*. New York: Greenwillow Books, 1978. Benny Rabbit stalls at bedtime. When he becomes afraid of an owl that he imagines to be in his closet, he and his father walk into the forest pretending to take the owl with them, feeding it and letting it go free. Then Benny is able to go to sleep. (Preschool)

Mayer, Mercer. *There's a Nightmare in My Closet*. New York: Dial Press, 1968. A little boy who is afraid of an imaginary monster in his closet decides to come to terms with it, first by shooting it with his toy gun and then by befriending it. (Preschool)

Morris, Terry Nell. *Goodnight, Dear Monster*. New York: Alfred A. Knopf, 1980. A picture story of a young boy who helps his teddy bear overcome his fear of a monster at night. (Toddler)

Viorst, Judith. *My Mama Says There Aren't Any Zombies, Ghosts, Vampires, Creatures, Demons, Monsters, Fiends, Goblins, or Things*. New York: Atheneum, 1978. A little boy, seeing that his mother is not always right, wonders if he can believe her when she tells him that the monsters he thinks he sees are not real. (Preschool)

Willoughby, Elaine Macmann. *Boris and the Monsters*. Boston: Houghton Mifflin, 1980. Boris's nighttime fears of monsters in his room disappear when he gets a puppy named Ivan the Terrible. But Ivan becomes scared and Boris ends up protecting him. (Preschool)

Early Morning Waking

Dennis, Wesley. *Flip and the Morning*. New York: Viking Press, 1951. Flip, a colt, gets up early in the morning and disturbs all the other animals who like to sleep late until he goes off quietly in the morning in search of the wood duck. (Preschool)

Kraus, Robert. *Milton the Early Riser*. New York: Windmill Books and E.P. Dutton, 1972. Milton the panda wakes early in the morning and must play alone while the other animals sleep. (Toddler)

Dreams

Allsburg, Chris Van. *Ben's Dream*. Boston: Houghton Mifflin, 1982. It is raining as Ben falls asleep reading a book on geography. He dreams of seeing the great landmarks of the world in the midst of a flood. (Preschool)

de Paola, Tomie. *When Everyone Was Fast Asleep*. New York: Holiday House,

1976. When everyone was fast asleep the Fog Maiden sent Token to take a brother and sister on a quiet pleasant dream adventure. (Preschool)

Donaldson, Lois. *Karl's Wooden Horse*. Chicago: Albert Whitman & Company, 1970. A simply told story about Karl's dreamland adventure on his new wooden horse. (Preschool)

Marzollo, Jean. *Close Your Eyes*. New York: Dial Press, 1978. If you close your eyes you can be anyplace you like in your dreams. This fact is described and illustrated very warmly. (Preschool)

Sendak, Maurice. *In the Night Kitchen*. New York: Harper & Row, 1970. Mickey goes to sleep then falls through the dark, out of his clothes into a dream of the night kitchen full of chubby chefs, and airplanes made of dough, and giant milk bottles. (Toddler)

Storm, Theodor. *Little John*. New York: Farrar, Straus & Giroux, 1972. A story of Little John's dreaming adventures in his trundle bed. (Preschool)

Wersba, Barbara. *Amanda Dreaming*. New York: Atheneum, 1973. Amanda's beautiful dreams are described in almost poetic prose and with surrealistic illustrations. (Elementary school)

Educational Books About Sleep and Dreams

Hirsch, S. Carl. *Theater of the Night: What We Do and Do Not Know About Dreams*. Chicago: Rand McNally, 1976. A scientific book on dreams for children. (Junior High School)

Kastner, Jonathan and Marianna. *Sleep—The Mysterious Third of Your Life*. New York: Harcourt Brace & World, 1968. A factual book on sleep, sleep research, and dreaming for children. (Junior High School)

Lindsay, Rae. *Sleep and Dreams*. New York: Franklin Watts, 1978. A scientific approach to sleep for children. (Elementary School)

Showers, Paul. *Sleep Is for Everyone*. New York: Thomas Y. Crowell, 1974. A simple description of sleep, what happens during sleep, and the consequences of not getting enough sleep. (Elementary School)

Silverstein, Alvin and Virginia. *Sleep and Dreams*. Philadelphia: J. B. Lippincott, 1974. A scientific approach to sleep for older children. (Junior High School)

Singer, David L. and Martin, William G. *Sleep On It: A Look at Sleep and Dreams*. Englewood Cliffs, New Jersey: Prentice-Hall, 1969. A book on sleep, sleep research, and dreams for children. (Junior High School)

Appendix B

Helpful Organizations

The Association of Sleep Disorders Centers
P.O. Box 2604
Del Mar, CA 92014
(619) 755-6556

This is an association of sleep disorders centers located primarily in the United States and Canada. The purpose of the organization is to maintain high standards in the developing field of sleep disorders medicine and to assure sharing and dissemination of knowledge. The central office can provide an up-to-date listing of sleep disorders centers in all parts of the country.

The American Narcolepsy Association
1139 Bush Street, Suite D
San Carlos, CA 94070-2477
(415) 591-7979

This is a non-profit association whose directors, advisors, and members include narcoleptic patients, sleep disorders medicine specialists, and other interested individuals. The aims of the association are to provide support and information to narcoleptic patients, to increase public awareness and understanding of the disorder, to encourage governmental funding for research, and to keep the medical community informed. The directors are particularly concerned with trying to shorten the length of time from onset of symptoms to diagnosis and start of treatment. And they want to do everything possible to help a newly diagnosed patient adjust to his or her problem. Local chapters also exist in many states. The national association can provide informative brochures, membership applications, and lists of local chapters.

Index

ABOUT THE AUTHOR

DR. RICHARD FERBER is widely recognized as the nation's leading authority in the field of children's sleep problems. Director of the Sleep Lab and the Center for Pediatric Sleep Disorders at Children's Hospital in Boston (Harvard University's pediatric teaching hospital), Dr. Ferber also teaches at Harvard Medical School and is a pediatrician.